YOU SHOULD HAVE BEEN HERE YESTERDAY

YOU SHOULD HAVE BEEN HERE

YESTERDAY

A Life in Television News

GARRICK UTLEY

PublicAffairs
New York

A portion of Chapter 20 originally appeared in the March/April 1997
edition of *Foreign Affairs*.

Published in the United States by PublicAffairs™,
a member of the Perseus Books Group.
All rights reserved.

Printed in the United States of America.

Book design by Mark McGarry, Texas Type & Book Works.
Set in Trump Mediäeval.

Library of Congress Cataloging-in-Publication Data
Utley, Garrick, 1939–
You should have been here yesterday : a life in television news / Garrick Utley.
p. cm.
Includes index.
ISBN 1–891620–94–0
1. Utley, Garrick, 1939– 2. Journalists—United States—Biography. I. Title.
PN4874.U89 2000
070'.92—dc12
[B]   00–029121

10 9 8 7 6 5 4 3 2

For Clifton and Frayn

CONTENTS

INTRODUCTION

HOW MANY of us recall the first time we awoke before the light of dawn when the world we were used to seeing was still wrapped in darkness.

And cold.

It was 4:45 on a winter morning when I felt my father gently shaking my shoulder. Normally, a seven-year-old would have rejected this parental intrusion and slipped down under the bed covers to return to the comforting embrace of a child's dreamland. But not on this morning. I washed my face, dressed quickly, and tiptoed down the stairs so as not to disturb my mother and two brothers, who were still asleep. This was not a father initiating his son in the ritual of early morning fishing or deer hunting; these were not the urban pursuits of a family living in a large house on the south side of Chicago. Instead, a different kind of father–son bonding was taking place. Dad was taking me to work.

Perhaps he thought it was time for me to see what he was doing when the family gathered around the breakfast table without the paterfamilias present. Or perhaps he recalled an incident four years earlier that had shown how disorienting the impact and illusion of a broadcaster's work can be. A family friend was sitting with my mother in the living room (so I would be told many decades later). The woman asked, "Garrick, where is your daddy?" Apparently I ran as quickly as my three-year-old legs could carry me to the large mahogany console radio that stood at one end of the room, pointed at it, and said, "He is in there."

And so he was. Clifton Utley was a Chicago newscaster and commentator whose voice and thoughts were heard through much of the Midwest, propelled by powerful 50,000-watt radio stations that penetrated homes with an intimate intensity that only television and, one day, the Internet would equal. If broadcasting was his craft, his passion was the world; a world that was a tangible presence in our home. During World War II our three-story turn-of-the-century house had resonated with a mixture of French and English when my parents took in three refugee children from France. Years later my mother, Frayn (who also worked as a broadcast journalist), would help supervise international student exchanges, as well as the visits of foreign government officials, teachers, and artists, to Chicago. My horizons, though, were not that distant in 1947. The nine-inch black-and-white RCA television set that would soon be delivered to our house had not yet arrived. Broadcasting still meant radio, and my father's 7:55 A.M. breakfast-time newscast commanded a large audience.

As my father drove our Studebaker along the Chicago lakefront, a winter gale was whipping down from Canada, hurling white-capped waves against the rocky breakwater. Dad explained what I would see on my first visit to the NBC newsroom and studios in Chicago. Radio news then, as now, was largely a one-person craft. Dad would collect the overnight national and international stories from the wire services and put together his five-minute newscast, which was squeezed between two morning music programs, one sponsored by a commuter rail line and the other by a local chain of clothing stores. But in those five minutes, with time out for a commercial, the midwesterners listening to WMAQ received their early morning ration of news. Along with their local newspaper, it was the only information of the nation and the world they would, or could, receive until evening, when the afternoon newspapers appeared and the early evening radio newscasts and commentators came on the air. It was life before television, before anyone conceived of an information society.

As in many homes, information arrived at our house each morning with a light thud at the front door. A newsboy would roll up the two morning Chicago newspapers, tuck in the ends to make them more aerodynamic, and then lob the papers from the sidewalk onto our front porch. For broader international coverage the *New York Times,* the *New York Herald Tribune,* and the *Christian Science Monitor* arrived by mail a day late. For regional news there was the *St. Louis Post-Dispatch* and the *Des Moines Register.* There were a few magazines and journals as well as the occasional foreign publication from Europe. And there were books, which offered knowledge if not current information. It was, for its time, an impressive massing of news, a time when the amount of news available was no greater than a journalist's ability to consume it. This mastery of the news by newscasters and commentators, so much greater than that of their listeners, who had even less access to information, gave early broadcast journalists an aura of exceptional authority. When that authority could be linked to the particular force of radio as a conveyor of the spoken word, it led to the rise of the commentators of the late 1930s and 1940s. H. V. Kaltenborn, Elmer Davis, Edward R. Murrow, Lowell Thomas, Gabriel Heater, and many others attracted large audiences, giving the news and then telling their audiences what they thought of it.

For a seven-year-old driving to work with his father for the first time, radio, with its disembodied voices floating out of a box, created a wondrous playground for the imagination. Now I was about to enter it. And yet there was a secret I dared not utter as Dad parked the two-door Studebaker and we entered the massive Merchandise Mart along the banks of the Chicago River and rode the elevator to the nineteenth floor, where the NBC studios were located. The excitement that had been building inside me was fueled by the knowledge, the tantalizing prospect, and the absolute, unshakable certainty that one of my young life's dreams was about to be splendidly fulfilled. I was going to meet Aunt Jemima.

I knew she would be there because she was there every morning. Aunt Jemima pancake mix was my father's sponsor, a logical and inevitable advertiser for a breakfast-time news program. I loved her rich voice, coated in the rolling cadence of a southern African-American woman. Although I couldn't see her, I knew what she looked like, for there she was on the red pancake mix box in the kitchen, her broad smiling face topped with a bandanna wrapped around her hair. Now the face on the box and the voice in the radio were about to become one before my eyes.

As we entered the newsroom, I was drawn to the long row of news agency teletype machines lined up against a wall, fascinated by the endless staccato clatter of keys striking the unwinding rolls of paper and the warning bells ringing as a story of particular urgency scrolled up and out of the machines of the Associated

Press, the United Press, and the International News Service. The wire services were the journalistic lifeblood of radio news. Their news was even fresher than the morning newspapers that lay strewn about on the coffee-stained desks.

I watched Dad devour his breakfast of coffee and a creamy sweet roll as he prepared his script. From time to time I glanced at the heavy, soundproofed door at the end of the room that led into the broadcast studio. Impatient, I wondered when Aunt Jemima would arrive. As 7:55 A.M. grew closer and she still had not appeared, I reasoned that since she was not a journalist she was probably in another room thinking about the succulent words and phrases she could offer that morning to persuade listeners to add her pancake mix to their shopping list.

At 7:53 my father picked up his scripts, took me by the hand, and led me through the heavy door into the small studio. In the middle of it was a table covered with a dark fabric and a microphone. On the far wall was a window behind which a technician was asking my father for a voice check. A minute later he was on the air, giving the morning news to a vast audience across Chicago and a broad swath of the Midwest. Sitting on a chair against a wall, I was filled with mounting anxiety. Where was Aunt Jemima? I knew her commercial came at the end of the news, and there was not much time left for her to get to the microphone. Suddenly a door on the far side of the studio opened and a woman walked in briskly, sat down across the table from my father, and laid some papers under the microphone. Something was terribly wrong. This was not Aunt Jemima. The woman was white, middle-aged, and, well, remarkably skinny. My father, however, gave no notice to this obvious mistake. He kept speaking and then ended with the words I heard every morning at the breakfast table, "And now here is a message from Aunt Jemima."

Introduction

And Aunt Jemima began speaking. Or rather this middle-aged, skinny, white, bandannaless impostor began speaking in that familiar and beloved black southern drawl. *What is going on here?* I thought. *This is not right, this is ...* I struggled for a word, but "illusion" lay beyond my seven-year-old grasp. When the program ended, my father asked me to come to the broadcast table to meet "Aunt Jemima," who was now speaking with the practiced voice of a professional actor. I tried not to show my disappointment, exchanged a few perfunctory words, shook hands, and left. As we drove home, Dad asked what I thought of the program. It was interesting, even exciting, I replied. I did not mention Aunt Jemima or the lesson that life had taught a young boy that morning: not everything filtered through the microphones, and later the cameras, of broadcasting is what it appears to be.

THERE IS no single story of broadcast news, just as there is no single story of a news event. There is only the rich mosaic of countless stories collected by journalists who, armed with cameras and microphones, videotape recorders and editing decks, egos and ambition, values and commitment, have gone out to cover the community, the nation, and the world and report at least some of what they have seen and learned to their audience. There is also the story of where they, myself included, have failed.

Stories form a narrative. In television news, it begins in the 1948 season with the first network newscasts, which were fifteen minutes long and were seen in only a few East Coast communities. What was born then is the continuing story of individuals working to serve the public interest (and their own), men (and, much later, women) constantly mastering new machines and technologies that would both enhance and limit the personal, human dimension of journalism.

Inevitably, this is a personal story. I have been fortunate not only to have spent most of a lifetime in television news but also to have entered it almost on the ground floor: six weeks before the start-up of the evening half hour network newscasts in 1963. From that beginning of television news, as we came to know it and watch it over more than three decades, I was one of many who were able to help build and shape these programs into the national institutions, which, arguably, have had a larger impact on the American public than any other deliverer of news has had or is likely to have in the fragmenting information world of the future. For more than thirty years in the calling, craft, and business of television news, I was privileged to enjoy the full flood of its successes and, yes, its eventual decline as competition from cable news channels and the Internet sliced off ever larger pieces of the network television audience while providing vastly more information and choice to the public.

There are some who lament the passing of the old order and the sense of order that the Cronkites, Huntleys, Brinkleys, and their successors provided — those who might say, "You should have been here yesterday." Nostalgia, however, can play sly tricks; memory tends to recall the best rather than the worst of any era. What follows is one reporter's attempt to look at the not-so-distant past and to the future; to judge whether the best in the fraternity of journalists, as well as those who use and weigh our work, is behind us or is somewhere out there in a confusing and rapidly evolving future.

I have chosen to leaven the broad arc of network television news with events I have witnessed. My debt of gratitude extends to countless colleagues who have shared and enriched these journalistic experiences. Translating them from the television world to the printed page at book length has been a new and invigorating challenge. My deep appreciation for seeing this project to completion goes to my publisher at PublicAffairs, Peter Osnos (a former foreign correspondent), the sharp eye and support of my editor, Geoff Shandler, and to the encouragement of Lynn Nesbit who has shown me how the best agent is a good friend. Of course, neither the book nor the life would have happened without those closest to me. My wife, Gertje, provided patient support and understanding as I stretched my writing muscles beyond the abbreviated length of a television news script. For too many years she understood and tolerated my long absences as I traveled to more than eighty countries in search of news; journeys that achieved full richness only when she could accompany me. My gratitude to her for sharing the continuing journey is immeasurable. From my parents, Frayn and Clifton Utley, there was not only love and support for a reporter's career, they also exposed me early to life and events beyond the immediate community, beyond the oceans. Without them, needless to say, none of these experiences would have happened.

Chapter 1

STARTING YOUNG

SUDDENLY THE VOICES of radio were no longer alone. Faces were there, pictures, images moving on a screen: the face and image of a man. He was seated behind a desk speaking to me, an eleven-year-old sitting in a living room, listening to and watching the news. Yes, watching it! I was alone, and not alone. At the same moment he was also speaking to an audience that was growing rapidly as communities across the nation plugged in to what would soon be transcontinental television.

The man behind the desk was nattily dressed for the black-and-white screen. There was, invariably, a carnation stuck in his boutonniere. On his head was a carefully placed hairpiece. And in front of him, on the front edge of the desk, his name was spelled out in all its John Cameron Swayze length. The desk, in a studio in New York City, was important. It was more than a prop on which to lay a script. Just as a lectern grants weight to a college professor delivering a lecture or a pulpit elevates a Sunday preacher pronouncing the Lord's message, the desk quickly became an essential symbol of authority for the television newscaster. It also provided a stage for objects we do not see on news programs today: an ashtray on the desk next to Swayze, and in the background a discreetly placed but highly visible carton of Camel cigarettes, the sponsor of the fifteen-minute newscast.

When the network newscasts were launched in the 1948–1949 season with Swayze on NBC and Douglas Edwards on CBS, neither was a major figure in broadcast news. Swayze had worked as a newscaster for NBC on the West Coast and had been brought to New York to deliver a morning network news broadcast on radio. But when the audience for his show began to decline, management told him he was through at NBC. Of course if he was interested, an executive told Swayze, there were some NBC people laying plans for television news. Perhaps he might talk with them. Swayze left the glamorous broadcasting heart of NBC in Rockefeller Center and took a taxi up to 106th street in East Harlem, where the future of television news was in its unglamorous incubation chamber. Swayze went to work covering the 1948 political conventions in Philadelphia, the first to be carried on television, and found his future. His particular gift was not his journalistic or writing skills or the carnation on his lapel, but his memory. He could memorize long passages of news without having to look down at his script, a valuable talent before the invention of the TelePrompTer.

That a job which entailed sitting behind a desk speaking words largely written by someone else while staring into a camera would one day be among the most coveted, richly compensated positions in broadcasting was a future not yet divined. The word "anchorman" had not yet been uttered. Swayze and Edwards were news-casters, not commentators. The senior news talents of radio, such as Edward R. Murrow and Eric Sevareid, were suspicious of television's ability to report news with the editorial depth they could provide with their writing and voices and, at times, their opinions. Nor did they feel comfortable with the new medium, suspecting, perhaps, that they would not be very good at it. Thus they left the door open for Swayze and Edwards.

Swayze's was not necessarily the image that the NBC news department preferred to present to the public, but his was the one the sponsor wanted, and in those early days in television the sponsor could even impose its brand on the title of the network newscast: the *Camel News Caravan*. Indeed, at the end of the broadcast the screen was filled with a close-up shot of a burning cigarette in an ashtray, its smoke curling up languidly as an announcer intoned that the program had been "produced for Camel cigarettes by NBC News." For those concerned with sponsor interference in the news content of the program, let us note that there were only three prohibitions: no live camel could be shown (real camels were dirty, the sponsor thought), no "no smoking" sign could appear on screen, and no cigars were permitted. When the producer of the *Camel News Caravan* pointed out in the early 1950s that such restrictions made it difficult to cover news of Winston Churchill as prime minister of Great Britain, Camel granted special dispensation for the Churchill cigar.

The income from the *Camel News Caravan* paid for the early development of NBC News. The tobacco industry was not yet treated as a public health hazard, and cigarette manufacturers were among the most visible advertisers on the television screen. Commercials showed doctors (or actors in white coats portraying doctors) assuring us of the benign qualities of tobacco, while popular singers in a recording studio testified that Camels did not damage their precious, income-earning throats. NBC News was not alone in giving cigarette companies free rein. In 1954 CBS made Walter Cronkite the host of a morning breakfast-time program to compete with NBC's young and successful *Today* program. One of the on-air duties of the (already) veteran newsman was to deliver commercials, including lighting up and puffing on a Winston cigarette. In his memoirs Cronkite writes of his discomfort in the role of journalist as pitchman, but the journalist's side won out on one issue. Instead of saying, "Winston tastes good like a cigarette should," he said, "Winston tastes good as a cigarette should." Whatever writer's satisfaction Cronkite may have taken from defending proper grammar, the victory was short-lived. The sponsor insisted that "like" would sell more cigarettes than "as." If Cronkite could not bring himself to speak the Winston lines correctly, they could find someone else to do it. And they did.

Today, network television time is too expensive for one company or one advertising budget to sponsor an entire program. But in the 1950s, in television's infancy, it was still affordable. Texaco sponsored Milton Berle, and Alcoa Aluminum funded Murrow's *See It Now* for several years. Oldsmobile put its brand on the CBS newscast just as Camel did on NBC news. The potential for conflicts of interest between the independence of journalists and the demands of a sponsor were not yet seen as conflicts. Or if they were, broadcast executives in a young industry were not so concerned as to reject the sponsor's money. In the early 1950s Americans were more enthralled by the novelty of television than suspicious of its power to influence.

And what were we seeing on the small screen during those early newscasts? There was war in Korea. The film was black-and-white and silent, and it showed little combat and few casualties.

At the end of each week NBC in New York sent a reel of collected news film to Chicago, where my father was now the leading television newscaster and commentator. He wanted to know which film stories had been seen by a national audience before he showed them again to his local viewers. Each weeknight I wrote out a detailed record of the film reports shown on the *Camel News Caravan*—my first reporting job and a condition for a modest increase in my weekly allowance. Growing up in the earliest trial-and-error years of television news, I was learning the craft by osmosis.

How good was the news coverage? No amount of nostalgia or yearning for some "golden era" of television can polish up what we were seeing, or not seeing, on the screen. In their fifteen minutes, the NBC and CBS newscasts offered skimpy reports. Most of them were brief film clips "voiced over" by a disembodied voice or excerpts of a news conference or an occasional interview with a political figure. All too often "reporting" a national or international event was nothing more than filming and then broadcasting a statement by a government official; the statement was the accepted story. But then, in the 1950s, the "credibility gap" that separated press, public, and government had not yet opened, and authority was not rigorously questioned. Television, like much of the written press, allowed Senator Joseph McCarthy to have a long, unimpeded run as he hurled accusations and ruined lives before anyone challenged him. The resonance that still surrounds the CBS *See It Now* program of Edward R. Murrow and Fred Friendly, which attacked McCarthy, is due not only to what it said but to the fact that it was the only program that dared to say it at the time.

Many of television's limitations and even shortcomings were understandable. It was a new medium. The technology was primitive. Visually, television offered little more than the newsreel, which was still playing at the local movie theater, although it was presented with new stories daily rather than once a week. The news film that was broadcast on television was actually provided by newsreel companies—Fox Movietone for NBC and Telenews for CBS. Like the newsreels, the news programs often ended with a feature about pets or the latest fashions; women's hats were a particular favorite. Aside from the war in Korea, television news did not pretend to cover the world in any depth. Indeed, John Cameron Swayze's most familiar words came near the end of the broadcast, when he would announce that it was now time to "hop-scotch the world for headlines," referring to important news stories for which no pictures were available. They would therefore be skipped over lightly. Critics did not complain. Neither they nor viewers expected much of substance to emerge from the new piece of furniture with the flickering screen in the living room. From the beginning television news was mainly a headline service, and a very limited one at that. If viewers wanted real news, in depth and breadth, they turned to the newspapers or the weekly news-magazines. Yet television did offer that one exciting, indisputable advance that made up for all its shortcomings: images of news events were coming into our living rooms. They moved and in doing so often moved us as they spoke to us. They were working their way into the marrow of our lives.

In 1951 the high point of my week came on Saturday afternoon when Dad would take me along to the NBC studios in Chicago as he prepared one of his news and commentary programs. If television technology was limited and news film scarce, the staff was minuscule. There were no copyboys to run the mundane errands in the newsroom, so I would climb on a chair to cut the news agency wire copy as it poured in from around the world on the teletype machines I had first encountered as a seven-year-old.

I was fascinated by the datelines and bylines of foreign correspondents in distant lands. I also pestered anyone I could find, asking questions about how broadcasting worked. Fortunately, there were some good role models at NBC in Chicago, including a disc jockey named Dave Garroway, who would become the first host of the *Today* show, an announcer, Hugh Downs, and my father's assistant—a young man making the transition from newspapers to television, John Chancellor. Our paths would cross again.

ON A SUNNY June morning in 1961, the president of Carleton College, in Northfield, Minnesota (a town that had succeeded magnificently in living up to its motto, Cows, Colleges and Contentment), shook my hand and handed me a diploma, which I took to mean that I was now a certified adult. I had spent four years absorbing a liberal arts education and working on the campus radio station as a newscaster and ultimately the news director. Not that it involved much work. Our only news lifeline to the world was a United Press teletype machine. It was provided free of charge by Lucky Strike cigarettes in exchange for Lucky Strike getting free sponsorship of all the news programs on station KARL. Did I feel any conflict of interest or even the slightest twinge of conscience as I read the Lucky Strike commercials that were mailed to us by the company's ad agency? Not the slightest. Our broadcasts were not heard beyond the college dormitories, but heck, we said to ourselves, we were following in the footsteps of the *Camel News Caravan* with John Cameron Swayze or Walter Cronkite puffing away on his Winston. Like NBC, our tiny station was not about to turn down a sponsor. It was a different era.

When I left Northfield, there was a world to face and a career to choose. The goal was clear—to become a foreign correspondent for a television network—and a plan had been worked out. I would study overseas for a year or two in order to learn a language or two. Then I would find a job as a "stringer" for an American newspaper to build up a portfolio of articles as well as experience. Then I would add a part-time job as a radio stringer for one of the networks, which would, in the fullness of time, lead to a position in television. There was only one obstacle to the success of this foolproof (I thought) plan. The United States was approaching the high noon of the Cold War. The building of the Berlin Wall was two months away, the Cuban missile crisis was a year off, and as a young man I faced the inescapable prospect of military service. The draft, and the two years it would take out of my young, "anxious to get going" life, hung over my head more as an inconvenience than the mortal threat or moral outrage it would become during the Vietnam War.

One afternoon shortly before graduation, luck, or perhaps coincidence (the two are not always distinguishable), intervened. A notice appeared on a college bulletin board announcing a new foreign language program offered by the U.S. Army Reserve. At the time, an alternative to the two-year draft was to perform six months' active duty followed by five and a half years of weekly reserve meetings. Under the proposed program, which was pinned to the bulletin board, the active duty would be lengthened to allow for one year of intensive language training at the Army Language School in Monterey, California, hardly a hardship post. When the language training was finished, so the notice promised, the members of this special language program would return to civilian status as reservists. If ever opportunity was writ large, it was on that bulletin board. Two days after graduation, I walked into the Fifth Army headquarters in Chicago, where a major cordially asked me to sit down and assured me that the army would like to teach me a language.

"How about Lithuanian?" he asked. I hesitated a moment, hoping he was joking. He wasn't. I cleared my throat, tried to hide my disappointment, and replied, "I was thinking of something a bit broader, like French or German."

"We're not offering those 'tourist' languages," he replied brusquely. "We need specialists in the exotic ones." I did not know what the military considered to be "exotic." "And don't forget," the major continued, "if you can speak Lithuanian, you have a leg up on Latvian." I acknowledged that a Baltic language might be of help were I planning on a political career that would one day culminate in my election as an alderman from one of Chicago's ethnic wards. But that was not how I saw my future.

The major paused and then opened the center drawer of his steel, military-issue desk. He pulled out a sheet of paper and studied it for a minute. "I'll be honest with you, Garrick. I think you are missing a rare opportunity with Lithuanian. However, we may be able to accommodate you. We have an opening in Polish." There was a silence in the room. We were eyeball-to-eyeball and the U.S. Army had blinked, at least a little. But my feeling of elation quickly gave way to doubt. Should I accept Polish? It was a serious offer. If I turned it down, I would still have the draft to face. Suddenly I was in my first job negotiation. "Polish is more interesting," I granted, "particularly if I plan to run for mayor of Chicago one day. But since my plans lie elsewhere…" The major shook his head. "I really don't know if we can help you. Just leave us your phone number. We'll call you if something else opens up."

The next two days were consumed by worry that I had made a terrible mistake. The growing prospect of the U.S. Army's Infantry School, and a possible winter posting on a hilltop along the Korean

DMZ, did not seem to be a better start to adult life than learning Polish. Three days later a telephone call brought welcome relief. The major was on the line, his voice brimming with confidence. "Garrick, I have good news. You can study Russian."

The eleven months at the language school were intensive and mentally exhausting. For six hours a day I spent military duty in small classrooms as patient instructors, many of them elderly human relics of the last days of the czar, drilled the rich beauty and brain-curdling complexities of the Russian language into me. As they did, I saw two doors opening. One led to a foreign language and a distant culture. The other offered a perspective of my own language and culture as viewed from another tongue, just like an astronaut who no longer views the earth in the same familiar way after seeing it from space.

In September 1962 military life ended. I took off my uniform, said good-by to early morning reveilles, let my hair grow longer, and took off for Europe. The first stop was Berlin and a year of graduate study at the Free University in the western part of the divided city. In Europe university students are left on a long academic leash, and I used mine to roam through the city's rich cultural life, as well as show up for assorted lectures and seminars on European history and international affairs. It was a last delicious fling with student life. When it ended in the summer of 1963, it was time to get serious about becoming a foreign correspondent. Opportunity was waiting for me in Brussels.

Chapter 2

INITIATION

I ARRIVED BY TRAIN, which, then as now, is the best way to travel in Europe. I traveled light, which is the best way to travel anywhere. In one hand I carried a suitcase, in the other a portable typewriter, and in the inside pocket of an ill-fitting sport jacket, a letter. The suitcase held the meager wardrobe of a twenty-three-year-old American. The letter, carefully folded in my pocket, was the chance I had hoped for: an offer from NBC News correspondent John Chancellor, a journalist of exceptional class and experience. He was inviting me to be his office assistant, coffee maker, bill payer, and NBC Radio stringer in Brussels. The pay was $62.50 a week, which, I was informed, was nonnegotiable. Still, I asked myself, what was money when I had a foot in the network door?

Only there was no door; there was not even an office.

Chancellor had arrived in Brussels a week before and had not yet found a suitable bureau. So we enjoyed the pleasures of an interim office—a table at an outdoor cafe, where each morning we met over coffee and croissants to read the newspapers and plan the day. I was soon relishing the style as well as the substance of journalism and was learning how both were about to change dramatically. NBC's evening newscast, the *Huntley-Brinkley Report,* and the *CBS Evening News with Walter Cronkite* were expanding from fifteen minutes to a half hour. Chancellor had been sent to Europe to provide the longer reports that the new program would demand. He explained that I was getting in on the ground floor of a new era in television news. A thirty-minute program each weekday evening promised more than twice the time to cover the news and offered new ways to present it. There would be as many as five film reports a night, each running two and a half minutes to five minutes. The possibilities seemed limitless. Television news was growing up.

By early September 1963, the half hour network news was on NBC and CBS. We had rented office space, and I found myself alone in it most of the time as Chancellor traveled across Europe in search of stories. There was a message in that activity, although I did not fully understand it at the time. The longer half hour format demanded that the correspondent travel to the location of the news event. This was better journalism, and it was also better television. Viewers wanted to see the reporter on the scene. Moreover, a three- or four-minute report had to be produced as well as reported. The correspondent as storyteller had to provide a narrative line—the requisite beginning, middle, and end to each report. These were new concepts in television news. Fortunately for me, in 1963, many radio journalists were still unable or unwilling to make the leap to the new medium, which provided an opportunity for a newcomer eager to learn how to work with pictures and sound as well as words. As I minded the NBC office in Brussels, offering occasional radio reports or submitting story ideas for television coverage, I wondered how long I would have to wait for my chance.

About six months, as it turned out. New York requested a brief report for NBC's *Huntley-Brinkley Report*. Length: forty-five seconds, on camera. Subject: the sale of chemical plants to the Soviet Union by Western European companies at a time when American firms were not allowed to compete for sales to the Communists. It was not exactly a burning issue of the day, so I realized that I was facing an audition. I hurriedly gathered more information on chemical plants than I thought any viewer would want to know, looked for a location with a suitable European background for my television debut, then stayed up until two A.M. writing a script.

The next morning I awoke with a case of opening-day jitters. I was starting at the very top of the profession on the *Huntley-Brinkley Report*, the most watched news program in the United States. If I failed, if the corporate mandarins back in New York turned their invisible thumbs down, I could only work my way down the professional ladder. I read the script again and was disappointed in what I found to be a report of marginal importance and certainly of no general interest. Still, I understood that what the faceless producers and executives in New York were looking for was simply whether a would-be correspondent in Brussels, whose face they did not know, would be "acceptable for television," to use the network language of the time. I looked nervously out the window on a gray March morning and hoped that rain would not interfere with the filming. As I dressed, I repeated the advice and admonition offered by John Chancellor: "Keep your sentences short, and your voice low." The plan was for a film crew from the NBC News bureau in London to arrive that afternoon. They would film my on camera "standup" and ship it on the overnight cargo flight to New York for broadcast the next evening.

The cameraman and his sound assistant arrived on time in Brussels, but unfortunately the camera and the rest of their equipment landed in Paris. For travelers lost luggage is an inconvenience, but for television news crews it brings work to a dead stop. An airline employee with a practiced, professional smile assured us the camera would be on the next plane from Paris. It was not. Then on the next flight, we were again assured. It was not. A call from our Paris office promised that it would be on the last flight arriving at 10:30 P.M., which would allow barely an hour to film before the departure of the midnight cargo flight. This dilemma at least left us time for a leisurely dinner. One of Belgium's virtues is its cooking. You can get a good meal anywhere, including the Brussels airport, which is about as demanding a test as exists. The cameraman, Chris Callery, his assistant, and I slipped into a corner table of the restaurant. My eyes, guided by my meager salary, searched for the budget special, the usual grilled steak with french fries. Chris, though, went right to the top of the menu, found fresh oysters, and ordered eighteen of them. "That will make up for the bother of all this waiting," he said with great relish. I was impressed. Television people obviously knew how to live well, at least on assignment and with an expense account.

We worked our way slowly through dinner as Chris told stories of wars he had covered in the Congo, South Yemen, and Cyprus. "Compared to that," I said, "it must be boring to film one short report by a novice reporter." "Not at all," he replied. "A few months ago they sent me from London to South America, and the only thing I shot was one lousy on camera standup with a correspondent. They want me to go—I go." He called it being a "fire-

14

man," but a fireman, I could see, who traveled the world first-class while eating oysters on the run.

Suddenly the stories stopped. Chris's healthy, tanned face had turned a sickly, pasty hue. Without a word he rose from his chair and walked rapidly to the men's room with as much dignity as he could muster. The oysters had struck. We now had no cameraman.

John Chancellor arrived to oversee my debut as the camera equipment finally turned up on the last flight. We maneuvered it through the customs bureaucracy and set it up, along with the lights, in a small passenger lounge across the hall from a conveniently located men's room. There would be no atmospheric European background, just a beige curtain in the room and a fake potted fern in front of it. We had no choice. Outside, the Sabena cargo plane was being prepared for its departure. We had half an hour, at the most, to film a good "take."

I stood in front of a television camera for the first time and rehearsed reading my script. I looked up and saw the camera lens. No longer was it a simple device for capturing a picture. Now it was an intimidating, impersonal object with all the warmth and reassurance of a rifle barrel aimed between my eyes. It was an alien creature that took but did not give back. Every television broadcaster has to face it—the lens—the only visual channel to reach the audience. You have to make it your friend or at the very least your tool. There is no way around it, only through it.

"Imagine you are speaking to a friend in Chicago," Chancellor suggested, sensing my unease. "Don't think of the millions of viewers watching. Think of one person." It didn't help. I saw only the cold, dark lens, and I heard awkward phrases spilling from my mouth that bore no resemblance to the crafted words in my script.

"Let's try it," Chancellor said, undeterred, as he crossed the hall to Chris's sanctuary, stuck his head in the door of the men's room, and shouted, "You're on!" Chris came out, still wan of face, focused the camera, and we tried the first take. No good. The sentences were short and declarative, but that was because my eyes were glued to the script. The camera was filming the top of my head.

And so it continued, much to the amusement of a small crowd that had gathered to watch the ordeal. Between each take Chris would retire to the men's room and return after a few minutes. Takes two, three, and four were better, but not good enough for Chancellor, who was watching my performance and his watch with equal intensity.

Take five was acceptable, but we needed one more to be sure that there were two good versions for the film editors in New York to choose from. Take nine did it. The soundman unloaded the film and ran with it to the waiting plane. Chris Callery turned off the lights and disappeared again across the hall. Chancellor and I found a bar nearby. We sat down on stools and each ordered a cognac. I felt glum.

Chancellor, though, was encouraged and offered some memorable advice for a beginner in television. "Forget what happened around you. Forget the bad takes. The audience will never see them," he said. "The only thing that counts on television is what ends up on the screen. I think you've made it."

Chapter 3

THE HIGHEST POWER

W HEN DID the United States become a television society?
Perhaps it was in 1951, when the coaxial cable linked the
nation with moving images from sea to shining sea. On CBS's *See
It Now* Ed Murrow presented to viewers a divided television
screen. On one half was a live picture of the Brooklyn Bridge, on
the other half we saw, also live, the Golden Gate Bridge in San
Francisco. The drama of the moment—the two images joined elec-
tronically—was etched in my mind. And so too was something
else, something about the power of this new technology. Although
Murrow offered eloquent comments on the implications of what
we were seeing, his words were superfluous; no commentary was
needed. The two pictures, visual bookends for the nation, spoke
for themselves.

And so did Lucille Ball. In 1951, while *See It Now* was illustrating the excitement and profundity of a nation linked by images, Ball and her husband, Desi Arnaz, launched *I Love Lucy* on CBS. Following in the footsteps of Milton Berle on NBC, *I Love Lucy* showed beyond doubt, or appeal, where and how the commercial power and wealth of television were to be mined. Nearly half a century later, at the millennium, Lucy and Ricky Ricardo and their neighbors, Fred and Ethel Mertz, are still a vivid, daily, black-and-white presence on commercial television. The few news programs of the caliber and consistency of the now legendary *See It Now* series, however, have been consigned to museum archives and nostalgic symposium discussions about the declining standards of television news. Reportorial rigor, however, requires an acknowledgment of why those great news series existed in the first place. *See It Now*, the pioneer of in-depth television reporting, flourished because of Ed Murrow's stature and also because of the fact that in the early 1950s there was space for it on the CBS schedule, which did not yet have enough successful entertainment programs to fill prime time. By the late 1950s, however, there were plenty of popular entertainment programs, and in 1958 *See It Now* went off the air. Entertainment was too lucrative for a network chieftain to give up prime financial time, on a regular basis, to lower-rated news or public affairs programs. In the direct, but condemning, words of CBS founder William Paley, when asked why news series were disappearing from the network, "the minute has gotten too expensive." But then no one imagined what would occur in 1959.

The quiz show scandals began with a simple and seductive idea: if an old radio quiz program called *The $64 Question* drew an audience, what would happen if a television sponsor offered a much bigger prize? CBS tried it and found out. *The $64,000 Question* and other copycat programs with even higher stakes attracted huge audiences (just as million dollar prizes would more than four decades later). As contestants appeared week after week and neared their big payoff moment, public thralldom to the drama became a national event. Contestants, unknown to the public when they were first led into the quiz show's "isolation booth" to answer the questions, became national figures. Then the bubble burst.

In the autumn of 1959, contestant Charles Van Doren confessed to a congressional committee that his winnings, $129,000 on the NBC program *Twenty-One,* were ill-gotten. The program's producers had fed him the questions in advance, justifying the exercise on the grounds that it was, after all, just an entertainment program. Members of the production team of *The $64,000 Question* testified to the committee that the sponsor, Revlon, had given instructions as to which contestants were dullards and should be gotten off the program and which ones should be allowed to continue. The scandals had nothing to do with television news. But soon they would have everything to do with it.

With their prestige and integrity in shambles, the networks feared not only the public's disillusioned reaction but also a government attempt to tighten the flaccid regulatory controls on television. Within weeks, CBS, which had just dumped *See It Now,* announced the creation of *CBS Reports,* and NBC weighed in with its own documentaries. These prime-time programs would run for years with topics ranging from domestic social issues, such as the exploitation of migrant workers, to stylish tours of the Kremlin and the Louvre. Thus the quiz show scandals, and the networks' reaction to them, provided solid financial and corporate backing for television journalists as the news divisions moved into a tumultuous decade. But salvation came for the wrong reasons: less to serve the public than to defend network television's privileged and increasingly profitable position in American life.

Today it may seem strange, or even quaint, to learn that in 1963, as the debut of the half hour evening newscasts approached, there were skeptics at the networks who wondered whether there would be enough news to fill thirty minutes of broadcast time. Yet the evening newscasts quickly became required viewing. The reason for their success was not to be found in the technology or even in the work of journalists, but in simple, unplanned, unforeseen coincidence, otherwise known as the 1960s. Within a year of the programs' debut, the civil rights movement was joined by other powerful story lines: the urban explosions from Watts to Detroit to New York City as blacks unleashed their frustration and fury and the counterculture movement as the children of white, middle-class Americans rebelled on campuses and in the streets, rebelling against a war, against their government, and against their parents.

It can be argued that 1963 was the year in which the United States finally became a television society, if news is the measure. In that year a Roper poll found, for the first time, that more Americans (55 percent) said television was their main source of news than those (53 percent) who said newspapers were. In November 1963 the assassination of John F. Kennedy and television's coverage of the nation's agony bonded viewers to the networks and to an event that came hurtling through the screen in a way it could never rise off a printed page. The seemingly endless parade of jarring events, from the freedom marches in the South to fighting in the Mekong Delta to protest on the steps of the Pentagon and eventually to the summit gathering of a generation in a farm field in Woodstock, New York, offered action, drama, and conflict. They were visual experiences filled with passionate voices made to order for the television screen, shocking, surprising, and striking the emotional nerve endings of the viewer in front of it. From the earliest *Mercury* liftoffs at Cape Canaveral to the *Apollo 11* landing on the lunar dust in 1969, television news was there. And the viewers were there in front of their screens at supper time, as night after night television news offered the one ingredient that the dramas, comedies, westerns, and sitcoms that followed in prime time could not hope to compete with: the drawing power of reality.

The 1960s and television news were made for each other. NBC and CBS quickly responded to the emotive stories and visual events with rapidly expanding news divisions fueled by what appeared to be unlimited network budgets. In contrast to the 1950s, news was now an affordable, even indispensable, loss leader. The motivation was a jumble of commercial, human, and journalistic concerns. Network executives, remembering their close call with the quiz show scandals and recognizing that their growing commercial bonanza from mass entertainment programming was due largely to the oligopoly they held at the pleasure of the Congress and the Federal Communications Commission, saw extensive news coverage as an effective public relations service. The same executives could also savor the personal influence and public esteem that came from running a network, and indeed a medium, that was demonstrating its new power with each evening newscast. Ultimately, though, there was a journalistic imperative for the expanded effort and money going into network news. The events of the 1960s were too big for the newest and most powerful medium in the land to ignore. For the charter members of the new age of television journalism it seemed like heaven. At NBC there was the edict known as "CBS plus thirty." Robert Kintner, president of the National Broadcasting Company, ordered that when NBC and CBS were covering live news events, including the national political conventions, NBC would stay on the air for half an hour after CBS News signed off. In network television, where time is money and entertainment earns more advertising dollars than news, it was the ultimate act of largesse. It was also shrewd. NBC understood that news coverage was defining the networks in the eyes of the public. Overseas news operations were expanded and each year ended on NBC and CBS with foreign correspondents flown home for lengthy, televised roundtable discussions of world events.

For those producing carefully crafted documentaries, instead of chasing the daily news, life was particularly good. Not only was network money available, but NBC and CBS decreed that all documentaries would be produced in-house. The rationale behind this was that a network news division needed to have direct control of the editorial content it was presenting to the public, since it was responsible for that content. A familiar tag line for news programs ran, "This program was produced by NBC News, which is solely responsible for its content." The decision to produce and control all news programming within the news divisions also served to enhance the size and budgets of the network news organizations. It excluded independent documentary filmmakers, who complained that they were being prevented from reaching a large audience, not only because the networks refused to carry their programs but also because, outside the networks, there was no way to reach a significant number of viewers. This made it difficult for the independent producers to raise money for projects that would be seen by few people. Not surprisingly, journalists at the networks did not see anything wrong with the system.

Was it too good to last? True, Ed Murrow was off the air and in 1965 his former *See It Now* producer, Fred Friendly, would quit as

CBS News president when the network chose to carry entertainment programs, including a rerun of *I Love Lucy*, instead of live coverage of Senate hearings on Vietnam. Network entertainment executives continued to grumble about the time news was taking from their programs, and even louder complaints came from the owners of local television stations affiliated with the networks, who were not happy to see their ratings and advertising revenue go down when a documentary replaced a popular entertainment program or a special news report delayed the *Tonight Show with Johnny Carson*. To the credit of the top network chiefs, these complaints and pressures were not passed on to the reporters and producers. We were able to get on with our work.

THE CAMERAMAN was having trouble setting his shot. He moved the heavy sound camera, mounted on a tripod, to the left of the young woman standing in front of him. Then he moved it to the right, but he was still unhappy. We were in a boutique in Oxford Street in London. The woman, who was modeling a dress she had just purchased, waited patiently for our interview to begin. Next to her, her husband, a London bus driver, with their year-old child in his arms, was clearly nervous about the family's imminent television exposure. Behind me and the cameraman, the store's public relations woman was pleased with the free publicity the new line of dresses was about to receive. She understood the problem facing the cameraman, literally facing him. The dress had no top. The standard head and chest framing of the interview would place the woman's exposed and amply developed breasts in the middle of television screens across America.

It was July 1964. Tastes and trends were being challenged on both sides of the Atlantic, and the topless dress, of fleeting fame, was one of the most attention-seeking, and attention-grabbing, stunts of the summer. What the audience in the United States saw on the *Today* show a few mornings later was the back of the woman and her infamous dress, and the face of a young NBC reporter trying, with great difficulty, to maintain eye contact with his interview subject.

This was not exactly what I had envisaged when I performed my audition in Brussels. Once NBC management had seen the film in New York and executives had decided that I was indeed "acceptable for television," I was sent to our London bureau. For two months I studied the basics of this new craft: how to write words to fit pictures, how to make pictures fit words, or ideally how to arrive at a marriage of the two to produce an informative and engaging television report.

My first assignment was unlikely to make the blood race. I was asked to prepare a piece for the *Huntley-Brinkley Report* on the discovery of vast natural gas deposits off the coast of Holland. That the North Sea would eventually yield a bonanza of oil was suspected but not yet confirmed. Still, the gas strikes alone, and what they meant for the Dutch, was a story worthy of coverage. I was joined by an essential element in any television story, an experienced camera team: the brothers Peter and Klaus Dehmel, who arrived from our Berlin bureau. They knew how to film a story. I needed only to provide them with the narrative, the building blocks of picturesque Dutch seaside communities, and interviews with geologists, small-town mayors, and residents whose lives would undoubtedly be enriched by the invisible gas that lay beneath the North Sea waters lapping the shore in front of them. We spent four days moving along the northern coast, and with each day I discovered not only that I was enjoying the work but also that I felt confident doing it. There were, however, certain conventions of a television news story that needed to be observed, as I was about to discover. On television even the most straight-forward story about natural gas (especially natural gas!) required an extra sizzle.

At the end of our Dutch wanderings, we reached Rotterdam. A producer from the *Huntley-Brinkley Report* flew in from London to supervise the final structuring of the story and my writing of the script. I had already fashioned a first draft that laid out the nec-essary facts and included a good cross-section of public comment from the Dutch burghers. As we sat down at a table in a hotel room, the producer, with a paternal smile, assured me that there is no script that cannot be improved. I was now in my first script conference. The producer had little trouble with the flow of my story. But the first time the word "gas" appeared in the first para-graph, he leaned over and wrote in "and oil."

"But this isn't a story about oil," I objected. The producer nod-ded his head and kept reading the script. Each time he encountered "gas" he added "oil." I protested again that no one had yet con-firmed the presence of oil in the North Sea. The producer put down his pencil, took off his glasses, and replied defensively that, yes, he knew that. His problem was that when he had first attempted to sell the story to his superiors in New York their reac-tion was less than enthusiastic. When he ginned up his pitch with the added possibility of oil, he sold the story. Oil carried an emo-tive punch that gas could not hope to equal.

"So, we have to put oil in the script," he said with finality. We did, wrapping the word gently in modifiers and couching it in spec-ulation. Oil, of course, was discovered in the North Sea, and today the great Rotterdam script debate seems of minuscule importance. But for a twenty-four-year-old apprentice reporter on his first big assignment it was a lesson. In print journalism a story that does not excite and hold attention is not a major problem, since the reader can turn to another article in the same newspaper or magazine. In television, a story that does not grab and hold attention can lead to the cardinal sin of losing a viewer to another channel. In those embryonic days of television news there was already a recognition of the built-in competitive need to make television news stories "sexier" or more dramatic, to make them good television as well as good journalism.

The extent to which journalists coming from a background in print or radio would have to adjust to the demands of television had been laid out in a lengthy memo to the NBC News staff. Its author was Reuven Frank, the founding producer of the half hour Huntley-Brinkley program. He described where the program and television were headed: "Every news story should, without any sacrifice of probity or responsibility, display the attributes of fiction, of drama. It should have structure and conflict, problem and denouement, rising action and falling action, a beginning, a middle and an end. These are not only the essentials of drama; they are the essentials of narrative. We are in the business of narrative because we are in the business of communication." Frank added, "The highest power of television journalism is not in the transmission of information, but in the transmission of experience." Nothing has proven him wrong.

ONE SLOW news day in the early summer of 1964, I was paging through the London tabloids—a dependable source of quaint, shocking, or simply ridiculous stories that rarely seem to burrow their way into the more respectable, if somewhat duller, press. A

London company was promoting the idea of using motor scooters to provide a taxi service to rush harried businessmen through congested city traffic. As an added inducement, the scooters were to be driven by attractive young women. On a lovely spring day we loaded a camera onto the back of a small truck. I mounted a scooter behind a blonde chauffeur and off we went, recording our interview as we zipped down the Mall in front of Buckingham Palace. I soon realized that I was being taken for a ride in more ways than one. The driver kept talking about her husband as the camera recorded our interview.

"Let's not talk about your husband," I shouted over the traffic as we rounded Trafalgar Square. "You are supposed to be young, pretty and, who knows, perhaps available. This is television."

"But my husband runs the public relations company which thought this up to promote the motor scooter. Isn't he clever?"

I had to agree that he was as we headed back toward Hyde Park. I was learning about the inherent, insatiable need television news has for interesting, amusing, and above all visual stories. I had learned that the people who had the stories needed television to communicate them, to push their products and causes. An unspoken alliance was being formed. In the case of the would-be (but never was) motor scooter taxi service, the changing of a few declarative sentences in the script to the conditional assuaged my journalistic conscience. And after the story was broadcast, we received requests for more "fun" stories.

London was a fertile place to do such pieces. The Beatles were at their peak and the Rolling Stones were emerging as a new, more edgy rock force. The stature of the royal family seemed inviolate, its members unaware of the power about to be unleashed by music, media, and the rebellion of the 1960s, which would eventually undermine established institutions that confused stolidity with solidity. Although Britain was fun, it was not where news, hot news, was happening. In the summer of 1964 the journalistic tide was swinging to Asia, to South Vietnam, where the United States and 15,000 American military advisers were backing a losing cause in the struggle against the Communist Vietcong. For television, the medium and the moment were about to meet.

Chapter 4

PICTURES OF WAR

T HE SAMPAN cut through the river's muddy water. Its small outboard motor offered the only sound as we glided downstream through flat, silent fields. Every few minutes we passed simple wooden houses standing precariously on high stilts along the water's edge. Under each house small, flat-bottomed boats were tied to one of the wooden supports like horses tethered to a hitching post. This was the Mekong Delta in eastern Cambodia in November 1964, the flood season, when sampans were the only means of travel.

I sat on a rough wooden plank in front, looking ahead to see what would appear around the next bend in the river whose green banks were beginning to narrow. As they did, the water struck out in random directions, forming channels and filling manmade canals that ran off across the rice fields. Behind me, in green army fatigues and polished black boots, sat the district police chief. Behind him were two Cambodian militiamen lazily smoking cigarettes, their carbines resting across their laps. Following in our wake was a second motorized sampan carrying an army lieutenant and six more soldiers with weapons. Next to me in the bow sat an American with sharply chiseled features, a receding hairline, and twenty years' experience in Asia. Grant Wolfkill was an NBC cameraman based in Hong Kong.

As we moved deeper into the delta and rounded each bend in the river, we drew closer to the border of South Vietnam, our eyes open for evidence of the Communist Vietcong on the Cambodian side of the border. Our destination was a small outpost called Banteay Chakrey. Even on the most detailed maps it was no more than a dot marking the remains of a small fort, a piece of colonial detritus abandoned by the French ten years earlier.

One month earlier an American special forces captain had been killed in a battle along a stream that formed the border. Reports said that the South Vietnamese government troops, with their American advisers, had been fired on from the Cambodian border post at Banteay Chakrey, that men dressed like Vietcong guerrillas had been seen running out of the fort, crossing to the Vietnamese side of a small river, where they captured the American. His body was later found floating in the reeds. The Vietcong, if that is who they were, then returned across the stream to the sanctuary of Cambodian territory.

Banteay Chakrey had been the site of several similar incidents, and Cambodia had kept the door firmly closed to prying foreign journalists. Now the door had been opened slightly for reporters who were invited to cover the celebration of Cambodia's eleventh anniversary of independence. Once in Phnom Penh, residing in the elegantly decaying splendor of the Hotel Royal, I asked our hosts and press minders to visit this isolated and mysterious border post. To no one's surprise we received noncommittal smiles and lengthy explanations of how difficult it would be to reach that remote area during the rainy season. Wouldn't we prefer to visit Angkor Wat, we were asked? We assured our hosts, and promised ourselves, that the magnificent temple ruins of the Khmer empire were high on our list, but news is news, and right now it was in a tiny fort on the border with South Vietnam.

It took some time for the Cambodian bureaucracy under the control of the country's mercurial ruler, Prince Norodom Siha-nouk, to decide whether we should be allowed to proceed to the border. We might find Vietcong, which would be embarrassing to the Cambodians, who denied that they allowed them sanctuary. On the other hand, we might see South Vietnamese troops crossing into Cambodia, which would support Prince Sihanouk's claim that his territory was being violated by the United States and its Saigon allies. Late one afternoon the decision was made. Our trip, once impossible, was now imminent. The next morning we left Phnom Penh at a quarter to six and drove eastward for two hours. Where the road ended, we transferred to a small boat with an inboard motor and headed downriver in a southeasterly direction for anoth-er hour and a half until we transferred again to the two sampans.

"You will see there are no Vietcong here!" The police chief's voice came from behind us in French as our eyes searched the pass-ing rice fields and particularly the houses standing along the water's edge. "Of course many of the farmers here are Vietnamese. They have lived on this side of the border for generations." And, I thought to myself, they all wear the same black shirt and trousers worn by the Vietcong, a natural camouflage for operating across a remote region, where ethnic Vietnamese and Cambodians could easily move back and forth across an ill-defined border.

We stopped at a small village built on slightly higher and drier ground to change to even smaller sampans for the final leg of the trip. The village had a dozen small structures, one woman, and about twenty men dressed in black, some carrying weapons and all armed with sullen faces aimed at us. Were they Vietcong? The police commissioner told us they were the local civil guard. I couldn't tell, but Wolfkill felt uneasy. Four years earlier, while covering the war in Laos for NBC News, he had been captured by the Communist forces and held prisoner for a year and a half, much of the time in squalid conditions in solitary confinement. It was an ordeal that nearly cost him his life and later led President Kennedy to award him the Medal of Freedom. The experience had left him with the gift of survival instinct. When we left the village, Grant spoke softly so as not to be overheard, saying that the silent hostility and the eyes drained of expression were the same he had experienced among his Pathet Lao and North Vietnamese captors. You could not prove that they were Vietcong, he said in a whisper, but he felt it. It made him nervous. And that made me nervous.

Earlier in the voyage, higher up the river, safely distanced from the border and the war, farmers had waved warmly as their children came running toward us, smiling and shouting as we glided slowly by. Now, as we approached the border and passed through more tiny hamlets, we saw men lurking in small homes, standing back in the shadows of doorways, acting as if they wanted to see us but didn't want us to see them. In one house Grant spotted at least ten men. Some were armed. One of our guides also saw the men and turned quickly to us to see whether we had observed them too. We gave no sign that we had.

We pushed on.

Pictures of War

I HAD FLOWN from London to Saigon four months earlier, in July 1964. The *Huntley-Brinkley Report* wanted a permanent correspondent based in South Vietnam. I was young, cheap, and available, and was given a six-week tryout assignment, which confirmed, if confirmation is necessary, the importance of timing in one's life. I arrived in Vietnam four weeks before the Gulf of Tonkin crisis, the real and imagined confrontations between North Vietnamese naval vessels and American destroyers that led to the first American air strikes against North Vietnam. It also led to the Senate resolution that handed the Johnson administration the authority for the military escalation that would lead to the nation's first lost war. The tryout had turned into an indefinite assignment, and now my baptism in war lay six hundred yards ahead as we approached the border post at Banteay Chakrey.

We could see and hear the shells exploding on the Vietnamese side of the border as we tied up at a landing alongside the fort and dashed inside. What we found was a collection of a few low, dilapidated buildings containing supplies and sleeping quarters, surrounded by earthen ramparts and rusting barbed wire fences. The entire square-shaped fortification was no more than fifty yards across. At each corner stood a concrete blockhouse. We raced for the closest one and climbed the narrow steps to the observation level. Standing under a protective roof and looking out through an opening, we could see the river at our feet marking the border. Across it, no more than thirty yards away, lay the flat, marshy Mekong Delta of South Vietnam. In the distance, hidden in the tall reeds, we could hear a battle raging. It was clear that the Vietnamese side of the river was held by the Vietcong, and we were told that an American special forces camp was located five miles away. As we looked through field glasses, we saw a line of soldiers in the distance, spread out left to right advancing toward us. The late morning sun was not quite overhead, and the figures were too far away to identify. Some, though, were clearly taller than the others. Grant and I were certain that they were Americans and that what we were watching was a Vietnamese army unit, with its U.S. advisers, trying to trap Vietcong guerrillas along the border. The shells falling in front of us were intended to cut off their escape back into Cambodia. It was exactly the type of operation that had led to the death of the American captain a month earlier. We had hit a news jackpot.

Suddenly the firing grew more intense. Shells from 105 mm howitzers located at the American/Vietnamese base five miles away came roaring in, landing with a dull thump in the mud or in the river, where they sent up explosive geysers of water. When the 105s fell silent, mortar shells began bursting in front of us. They were being fired by the South Vietnamese troops in the field, three shells in sequence, then a pause, then three more—the textbook procedure American advisers had drilled into the Vietnamese. After forty-five minutes the shooting stopped. We climbed down from the tower and went out into the yard for a sandwich lunch. The police commissioner commandeered a tattered, reclining beach chair, placed himself in the shade of a tree, and proclaimed happily, "You see, there are no Vietcong here. But the Americans and Vietnamese attack our country. You will show that in your country." The last part of his speech sounded like an order. I replied that we were certainly going to show what we had filmed, but as Grant and I walked around the fort we faced a perplexing question: what were we actually seeing? There were about forty men within the perimeter of the fort, an unimpressive collection of farmers who had been issued old weapons. One of the militiamen was in a foxhole with a machine gun. When we went to film him, he had to be shown how to handle the weapon.

I walked back to where the police commissioner was still sitting. "This is the first time you have been shot at?" he asked. I acknowledged it was. "Well, it is ironic that the first shells fired at you are American." He made a stab at an ironic smile to match his words and I had to agree he was right. But the mystery of Banteay Chakrey was not over. As we talked and finished our lunch, we heard the baritone resonance of a 105 mm howitzer firing in the distance, across the river. Conversation stopped and all movement froze, including the chewing of our half-eaten sandwiches. We waited for the next sound, the whine of the shell racing closer, growing louder as it roared over us and landed with an earth-shaking blast in the dry ground just behind the fort. A second and a third shell followed quickly, then a fourth and a fifth. I sprawled on the ground next to Grant as he tried to film the barrage with a small hand camera. The attack continued for approximately three minutes, the shells landing around the perimeter fence but not in the fort itself.

When the shelling stopped, we gathered our equipment and hurriedly climbed into the sampans, which fortunately had not been hit, and began the long trip back to Phnom Penh. As we worked our way slowly upstream, I tried to sort out what we had just lived through. The border clash and the artillery rounds falling around us were real. But the Cambodians inside the fort, who knew so little about their weapons, were suspect, most likely extras cast in a special performance staged for us and our cameras. There was more to the story to be reported.

So we tried the other side.

TEN DAYS LATER we sat in the mess hall of a U.S. Special Forces camp in South Vietnam. The distant silhouetted figures we had watched coming across the flooded delta now had faces and names and were seated across from us: an American captain and two sergeants.

"Were you really inside the fort?" the captain asked in disbelief. "Boy, we draw a lot of fire from there. So do the choppers when they fly close to the border. There are two antiaircraft positions in the bushes on each side of the place." We told them what we had seen, which wasn't much.

"Did you see any Russian advisers?" We shook our heads and added that with the low level of fighting, just skirmishes, Russian advisers would seem very unlikely. "Well, we've gotten reports from our agents over there that two Russian advisers were seen at the post. We think they are bringing in new weapons; mortars, probably."

"Was that a week ago Friday, the day of your firefight?" I asked. The captain turned to look at a calendar hanging on the mess hall wall. "Yeah, that was it." Grant Wolfkill drank the last of his coffee, put the mug down, and wiped his mouth with a paper napkin from the aluminum dispenser on the table. "Well, I think you're looking at your two Russian advisers. The mortar was the case for our camera tripod."

"Just shows you can never be sure of what you're getting in the agent reports," one of the sergeants said with a laugh. As we sat around the table, we let our collective imagination play with how the report could take on a life of its own: it had been passed on to Saigon for further analysis and then cabled to Washington, where it would be mentioned in a Pentagon strategy session (as an unconfirmed sighting, of course) and then communicated to the White House as one line in the daily Vietnam status report, where it might be leaked (no longer as an unconfirmed sighting) to a reporter who would publish the item, which would then become the subject of debate in Congress, which had to decide whether to increase aid to South Vietnam in order to stop Communist expansion, which now included Russian advisers moving into the Mekong Delta.

The mess hall was a small room at the end of a long wooden barrack with a concrete floor and screens, instead of windows, to keep out flies while allowing in what slight, precious breeze the delta offered. Similar barracks on the compound housed 160 Vietnamese soldiers. They were not part of the regular South Vietnamese army but were men from the local area who, so the theory went, would fight well because they were defending their homes. Many of the soldiers had carried the theory a natural step farther by bringing their wives and children into the camp and making it their home. The laundry hanging on lines to dry and the women cooking meals of rice and fermented fish sauce gave a touch of domesticity to a war camp. And war was as much a part of daily life as the laundry hanging out back. It had been so for fifteen years and would be for another ten. For the Americans, the war was a one-year assignment. For the Vietnamese, it was an indefinite sentence that could be shortened only by death or a debilitating wound.

While we were at the special forces camp, I began to understand how television was going to make it impossible for Americans to escape the war in Vietnam and what that would mean for television news and those watching it. It was not only the camera and the images recorded on a thin 16 mm–wide strip of film and coated with an assortment of chemicals that gave us a privileged power in reporting the war. Of equal importance was the free access we had. There was no formal censorship by either the South Vietnamese or the Americans (and there would be none for the duration of the fighting). This was a new freedom. Until the coup and murder of President Ngo Dinh Diem in 1963, television journalists had been kept under strict surveillance by the Diem government and were limited in their ability to work outside Saigon. The extent to which media control and manipulation were exercised was told to me by Grant Wolfkill during our stay at the special forces camp in the Mekong Delta. Two years earlier, he had been in the delta working on a story. It had taken the NBC reporter some time to obtain permission to film, which was finally granted under the strict condition that South Vietnamese government officials would accompany the camera team and determine with whom interviews could be conducted. A request was made to film an interview with a farmer. One was duly produced, and the interview was conducted in a rice paddy with the government escort serving as interpreter. Several weeks later, according to Wolfkill, the film was edited back in the United States for broadcast. NBC hired an interpreter to check the interview in Vietnamese. She discovered that the farmer in the Mekong Delta was merely counting 1, 2, 3, 4 ... up to ten, and then 10, 9, 8, 7, 6 ... back to one, on the instructions of the helpful government escort, who had told the farmer to keep counting while he provided the appropriate responses to the reporter's questions.

Now, at the end of 1964, with Diem dead and more compliant political leaders in Saigon, not only could we ask our own unrestricted questions, but we could provide our own interpreters and get uncensored answers. We could also go into combat with an ease that was at first surprising and then frightening. Late one afternoon the American captain announced that the next morning there would be another operation moving up to the Cambodian border and invited us to come along with our cameras. We accepted, though with little enthusiasm. We had come too close for comfort, or safety, in the recent battle there. But an hour before sunrise the next morning we joined the Americans and the Vietnamese militiamen. As the eastern horizon showed the first traces of light, Grant muttered the mantra of war correspondents and photographers—there is no story in the world worth getting shot for—an observation of such elemental truth that it has always amazed me that journalists still go out risking their lives to get a story or a picture. But there we were, the two of us doing what we did not have to do, because we both knew we had a rare opportunity to show both sides of a war—to combine the scenes we had filmed in Cambodia with what we would see this morning. In Vietnam you played the odds, and the odds lengthened when we discovered that it was to be an amphibious operation, and a primitive one at that.

Approximately thirty small sampans were drawn up next to the camp. Soldiers were climbing into them, three to four men in each, with a fifth man standing at the rear holding a long pole that he would use to propel the boat through the flooded fields. Radio equipment was loaded onto one sampan. In two others small mortars were erected with twenty-one rounds of shells stacked neatly in the bow. Grant and I quickly saw the problem. The lack of space meant we would not be able to take our large sound camera with us. It was the standard television news camera—highly reliable but also bulky and heavy. It was designed for stories where you could drive up in a station wagon, unload the camera, and start shooting from a tripod. That worked well back home in the United States, but the flooded fields of the Mekong Delta were not exactly tailgate country.

We left the sound camera behind and set out with a small hand-wind camera. It was to television news what the DC-3 was to aviation: old, simple, and dependable, but limited. It would give you pictures but no sound. I carried a tape recorder that would record sound, but it could not be synchronized with the film. As long as

I was recording general background noise, shooting, shouting, the lapping of the water against the side of the sampans, there was no problem. The only thing we could not record was the most important sound of all: a person speaking on camera.

We were exposed and vulnerable as our flotilla of sampans set out. If we ran into an ambush, we would have no place to hide except by leaping into the shallow water, which conjured up comic book images of hunted men hiding under water breathing air through hollow reeds. Neither Grant nor I nurtured any desire to be in the first wave of sampans, so we hung back next to one of the boats with a mortar and an American sergeant whose job it was to aim it. The objective was a small hamlet near the border a mile north of Banteay Chakrey, which, we were told, was frequently used by the Vietcong. As we approached the settlement, hidden in the shade of some trees, shooting erupted. It had the staccato sound of firecrackers and lasted for less than a minute as the few defenders, presumably Vietcong, withdrew across the river into Cambodia.

We entered the settlement and found a dozen or so women, children, and old men. A search of the few simple homes produced no evidence that the Vietcong had been using the settlement as a base. The end of the mission, though, was just the beginning of a deeper story. The South Vietnamese commander was about to order his men to withdraw when the American captain walked up to him and said firmly that the homes should be burned to the ground. The Vietnamese commander objected. Speaking through an interpreter, he explained that even if the Vietcong passed through the settlement, it was clearly not a Vietcong base. The modest structures were the homes of these people. The American understood that but argued that Communist guerrillas were finding shelter there, and therefore the settlement must be destroyed.

The debate went on for about ten minutes while an elderly woman stood watching and listening, apprehension etched in her face, waiting for the fate of her home to be decided. It was a candid debate, the essence of the larger one that would soon seize the United States. After several minutes of arguing the American captain prevailed.

As flames marched across the thatched roofs and the houses were reduced to charred wood, I felt anger stirring in me. I was angry at myself as the reporter as spectator, as a distanced observer trained not to intervene in the news but merely to tag along and record it. Slowly the anger turned into frustration, a frustration that we could not report fully what happened in that tiny Mekong Delta hamlet because we could not communicate the feelings and emotions of the moment. We could not capture the sound and the passion in the voices that were at the heart of this human experience so distant from the well-appointed policymaking chambers of Washington. Yes, our silent film would show the tall, lean captain, and the short, wiry South Vietnamese commander arguing. My narration, however, would have to explain what they were arguing about. The facts and the context would be broadcast; this journalist would do his duty. But at that moment I understood how television, its power and most definitely its potential, was about much more than facts and context. It was, and is, about experience, which ignites emotion. Standing in the tiny hamlet surrounded by destroyed homes and limited by our primitive equipment, we were little better than silent movies.

When I returned to Saigon to write the script for our border story, I felt a growing sense of unease that we were falling short in our coverage of the war. A lively correspondence with New York followed via telex and letter. In a few months, by the time the first major battles involving American forces erupted, the networks had developed lighter sound cameras with color film and rushed them into the field. Now the human sounds of war could flood into American living rooms, as well as the pictures—the war, as the NBC slogan promised, in "living color." The camera, with film and sound, had become the reporter of experience. All that was left for the correspondents and producers and camera teams to do was point the lens and the microphone.

Chapter 5

THE CAMERA RULES

" I AM A CAMERA." This intriguing identification was made by
Christopher Isherwood in his intimate and insightful stories of
life in Berlin in the 1930s, the lives of individuals played out
against the backdrop of Europe's march toward war. For Isherwood
the camera was a wonderful, comforting metaphor. It allowed him
to keep his emotional distance from those he was writing about. It
also played on the belief that the camera gives a stamp of validity
and truth to the images it produces, precisely because it is mechanical and therefore is thought to be immune to the subjective human
pollutants of the interpretive artist or politically engaged reporter.
The camera, after all, doesn't lie. Or is not supposed to.

In those early months of the war in Vietnam it became clear
that the camera and microphone were the true reporters of experience and that we correspondents were largely becoming caption

43

writers of combat scenes. Indeed, as American involvement grew rapidly in 1965, NBC executives in New York briefly considered keeping all of the network correspondents in Vietnam in the office in Saigon to merely write voice-over narration for the film that our small, but growing, army of cameramen would send back from the battle zones. The thought behind it was that the pictures did not need reporting, but only helpful information to describe what the viewer was seeing. Fortunately, this misguided thinking was not implemented. Had it been, the reporters in Saigon would never have accepted it.

In the early months of the war, reporters and camera teams knew that we were helping to write the first edition textbook for television news. And we did it the way journalists usually do, by improvising on the fly. We did not sit around and discuss the rules of visual communication that history and human nature were imposing on us, although subconsciously we may have been aware of them. The importance of symbols and the simplicity of message when trying to communicate constituted rule number one, which had been recognized from the days of the earliest mass media. The painters of the Middle Ages and the Renaissance kept their message simple by upholding the established religious and political order of the day with renderings of Christ or the Madonna with Child. Eventually, the patrons of the arts (the establishment) would commission scenes of historic events, battles won, and portraits of themselves, the rich and powerful. (Losers did not commission paintings or erect monuments to their failures.) With time, the camera came along, making the visual image accessible, inexpensive, and therefore democratic. True, the camera, like speech, could be controlled for a while. But a large part of the drama of the second half of the twentieth century has been the story of the holders of authority (and therefore power) losing their influence (and power) as they lost their control of the visual message. Vietnam merely exposed and thus accelerated that loss. The question I and my colleagues had to ask was, Were we losing control too? We had been handed new tools that would make journalists more influential and therefore more powerful than ever. Yet unlike print or radio reporters, television correspondents would no longer be the exclusive eyes and ears and "voices" of a story. We had to share the stage with the camera and its images. Some journalists' egos found that difficult to accept.

On one of my brief visits to New York for meetings, an executive at NBC News who was responsible for our foreign coverage invited me into his office. I had just completed my initial assignment in Saigon and had agreed to return to Asia to continue covering the war. The executive closed the door behind him so we could talk in private. I expected to be given details of NBC's plans in Vietnam or advice on the types of stories in which producers in New York were interested. Instead, the executive admitted he knew nothing about Asia and had to learn fast. What he really wanted to know was how long it would take to send a film crew to Saigon from our bureau in Hong Kong compared to Tokyo. He was surprised to learn that Tokyo was much farther away.

I cite this encounter not to add to the folklore of how a home office can be removed from what is happening in the field, but to celebrate it. The lack of knowledge back home about Asia and Vietnam was a major help for those of us reporting the war. It brought a blessed absence of second-guessing and preconceived ideas that producers and editors often overtly or subtly direct at their reporters on the scene. Today, with satellite communication and cellular telephones, a network correspondent is rarely out of reach of a producer in the New York office offering suggestions on how to trim a report to a minute and a half so that it will fit into the program, or even telling the reporter in the field how the story should be shaped and written. Fortunately, in the early television days in South Vietnam there was no telephone contact with New York. There were no satellites providing same day or live coverage of an event. When we finished our reports, we put the film, along with an audio tape of the recorded script, in a bag and shipped it on a Pan Am flight that ambled across the Pacific from Saigon to Manila, Guam, and Honolulu before reaching Los Angeles or San Francisco. In a rush, and with considerable luck, a report could be on the air twenty-four hours after we sent it off, although usually it appeared two or three days later. Left to our own devices, we devoted most of our work to background reports that tried to explain the tragic, bizarre, and sometimes surrealistic events in Vietnam to an American public that was becoming increasingly concerned about what Americans were doing in that small country on the other side of the world.

Not that we were that many. Most of the American press corps could fit around a couple of tables pushed together for lunch at Bodard's Coffee Shop on Saigon's Tu Do Street. There were journalistic veterans from World War II, as well as the still wet-behind-the-ears generation, and in 1965 it was evident that television news had not yet quite come of age. Print reporting still claimed a journalistic stature that the camera had not replaced. (One morning, while I was standing in the lobby of the Caravelle Hotel with Bernard Kalb of CBS News, an American embassy official came up to introduce himself. Bernie, in his outgoing, gregarious manner, shot out his hand. "Hi, I'm Bernie Kalb of CBS News," he said, and then added with the defensive tone of an apology, "but I used to be with the *New York Times*.")

In late 1964, CBS News was still rotating its correspondents in from Hong Kong and Tokyo. Its first Saigon-based reporter, Morley Safer, wouldn't arrive until early 1965. But CBS did have a proper bureau, a corner suite in the Caravelle Hotel that I envied. For four months I had been working out of my small hotel room aided by a Vietnamese cameraman, a driver, and an American freelance reporter who covered the daily radio broadcasts. One morning in December 1964 I received a telex from New York that I took as confirmation that Vietnam had finally been elevated to the status of a major story: authorization to rent a two-room corner suite, as well as an additional connecting room, and make it our bureau. The Caravelle's manager said I could have the third floor suite in a few days when a Mr. Luce checked out. Henry Luce, founder and ruler of the powerful Time-Life magazine empire, had come to Saigon to learn firsthand what was happening. He was given a whirlwind VIP tour of the country, met with Vietnamese leaders, dined with the ambassador, and was briefed by the top American generals. My room was next to Luce's suite and on the day of his departure, shortly after lunch, I hovered in the hallway ready to take immediate occupancy. As Luce left his room, I introduced myself and we chatted for a moment as he waited for the elevator. "What do you think of the situation here?" I asked this titan of American journalism. "I came with some pretty good ideas on what needs to be done," he said. Then he added with a shake of his head as he stepped into the elevator, "But now I'm pretty confused. It is all confusing." The elevator door closed. I moved into the suite, encouraged that a magazine mogul of Luce's influence and power was so open-minded. There was, however, no confusion or public doubt when Luce returned to New York and handed down his verdict. Three weeks later *Time* published a cover story on Vietnam entitled "The Tide Turns," a hymn of optimism that the United States would prevail. That bothered me a lot. It bothered *Time* correspondents in Saigon whose experience and reporting for the cover story were ignored. It should have bothered Luce, even if it was his magazine.

One serious problem facing American journalists in South Vietnam was the inevitable cultural barrier between us and the Vietnamese, and particularly the most important element in that barrier, language. Few Americans in or out of uniform had even a minimal conversational grasp of the complexities of Vietnamese. Educated Vietnamese, officers, and government officials spoke the French of their former colonial rulers, and many were quickly learning English. But even with the aid of interpreters poor communication could be tragic on the battlefield, obfuscatory in meetings between civilian officials, and sometimes embarrassing in social encounters—as in the "flower incident."

Jim Robinson was an "old Asia hand" who had taught school in China before the Communists had come to power. He was also NBC's correspondent in Hong Kong. At the end of 1964, as the military and political prospects of South Vietnam were looking increasingly bleak, he came to Saigon.

Early one morning, Jim came into the office looking as if he had had a long, though not necessarily unpleasant, night. He had met an attractive Canadian journalist, he told me, who was also passing through Saigon, and had invited her to dinner. They had followed the customary circuit of a night on the town, beginning in a French restaurant and then proceeding on to the Moulin Rouge in the Chinese quarter of the city, an old nightclub known for its raucous music, watery drinks, and seedy floor show.

"I don't know what happened," Jim said, as he leaned back on the couch trying to put together the pieces of the night before.

"Did something happen?" I asked.

"I have no idea. The last thing I can remember is being at the Moulin Rouge, then waking up here in bed. Alone." Jim continued, "I don't even know whether I took her back to her hotel."

"Or whether she brought you back here," I suggested.

Jim shook his head, but his sense of gallantry soon overcame his bewilderment, and he sat down to write a letter to his new-found, and perhaps now lost, friend. He thanked her for the evening and confessed that he could not recall how it ended. If he had behaved in any improper way, he wanted to assure her, he apologized for his behavior and would she please accept the small gift that he was enclosing as an expression of his sentiments.

Jim sealed the letter in an envelope, addressed it, and turned to our Vietnamese driver, Dang Khac Hoang, whom we called "Mr. Long." He spoke some French but little English, and you had to be very clear to give him specific instructions, which Jim was careful to do. He handed Long the letter and about two dollars' worth of South Vietnamese piasters, which would buy a nice bouquet of flowers down at the flower market a block away. Jim insisted that they should be freshly cut and that Long should take them and the letter to the lady at the Continental Hotel across the square.

Long left, and we carried on with our work. After lunch, when we returned to the office, Jim asked Long whether he had delivered the letter?

"Yes, yes, it's all okay," he replied with a satisfied smile.

"And you got some nice flowers?" Jim asked a bit warily.

"No had time for flowers. Had to ship film, go to airport," he said, still smiling.

"Oh, well," said Jim. "So, what did you do with the money?"

"No problem," Long's smile now extended from ear to ear, though Jim could not tell whether it was from embarrassment or pride at his presence of mind.

"No problem. I give money to the lady."

Chapter 6

A LAND OF THE
ETERNAL PRESENT

HALF THE FUN and adventure of Laos was getting there. If
you were in a hurry, the trip from Saigon could be made in
the relative comfort of an old Air Vietnam DC-6, which made the
run twice a week, or in the primitive confines of a DC-3, which
was the flagship of Royal Air Laos. I was in a hurry that day in
January 1965. There had been reports of renewed fighting in Laos
among the private armies of the royal brothers and half brothers
who were constantly vying for power. News reports from Laos, I
knew, were usually little more than unconfirmed rumors that had
seeped into the capital town, Vientiane, and had caused enough
concern or gossip among the local population for an AP, UPI, or
Reuters journalist to put a story on the news wire. I was anxious
to experience the promised mystical qualities of Laos, and even a

questionable story was a good excuse to go. Unfortunately, the only flight the next day was the DC-3. Fortunately it was full, and so we turned to Plan B, which came highly recommended: fly to Bangkok and take the night train to Laos.

When television news crews set out on a lengthy trip to some remote destination, they take on the appearance of a small safari. Even in the technically less sophisticated prevideotape years, the camera, tripod, sound equipment, lights, and cables, as well as a large provision of film, added up to a dozen cases or more of baggage. All of that, me, and the cameraman were jammed into two minisized taxis, with our knees tucked under our chins, when we pulled up to the Bangkok railroad station.

The first problem was getting the ticket for the train, which left at 7:30 that night. There was only one sleeping car, and I had been told that if we wanted to avoid the dubious experience of spending the night sitting bolt upright, jammed in among passengers, dogs, and assorted ducks and chickens, a sleeping compartment was an absolute necessity. We assaulted the ticket window but were rebuffed by an uncomprehending face and eyes that said they would like to help, but not in English. An attempt at sign language didn't work either, nor did writing out our plea. One of the baggage carriers who were following us motioned to the stationmaster's office across the large terminal hall. There, sitting behind a massive desk with an aura of serene calm and resembling a sculpted Buddha, the stationmaster, who spoke English, listened to our story, nodded his head in agreement, and personally sold us two berths on the sleeping car for that night. We thanked him with handshakes and smiles all around and were told where we could weigh our luggage. In Thailand, it seems, there is, or was, such a thing as excess baggage on trains. You were allowed so many pounds and then, as with the airlines, you started paying overweight. Or so we were told.

At precisely 7:30 P.M. the train creaked out of the station, slowly picking up speed on its narrow gauge tracks. We passed by simple apartments offering candid rear window views of families at supper, which gave way to suburbs with luxurious houses in wide, shaded streets. Finally the city smells were swept out of the open window by the fresh air of the flat, green countryside, with its dirt roads and widely scattered farmhouses.

We had bought sandwiches and beer at the station and devoured them as we watched the lingering daylight slide into a sultry night. Somewhere on the train there was a dining car, but no one in our sleeping car went looking for it. Instead, every half hour the train slowed down and came to a stop with a final jolt in the middle of nowhere: no station, no lights. Outside, in the dark, we heard voices as scores of children appeared in a rush, running up alongside the cars hawking cold drinks, coconut, dried fish, rice, and fruit. In three minutes the passengers were refueled and the train continued, until the next stop where the scene was repeated. Through the night, the warm air swished by the compartment window as we headed north to Nongkai, the town on the Thai side of the Mekong River.

Early the next morning we found the dining car, and there was time for a breakfast of bacon and eggs and something that neither looked nor tasted like coffee. At Nongkai everyone got out. It was the end of the line. Ahead of us flowed the Mekong River and on the opposite side was the lush jungle foliage of Laos ready to swallow us up. We crossed the river in a small boat and landed in a different world.

Every morning at seven a muffled gong rang at the main pagoda in Vientiane. The large, heavy gate swung slowly open as several hundred monks clad in bright orange robes slipped quietly out. They separated quickly into groups of five or six and headed down the nearly deserted streets. The monks would stop when a woman or an elderly man came out of a store or home, knelt down, and offered a bowl of rice. Offering food to the monks, as the first act of the day, was part of the daily routine in a land in which little seemed to change.

Some countries are known for the distinction of their people, others for beautiful scenery, a few for former greatness. Laos's attraction was that time seemed to stand still: there was no past, or so it seemed, just as there was no future. Laos, a friend told me, was the land of the eternal present; all that mattered was today. Even in the capital, Vientiane, life barely crept ahead. Along the unpaved main street Indian Sikhs, in their turbans, stood patiently outside their shops waiting for a customer to pass by. Drivers of three-wheeled pedicab taxis searched languidly for a fare while battered army trucks clanked down the dusty street carrying their loads of sleepy-eyed soldiers. The only excitement came when the city's fire engine raced by with its bell clanging, sending shoppers, dogs, and monks carrying sun umbrellas scurrying for cover. A normal day in Vientiane was divided into long periods of time for eating and sleeping, with a little work thrown in to break the monotony. Among Westerners, an invitation to dinner was rarely extended, or expected, before 4:00 P.M. of the same day.

Not only were there no roads leading to the outside world, but there were no individual telephone lines. International communication required strolling down to the telephone office and impressing on the agent, with a small bribe, the importance and absolute urgency of the cable message you wanted sent to your home office. Happily there wasn't much news to send. Laos was controlled by three political factions, each with its own princely leader and army. There was the centrist prime minister, Prince Souvonna Phouma, the left-wing faction of Prince Souvanavong, backed by

North Vietnam, and the right-wing Prince Phoumi Nosovan. The rivalries were all in the family but were assuming greater importance as North Vietnam turned eastern Laos into a network of infiltration routes to South Vietnam—the Ho Chi Minh Trail.

The relaxed nature of Laos extended to television news, not that there was any television to watch. The American networks did not feel the story was worth covering on a full-time basis and as a result there was only one news cameraman in the country, a Lao who hired himself out to NBC and CBS and a host of other TV agencies. Since he had the market to himself, he would cover a story by shooting one roll of film for NBC, a second for CBS, and so on for his other clients. Neither the idea of competition nor the concept of conflict of interest had any place in his life.

The Constellation Hotel, where I stayed, like any good press hangout, was longer on atmosphere than comfort. It was run by an industrious Frenchman, Maurice, who seemed to be the source of any product or information you might need. He had grown up in French Indochina and his daughter, now fifteen, was becoming a beautiful young woman. Over a late afternoon Pernod and water, Maurice thought aloud that perhaps it was time to move his family to France, a place he did not know and had not even visited. But he acknowledged, with an air of resignation mixed with an acceptance of his life's path, that it would be hard for a former colonial, and now ex-colonial, to leave. Laos was a way of life that exerted its own gravitational force.

In the evening a strange band of Westerners gathered in the plain lobby of the Constellation, which opened to the street. There were a few journalists working as newspaper stringers or part-time employees of news agencies, CIA bush pilots, and ex–French Foreign Legionnaires, some of whom were German with SS still written in their manner. Stories were told and legends polished of old wars and daring exploits. The men played their games of dice while the women tried to keep their children from running into the street and talked about the latest fashions displayed in the week-old illustrated magazine that had arrived from Bangkok that afternoon. Not only was there no television to watch, there were no movie theaters. Entertainment was simply spending time talking, without asking too many questions about a person's past. Vietnam, and the war just across the border, seemed remote. The quality of the latest opium crop was of more immediate interest.

More than a business, opium was part of life. One night after dinner an American journalist living in Laos insisted that I not leave the country without having tried its most famous and profitable product. As we walked through the back streets of Vientiane to my initiation, I conjured up what I expected to find: a dimly lit room with oil lamps, the air heavy with smoke, and men lying on their sides, silently inhaling smoke through their long pipes, their minds lost in a drugged reverie.

I was not disappointed. The room had a low ceiling and just enough space for seven men to lie on their sides in a circle. In the center of the circle an elderly Lao with wrinkles etched deeply around impassive eyes prepared the pipes. He heated small balls of the brown sticky opium over a flame and then quietly inserted them into the long-stemmed pipe. My guide explained that I should smoke no more than three pipes this first evening. With the first pipe I knew I was in trouble.

The stem was wide, perhaps an inch in diameter. In the center of it was a tiny opening through which the opium smoke made its long passage up the pipe. It required pursing your lips around the opening to make the seal airtight and then slowly inhaling the opium in one long breath. From the moment the opium was placed in the pipe, I was told I had about fifteen seconds to smoke it. I made a mess of the first pipe. I couldn't get my lips to close tightly around the hole, and I assumed in my nervousness that all the opium was going up in smoke from the pipe bowl, rather than into me. I felt clumsy and embarrassed among the opium veterans lying on their sides, calmly and slowly inhaling. The next several pipes repeated the same failure. Finally, I gave up out of frustration as well as consideration for the old man who had been patiently preparing my pipes, twelve in all. I feared the experience was a total loss.

Back in the hotel my body informed me that it had not all been in vain. I had inhaled, a lot. I woke up in the middle of the night feeling wretched, as sick as I had ever been, and spent the next day flat on my back on my bed watching the ceiling fan rotating slowly above, imploring it to turn faster to provide some marginal relief from the heat outside. But like everything else in Laos it was set for one speed, languid. The opium that had taken possession of the body released it reluctantly.

After one week, I decided I had sampled the essence of Laos and had learned the true lesson of the place—the narcotic was not what you smoked in pipes but rather the land's magnificent isolation and its sense of time suspended. It could be addictive to Westerners, yet just a few miles to the east the flow of soldiers and war materiel from North Vietnam to the South was increasing rapidly. The United States was about to send its first combat troops into the war to hold off the looming collapse of the Saigon government and its own failure in its fight against communism. It was time to get back to work.

Chapter 7

THE MONK'S TALE

LATE ONE AFTERNOON in Saigon, Vo Huynh, our star cameraman, came into the office, closed the door behind himself,
and said he had something important to talk about. "Here is the
story," he said as we sat down with a couple of soft drinks. "The
monks are going to start burning themselves."

Huynh was from North Vietnam and had moved south like a
million other refugees who did not want to live under the
Communists. He was our principal cameraman in Saigon, someone who would time and again plunge into combat to get the best
close-up pictures of action. But he also had excellent contacts in
the Vietnamese army and government and, as it now turned out,
in the Buddhist political movement.

"The monks are going to start burning themselves again to put
pressure on the government," he continued. I nodded, not totally

surprised. "And they want us to televise their suicides." I starred at him, dumbstruck. A year and a half earlier, monks had sat in the street, poured gasoline over themselves, and lit a match. The still pictures of the immolations, the flames leaping from the stoic figures sitting in their position of prayer, had shocked international opinion and helped bring down the American-backed government of Ngo Dinh Diem. Now the Buddhists were bidding for power for themselves, trying to topple the country's weak civilian leaders. American officials were worried that the Buddhists might try to negotiate an end to the war with North Vietnam, something neither the Saigon government nor the United States was prepared to accept.

Vo Huynh had spoken with Buddhist leaders. Their reasoning was clear. If still photos of monks killing themselves had shaken the world and contributed to the American abandonment of the Diem regime, how much more powerful television pictures would be. It was a remarkable insight given that there was, at the time, no television to be seen in South Vietnam. The monks were acting on a purely abstract concept. Huynh had been told that the first monk prepared to burn himself was willing to be interviewed. We could have the interview as an exclusive but must not broadcast it until after the monk had committed suicide. The Buddhists would also tell us when and where the self-immolation would occur so that we would be able to set up our camera to film it.

There we were, a television reporter and a cameraman discussing an exclusive story that would reverberate around the world. We were also being manipulated. We had to confront a question that television journalists will have to face for as long as there is television and people seek to use it for their own ends: should I cover a demonstration or an event that may not occur if I do not cover it? But if I didn't interview the would-be Buddhist martyr, would CBS or ABC get the exclusive? And would New York care about my moral reservations while watching flames leaping over the robed figure who was now appearing on a competing network? I told Huynh to set up the interview. We could worry about the ethics of filming a suicide later.

The next day, we drove to the An Quang Pagoda and were led into a small office and told to wait. A moment later the door opened and a young man with a boy's face under a shaven skull came in quietly and sat down. He showed no emotion when I asked him, as Huynh operated the camera and interpreted, why he was prepared to sit down in a street, pour gasoline over his body, light a match, and end his life. The answers came out mechanically as if programmed. "The government's actions left no alternative ... a single human sacrifice was a small price for a higher calling." There was no prompting or cueing. More likely, I suspected, there had been much prompting and indoctrination before the young monk was led before our camera. When we finished the interview, one of the senior monks showed us out, assuring us that he would let us know if and when it became necessary for the young man to take his life. "You will certainly want to be there," he said. "Of course," I replied.

Of course? What business did any journalist have being used by a group or an individual trying to advance himself, particularly when a human life was at stake? I thought about that as we drove back to the bureau. Then the counterargument intruded: what right did I, as a reporter in Vietnam, have to ignore an event that probably would take place whether or not an NBC camera filmed it? The Buddhists had demonstrated ample proof of their willingness to immolate themselves.

Today I would not agree to the deal we were tacitly making with the young monk at the An Quang Pagoda. Rifling through my old papers, trying to freshen my memory of the Vietnam years, I found a script dated January 27, 1965. I had no recollection of having written it and yet there it was: the story of the young monk to be broadcast after his death.

This was Thich Thong Hanh. A Buddhist monk. He was born twenty six years ago in a small village in Phu Yen province, 200 miles north east of Saigon.

He grew up in a very religious family. Had he stayed in his village, he probably would have become a farmer, or perhaps a tradesman.

But ten years ago, Thich Thong Hanh decided he wanted to become a monk. He was accepted and his life became one of simplicity, meditation and self discipline.

In the security of the pagoda his daily routine was built around prayer. The outside turmoil of a country at war didn't enter his world of peace and meditation. That is until a little over a year ago when politics invaded his world of religion.

Under the rule of Ngo Dinh Diem South Vietnam's Buddhists were oppressed. Once passive monks became militant enemies of the government, their agitation helped to sweep Diem from power.

Now, over a year later many of the same Buddhists, like Thich Thong Hanh claim that Prime Minister Tran Van Houng is persecuting them. Their campaign against the government has been worked out step by step.

First, there were protests, then mass rallies, and then violent demonstrations. All failed. So it was decided that the supreme step must be taken: A monk would burn himself to death.

Thich Thong Hanh volunteered.

The young monk explains his decision simply and directly. He does not consider himself a martyr, and does not want to become one. He sincerely believes that his religion is being persecuted. All else has failed, he says, so the ultimate protest must be made ... the sacrifice of a human life.

On January 27th, Thich Thong Hanh prepared for his final ordeal. One of his last acts was a letter to Prime Minister Houng stating again his opposition to the government and the reasons for giving his life in protest.

To the westerner, Thich Thong Hanh's act may seem to be a futile and wanton self sacrifice of a human life. There is also a real question whether the religious persecution he was protesting against even exists in South Vietnam. What is important is that there are many in South Vietnam who will come to regard Thich Thong Hanh's act as the supreme sacrifice, and respect a person who could live and die for a faith.

Garrick Utley, NBC News, Saigon.

The script told the basic facts as told to us by the monk. Its tone was deliberately light on emotion; the event and pictures would provide that. It was a script that finally, to my great relief, was never broadcast. While I wrestled with the question as to whether we should cover the suicide, there was yet another military coup in Saigon and another change of government, which appeased the Buddhists, who abandoned their political campaign. Today I like to think that Thich Thong Hanh, the young monk who sat in front of our camera with his composed demeanor and spoke through us to his intended audience in living rooms across America about why he was prepared to sacrifice his life in flames, is now enjoying a tranquil middle age. But he still haunts me.

ONE SULTRY afternoon while I was savoring a lemonade in a cafe in Saigon, a group of half a dozen American servicemen came in and seated themselves at the next table. I noticed that their unit patch, worn on the sleeve, bore a motto that went daringly beyond the usual bravado of the morale-raising slogans in the military: "Complete Success, or Total Failure." Curious about this fatalistic, and even nihilistic, view of life, I asked the soldiers what their specialty was. A sergeant leaned over and replied, with scrupulous logic, "bomb disposal."

The motto was a good definition of any country's entry into war. But a giant question mark hovered over the concept of "complete success" as the first U.S. combat troops hit the beach on March 8, 1965. The troops were Marines and the beach was at Da Nang in the northern part of South Vietnam, the site of a major air base the Americans were assigned to protect. The United States was going to war and we were doing it with our eyes wide open and the cameras running.

The arrival of American combat troops in South Vietnam immediately changed the nature of the story and the way television covered it. During the preceding eight months the growing band of television correspondents had been able to roam and report as we saw fit. Back in the news division headquarters in New York, Vietnam was seen as a foreign story of growing but not yet dominant American concern. Now, with U.S. troops arriving every week, Vietnam had turned much more American and was becoming a domestic story that happened to be taking place halfway around the world. On this "American" story producers in New York considered themselves experts. Soon requests began to pour in for specific reports tailored to one angle or another of the American presence. One morning I received a congratulatory telex from a producer in New York for whom I had prepared a report on the implications of the American military buildup. "Excellent report, just what I had in mind," he wrote. I was flattered by the first half of the message and bothered by the second.

One of the challenges facing foreign correspondents is their relationship with producers or editors in the home office. Months or even a year may pass without us seeing each other face-to-face, yet we are intrinsically dependent on each other. The correspondent gathers information and fashions it into a story. The television news producer then takes several reports and fashions them into a news program that is accurate and, he or she hopes, interesting enough to attract an audience. The correspondent and the producer are both journalists, each doing a job. But inevitably they will have different perspectives and priorities. In the best of circumstances there is mutual respect and confidence between the two and the system works well. Indeed, one of the principal responsibilities of a foreign correspondent is not only to inform the viewer or reader but also to advise and guide the home office in its editorial decisions. In turn, correspondents can benefit from the larger news perspective, particularly ideas for stories that answer the questions people at home are asking. The danger arises when a producer suggests a story with a preconceived idea, if only subconsciously, of what he or she wants to see in the finished report. A correspondent aware of that, or at least suspecting it, may in turn subconsciously tailor a report to impress the home office rather than the larger public beyond the producer's desk. The ultimate accolade then becomes, "Excellent report, just what I had in mind."

As American combat troops flowed into South Vietnam in the summer of 1965, so did more network correspondents and camera teams. Soon our suite in the Caravelle was hopelessly overcrowded. When I heard that the West German embassy was moving out of an office building across the square, I rented the space, although it was more than we needed and the rent was higher than our executives in New York wanted to pay. I also worried that by being the first network to move out of the Caravelle we would miss the tips and rumors that gravitated to the hotel like metal filings to a magnet. The ideal solution was to split the new office space and convince the Associated Press to move in with us. As subscribers to the AP, we would have twenty-four-hour access to their news wire and would be able to trade information with their larger staff spread across the country. Fortunately, the AP needed more space too and accepted the offer. I was able to sleep better at night in apartments I rented for Vo Huynh and myself one floor above the office, knowing we were less vulnerable to being scooped by the competition.

Late one night I strolled into the AP office and found a colleague, Michel Renard, reading a telex with growing exasperation. Renard was a Belgian born in Katanga Province of the former (and once again) Congo. One of his prize possessions was a Katanga passport issued when that province, richly blessed with minerals, had tried to assert its independence after the Belgians had pulled out of their ill-prepared and soon-to-collapse colony. The Katanga passport didn't get Renard far, but a Belgian passport and a camera took him from one war to the next, and finally to Saigon. As a freelance photographer he was in demand, and the telex he was reading had just arrived from a national weekly newsmagazine in New York City. The magazine needed a color cover picture for its next edition, needed it to be shipped in forty-eight hours, and had spelled out what it should show: "Want close up American GI, with helmet, with couple of days' beard growth, in jungle, with tired eyes looking warily to one side."

"Christ," said Renard, "they should shoot the bloody thing in Hollywood." He knew, of course, exactly what the magazine wanted to splash on its cover and why it couldn't be shot in Hollywood. This was news. The soldier had to be genuine and so did the helmet, the beard, and the jungle. But if Renard asked the GI to look "warily to one side," would that be journalism or dramatic license, even staging? Staging was out of the question, but dramatic license was becoming a harder line to draw. How, I wondered, could any editor, reporter, or photographer want or need a dramatically "enhanced" picture amid the real drama and trauma that were happening around us? The answer, as I had learned in the cable from the television producer in New York, was the often intrinsic desire (or commercial need) of print editors and television producers to shape reality in order to create an even sharper tone or edge in their publications and programs—reality as the source and stuff of produced drama.

There was, however, one area in which producers and, above all, network executives applied no pressure and, indeed, deserved a medal for valor. They constantly, and often bravely, shielded the reporters in the field from the growing pressures and criticism in Washington directed at the news coverage of the war. "Whose side are you on?" had become a familiar question from government officials as journalists' reports questioned the wisdom of the deepening American commitment in Vietnam. From World War I through the Korean War, there had never been any question as to "whose side" the press had been on. The lines in those conflicts had been clearly drawn, both on the battlefield and in the justness of the cause. In World War II, leading journalists went to Washington to work for the Office of War Information, the government agency created to manage and monitor the information flow from the front line to the living room. One of the most respected commentators on radio, Elmer Davis, gave up his program to become the director of the O.W.I. Vietnam was different, not only because of the lack of censorship but also because the issues were never as clear-cut as they had been in the wars Americans had previously fought in. Ho Chi Minh was a Communist, but he was also a legitimate nationalist with a large popular following. The South Vietnamese government was hardly democratic, and even if a moral case for American involvement could be made (and was made), there was still the grave question of the wisdom of it.

One of the most intense confrontations between government and press occurred in July 1965 at the home of Barry Zorthian, the senior American spokesman in Saigon. Journalists were served drinks in the spacious living room of his villa and then sat down to talk with his guest, who had just arrived from Washington: Pentagon spokesman Arthur Sylvester. Sylvester not only represented the official U.S. government position on Vietnam (that was his job), but he also represented a different generation and mind-set than had been involved in World War II and Korea. As the evening progressed, polite conversation and discussion turned caustic as Sylvester began to lecture the reporters on what our duty was as Americans as opposed to how we saw our duty as journalists. Sylvester argued patriotism (being "on the team") as an ethical priority while the reporters argued facts—the truth as an ethical patriotism. As the evening grew later and the emotional temperature grew hotter, it was clear that there would be no meeting of the minds. Morley Safer simply gave up and walked out of the room, slamming the screen door behind him. The reverberating sound was a coda to the evening and to Sylvester's failure to get us, in his words, "on the team."

As the American military buildup continued, the casualties began to mount. They were not all from combat.

THE CHILLS came first.

As I lay in bed, I felt my body grow cool and then suddenly, numbingly cold. My teeth began chattering. Then my entire body shook uncontrollably. The tall French windows in my bedroom were wide open. From below, Saigon street noise drifted up five floors and into my apartment. It was a hot summer afternoon, siesta time for the Vietnamese. In the cafe around the corner I knew that the usual group of Frenchmen dressed in white shorts would be continuing the routine of their postcolonial lives, sitting at their corner table under a ceiling fan, sipping their lemonades, and reading three-day-old Paris newspapers, the latest journals to arrive from the homeland. The warmth that enveloped them was for me a distant land. Neither the pajamas I wore nor the blankets nor the wet heat in the mid-nineties had the slightest effect on the wracking cold that surged through my body. Then it stopped as quickly as it had started. I lay in bed, baffled by what had hit me, when sweat suddenly began to pour from my body. I felt so weak I could barely manage to get up to close the windows and turn the air conditioner on high. It rattled and banged as chilled air poured into the room. It didn't help. An unquenchable heat inside me soaked my pajamas as I lay on top of the bed, the blankets kicked off on the floor. After persisting for half an hour, the heat too suddenly passed.

I regained a measure of lucidity and called the NBC office and asked the driver to bring the office car to take me to the hospital. We worked our way slowly through the late afternoon Saigon traffic, which had its own class system; the small blue and white taxis cut in front of us with impunity while we honked impatiently at the cyclo drivers on their three-wheeled vehicles, pedaling impassively ahead of us. I searched for the cause of what had hit me. Two weeks before I had gone out on a three-day patrol with a Marine Corps platoon near Da Nang. The first night we had slept along the banks of a stream, and I wondered whether I had caught malaria, although I had not heard of any malaria cases in Vietnam. When we reached the U.S. Naval Hospital, which took in American journalists, I was directed to a young doctor, a navy lieutenant, in a receiving room. He sat behind a table wearing crisp white trousers and a short-sleeved shirt. I explained my symptoms, told of the marine patrol, and suggested I might have malaria.

"No, there is no malaria in Vietnam," the young lieutenant assured me. "You have dengue fever; it has the same symptoms as malaria. The good news is that it's not dangerous," he said with an affected air of nonchalance. "The bad news is that there is no cure for it. It may take ten to twelve days for it to run its course." He told me to go to bed, take aspirin, and shake and sweat out the fever.

I took his assurances and a family-sized bottle of aspirin home with me. For the next two bedridden weeks I shook and sweated and waited for nature to perform its healing process. When it didn't, I decided that a second medical opinion was in order. I drove again through the Saigon traffic to the navy hospital, limped again into the receiving room, and found the same lieutenant on duty. After losing two weeks to my ordeal, I no longer looked on his white trousers and crisply ironed short-sleeved shirt as a symbol of cool authority.

"Back again," he said with a wary smile and considerably less confidence in his voice.

"Yes," I replied, "and your dengue fever is not living up to its reputation."

"That's interesting. I guess I'll have to give you a blood test," he said. I offered no comment as to why he had not bothered with this most basic of medical tests on my first visit. He stuck a needle into my arm and pulled out a sizable quantity of blood, which he then poured into a tube. "Just have a seat," he said, as he disappeared with the test tube into an adjoining room. "We'll have the results in about twenty minutes."

It was more like an hour. When he returned, the lieutenant seemed worried. "Mr. Utley, you have malaria," he announced, with due solemnity. "In fact, it is a bad case of falciparum malaria." I was tempted to offer some tart observation but kept my silence as the doctor continued.

"Fortunately, your malaria is not fatal."

"I am relieved to hear that, but how do you know?" I asked.

"Because you are still alive," he replied.

There was a momentary silence in the room as we absorbed the magnitude of his medical insight. "That makes me feel a little better," I tried to say dryly.

"Well, you will soon feel better because we can treat malaria." He gave me an envelope filled with two kinds of capsules. "Here, take these. In three days your symptoms will be gone. Then come back and see me."

I returned home, and in three days the medicine accomplished its promised miracle. The chills and fever diminished gradually and then stopped completely. I felt I was ready to rejoin the human race when I walked into the doctor's office for the third time.

"How are you doing now?" He greeted me with what appeared to be self-satisfaction, or perhaps sheer relief, over my recovery.

"Weak, but well," I replied.

"Excellent. Now I want to put you in the hospital."

I looked at him in disbelief and some irritation. "Look," I said, "I walked in here with a serious illness, possibly even a fatal one for which you didn't even test me. You gave a facile diagnosis and then said I am alive purely by good luck. Then you cure me and now you want to put me in the hospital?"

"It may seem we are doing things backward here," the lieutenant acknowledged, "but in the last two weeks we've been getting a lot of malaria cases among the combat units arriving in the country." The military had not expected a malaria problem. Now it had one, and tests were being run on everyone who had been hit by the disease. The lieutenant smiled as he showed me the way out. "You're one of the first. Congratulations."

I checked into the hospital, reasoning it was as good a place as any to rest and get my strength back. My appetite was reviving, and the promise of American T-bone steaks and milkshakes seemed to be a fair trade for my contribution to military medicine.

At 6:00 A.M. on my first morning in the hospital ward, I was awakened by a navy corpsman whose bedside manner was as pointed as the large syringe he held. "Time for your daily blood count," he said as the needle went into my stiffened arm. "We have to see how those corpuscles are behaving." In less than a minute he and my blood were gone. An hour later I had finished breakfast and was reading the morning *Saigon Post* when two army officers appeared at my bedside. The colonel introduced himself and his colleague, a major who was opening a black bag and pulling out a syringe that looked even larger than the one wielded by the navy corpsman.

"Mr. Utley, we have just arrived in Saigon on a crash program because of the malaria problem. We'd like to take some of your blood." The major advanced toward me with the needle as I offered a feeble protest. "But I just had a blood sample taken an hour ago." "I know," he replied, "that was the navy's research. In the army we have our own program." The needle was in and the blood was coming out before the colonel finished speaking. "There now," he said as he applied a Band-Aid over the second puncture mark. "You can relax for the rest of the day. We'll see you tomorrow morning." The major snapped shut his black bag and the two officers started to leave. "Hey wait," I shouted, "is the air force going to come around with its program too?" "Wouldn't be surprised," the colonel said as he walked out of the ward.

I never found out about the air force. That night Vietcong terrorists attacked the My-Cong floating restaurant in Saigon's harbor, a favorite dining place for Americans. It was a brutal attack. A small bomb went off on the restaurant boat itself, killing and wounding a few Americans. Then, as the rest of the diners rushed off the boat to supposed safety, a claymore mine filled with shrapnel and attached to a bicycle parked on the shore was detonated, killing and wounding more. I was about to fall asleep in the hospital ward when a navy corpsman rushed in and told me to get dressed and clear out of the hospital immediately. My bed was needed. A few minutes later I was on the street and hailed a passing cyclo driver. As I climbed onto the passenger seat, I still felt weak from the malaria, and my mind was on the restaurant. I had called the office to make sure that our camera teams and a reporter were covering the attack. Now, as the old Vietnamese pedaled behind me in the muggy night air, ambulances, with their sirens wailing, raced by in the opposite direction delivering the wounded to the hospital.

It was a twenty-minute ride to my apartment. The night-time traffic was light, which allowed the driver to maintain a steady rhythm. I heard a light "click" with each turn of the pedal, as well as his breathing a few inches behind my ear. Neither was forced but functioned in a long practiced harmony. I wanted to talk to him, taxis, of whatever form, being one of the few places where it seems acceptable to conduct aimless conversations with total strangers. But I spoke not a word of Vietnamese and he, no English or French. We rolled though the Saigon night, two men alien to each other, unable to communicate. As more ambulances sped by, I wondered whether one of them was carrying a friend. I also began thinking of how much more of the Vietnam War I wanted to take.

You Should Have Been Here Yesterday

IF THERE was to be a moment of journalistic as well as military truth in Vietnam, it came, for me, on a gray morning in November 1965 in the central highlands at An Kay at the headquarters of the First Air Cavalry Division. For Robert McNamara, I suspect, it was to be a moment of truth too, no doubt one of many uncomfortable moments. I stood outside a tent waiting for the secretary of defense to arrive to check personally on the progress of the war. Inside the tent intelligence officers had arranged their maps and charts and had rehearsed their presentation. It would be straightforward, they had told me. Despite heavy American bombing of North Vietnam and the infiltration routes into South Vietnam, the amount of war materiel and the number of soldiers moving south were growing rapidly. This was not the direction that events, in McNamara's rational view, were supposed to be taking. The facts challenged the theory behind the bombing, and indeed the war itself, that infiltration could be cut and North Vietnam compelled to give up. Thirty minutes of McNamara's precise schedule had been allocated for the intelligence briefing. A small group of reporters stood outside the tent and waited. A half hour passed, then an hour. When McNamara finally emerged from the briefing after nearly an hour and a half, he bore the expression reporters like to describe as "grim faced." McNamara spoke to us of the hard reality in Vietnam. He acknowledged, for the first time publicly, that there would be no quick end to this war. There was, it turned out, no light at the end of the tunnel. Indeed, there was no assurance that the tunnel even had an exit.

A few days earlier in the Ia Drang valley, not many miles from where the intelligence briefing had taken place, a brutal battle had been fought. It was the first of the bloody clashes that would characterize the American combat role in the Vietnam conflict: battles in which victory was measured not by captured territory but by the most hideous of measurements—the body count—as if military success and failure could still be quantified by numbers of lives ended. For several days the battle raged in the valley. When it ended, the North Vietnamese and NBC had lost. Our camera crews had gone into the thick of the fighting but couldn't see or film the story for the trees, the heavy jungle foliage hiding much of the fighting. The CBS crew had stayed back at an airfield and interviewed wounded American soldiers as they were brought out of the battle zone on medevac helicopters. Their stories told on camera, often while the soldiers were lying on stretchers, were more graphic, more immediate, and more personal than our film at the front. They had captured the true drama—the horror of battle in the voices as well as the appearance of the wounded Americans—and that is the way it came over on television back home. Unhappy messages from New York, or "rockets," as they were called, rained down on us, leaving no doubt as to how we had been mauled by the competition. I felt terrible. Our cameramen had exposed themselves to much greater danger than the CBS teams but had come back with much less. It was a hard, critical lesson: in television the story may not be where the event happens but where it is being told with the greatest visual and emotional impact.

There would be other battles, other opportunities to recoup, which was becoming part of the problem. When we proposed a series of in-depth background reports to New York, the response was to the point: don't let it interfere with the "bang-bang" coverage of war. Much of the Vietnam reporting, like the war itself, had switched to automatic pilot and would remain there for years to come. After spending a year and a half in South Vietnam, I asked the NBC executives in New York if I could leave Vietnam by Christmas 1965. But I did not want to leave with the defeat of Ia Drang hanging over our team.

You Should Have Been Here Yesterday

Late one afternoon, a few days before my departure from the country and the war, I was in the office cleaning out my files when a call came through from Da Nang, at the northern end of South Vietnam. Over a bad connection, which had been routed through a patchwork of military switchboards, came the barely discernible voice of Dean Brelis, one of our correspondents. He told an incredible story, or rather a totally credible story, that he had just filmed. He had been at the marine hospital when a lieutenant colonel was brought in who had had his leg shattered by ground fire while flying on a helicopter mission. The leg had to be amputated. Brelis was given permission by the colonel, who was lucid, to film the operation. As the camera peered over the backs of the surgeons, the colonel gave a running commentary. He had been flying over a village known to be controlled by the Vietcong, but when he saw civilians below he didn't want to open fire. He couldn't shoot at women and children, he said, as he lay on the operating table under local anesthesia. But ground fire from a hidden position had ripped into the helicopter and through the colonel's leg. He spoke coherently, even eloquently, as his lower leg was removed. It was personal, it was emotional, it was in color and sound. It was war and television in their mutual embrace. Television needed to film what was happening on that operating table, and the marine colonel wanted to talk on television about what had happened to him; he needed his story to be heard, his loss witnessed and validated. Here was one of the most unanticipated powers of television: that of a healer to those who appeared on it, who would bare their leg, and eventually their souls and confessions, in the public arena. The glare of the television lights was not something to run from. The camera would become an irresistible force that attracted people like the proverbial moths to the flame. The amputation of the colonel's leg was some of the most dramatic film to come out of Vietnam. It was time to move on.

Chapter 8

SHIFTING VISIONS

ON MY OFFICE wall hangs a front page of the *New York Times*. Unlike most front pages tacked to a den wall or folded carefully away in a scrapbook to be revisited every few years, this one does not mark a birthday or commemorate a wedding. Nor does it proclaim in towering, dramatic headlines an event of historic dimensions and indelible memory. But there is a story in there, and a healthy admonishment for journalists who report the present with impressive clarity while missing the implications for the future by the proverbial country mile.

The date on the front page is April 8, 1927.

It was less than a year after the National Broadcasting Company had begun to link radio stations across the nation into something called a radio network. CBS added its initials to the airwaves that year, but radio was still a decade away from providing listeners with a dependable source of news. In 1927 newspapers were the only source of news and for the readers of the *New York Times* on that April morning (it was a Friday), the world seemed to be a reasonably safe, contented place. The twenties were still roaring and the stock market was rising. Black Friday, Hitler, a second world war, the Holocaust, and the nuclear age lay far beyond the horizon of the imagination. The lead story on the far right-hand column came from China, where police had raided and searched the offices of the Soviet consulate, which was located in the French Concession, one of the outposts of European imperial and commercial power in Asia. From North Carolina came the story of a man facing a judge on a charge of assaulting a woman. The judge offered the defendant a choice no longer available in our courts: a sentence of two years' labor on the roads or banishment from the state. The defendant, to no one's surprise, chose exile from North Carolina and, it was believed, would move across the state line to Virginia.

Then there was the real and lasting news of the day, at least as we look back on that front page. On the left-hand side a two-column headline announced an experiment:

"FAR OFF SPEAKERS SEEN AS WELL AS HEARD IN TEST OF TELEVISION."

Beneath the large, dark type came a column of smaller subheadlines extending halfway down the page.

"LIKE A PHOTO COME TO LIFE."

"HOOVER'S FACE PLAINLY IMAGED AS HE SPEAKS IN WASHINGTON."

"THE FIRST TIME IN HISTORY."

"PICTURES ARE FLASHED BY WIRE AND RADIO SYNCHRONIZING WITH SPEAKER'S VOICE."

And then, in one of the memorable howlers of journalism, "COMMERCIAL USE IN DOUBT."

A GOOD MEASURE of sympathy is due the unnamed *Times* reporter who had only the vaguest clue of the future he was staring at as he watched the test broadcast at the Bell Laboratories of AT&T, watched as the jerky picture was transmitted at eighteen images a second from Washington to New York City. But he recognized some of the new forces at work on the flickering screen. After Secretary of Commerce Herbert Hoover finished speaking, a Mr. Nelson of AT&T appeared from Washington to explain the technical process. "Mr. Nelson had a good television face, he screened well as he talked," the reporter noted, an observation not made of Secretary Hoover.

And what of its "commercial use"? "The commercial future of television, if it has one, is thought to be largely in public entertainment," the reporter wrote, "super newsreels flashed before audiences at the moment of occurrence, together with dramatic and musical acts shot on the ether waves in sound and picture at the instant they are taking place in the studio."

It was, in the end, a pretty good forecast. Of course the *Times* reporter did not foresee the commercial clutter that would also be shot on the ether waves. Nor could he foresee the reach of satellites and the impact of global communications. But he did look beyond the technology and grasp the essence of television: the human factor, the roll of personality and presence, the face that "screened well" that would be at the heart of television's ability to communicate.

He also foresaw those "super newsreels."

Nearly four decades later they were known as the *CBS Evening News with Walter Cronkite* and the *Huntley-Brinkley Report* on NBC. Together, they were, in the eyes and minds of American television viewers, the masters of the news universe. ABC News, with a series of anchors, including a young Peter Jennings, offered only token competition; its turn would come later.

In January 1966, NBC and CBS were exciting places to work. Amid the growing war in Vietnam and the domestic upheavals at home, Huntley, Brinkley, and Cronkite, and the news divisions they represented, offered an aura of stability and authority; they had become the new electronic central nervous system of news that a large audience looked to. There was little competition. Radio had withered as a serious source of news, and the choice of daily newspapers, particularly afternoon editions, was shriveling as readers chose to get their news from television. Through the first half of the 1960s, the public had shown a marked preference for the *Huntley-Brinkley Report* over the *CBS Evening News*. Why this was about to change offered one of the first insights into the shifting fates of the network television newscasts.

In early 1966, the ratings mania was not yet a public spectacle or a major concern to a network into whose treasury ample advertising dollars were flowing. Whether it was in first or second place in the network news competition mattered little. The audience, however, was becoming more aware of the differences between the two newscasts, and viewers were turning from NBC to CBS. For nearly a decade, NBC had developed and then defined a fresh tone for network news. Much of this success was due to the now legendary teaming of Chet Huntley, as the traditionally sober, authoritative newscaster, with David Brinkley in the role of the young, witty, and insightful wordsmith whose comments carried that rare and irresistible quality: the ring of truth. Some competitors at CBS tried to belittle Brinkley's impact by calling it "jukebox journalism," but the public didn't care. It liked what it heard and believed what it saw, and there was little CBS News could do about it. In addition to the *Huntley-Brinkley Report*, NBC had built a formidable news organization with a small but high-quality stable of senior correspondents, including Frank McGee, John Chancellor, Sander Vanocur, and Edwin Newman. But unlike CBS, which still drew sustenance and a sense of purpose from the legacy of the Edward R. Murrow era, NBC was not a "correspondents" network. Rather, it was driven by the vision and control of program producers who saw the correspondents as important elements in the newscasts but not as decisive or indispensable players. This was possible because of the personalities and talents of Huntley and Brinkley, who could carry their nightly half hour program as well as NBC's coverage of political conventions, election nights, and other special news coverage. Indeed, the *Huntley-Brinkley Report* was a more polished news program than the *CBS Evening News*, written with more articulate turns of phrase and better edited in its film reports from correspondents in the field. But in this successful formula was the seed of its own eventual decline.

Any endeavor that has enjoyed long success is threatened by that subtle human infection known as self-satisfaction. There is also the unpleasant fact that cycles do change, slowly at first, then with a swift decisiveness that announces that one era has ended and a new one has succeeded it. And no appeal is possible. By the end of the first year of the American military escalation in Vietnam, the ascendancy of the *CBS Evening News* was well under way. Part of the reason was that after nearly ten years on the air, the Huntley-Brinkley style had lost some of its freshness. It was a program rooted in the more placid 1950s.

By the mid-1960s, though, the news from the Mekong Delta to

university campuses and the inner city had become more contentious; it had become "harder" news. While the *Huntley-Brinkley Report* had coated its journalistic substance with a distinctive style, the *CBS Evening News* was, from its beginning, a no-frills hard news program. This was rooted in the CBS news tradition, but it also reflected the instincts of Walter Cronkite, who had spent his formative years as a wire service reporter covering the end of World War II and the birth of the Cold War. Cronkite's style was no style; the writing on his program (from an NBC perspective) was mostly pedestrian, the news coverage a simple listing and reporting of the day's top stories. But by the mid-1960s that is what viewers wanted. While NBC was relying on Chet and David to pull in the viewers, CBS had built a long bench of highly skilled and prominently featured correspondents: Dan Rather at the White House, Roger Mudd covering Capitol Hill, Marvin Kalb at the State Department, and Morley Safer in South Vietnam. Each night at the beginning of the news, CBS would list the reporters who would appear on the program. The message to the viewers was easily absorbed. If they wanted style and wit with the news, they could still turn to NBC. If they wanted straight news, CBS was the place to be.

At NBC, the audience shift to CBS was a difficult lesson to accept or even understand. During its years at the top, NBC had excelled in almost every facet of television news except the core one—consistently being the fastest and most aggressive news network. To be beaten on a story by CBS was a disappointment but rarely a cause of great concern at NBC. After all, it had the news audience. But by 1966 it no longer had the largest audience. CBS and Walter Cronkite were at the beginning of their long run of dominance in the ratings that would endure for nearly twenty years.

But we are getting ahead of our story.

Chapter 9

MOVING ON

B OMBAY. FEBRUARY 1966.

The old freighter was lost among the larger ships tied up at the dock. It had the air of a plain girl or an awkward boy at a school party, half hiding in the corner, feeling ill at ease and out of place. A searching eye caught paint peeling along the railings. On the bow of the waterline there was the acne of rust. It was a ship whose name I have long forgotten, whose log book, no doubt, was filled with adventurous stories of violent storms at sea and port calls to exotic lands, but whose fate was to end up as a tramp steamer plying the coastal routes of a Third World continent.

The freighter had just sailed from Galveston, Texas, across the Atlantic, through the Mediterranean, down the Suez Canal, and finally across the Indian Ocean to Bombay, where now cranes were unloading large pallets stacked with sacks of American wheat.

Saigon was two months behind me and I had come to India to report on the famine that had struck the subcontinent. The emergency grain shipments were part of an international relief effort. The American embassy in New Delhi had alerted me to the ship's arrival, and the Indian government, after considerable bureaucratic haggling, had given permission to film the unloading of the food. In the United States it would not have been a problem. But India considered its ports to be military installations, and there was a well-developed suspicion, as well as bureaucratic paranoia, that anyone with a camera was a potential spy. We were strictly told that we could film the American freighter and nothing else. A young man from the port authority office was sent along with us to make sure we behaved.

After filming from the dock, I asked our guide if he had any objection if we went on board the ship to film the unloading from a different angle and to speak to the American crew. He was not prepared for this unexpected deviation from his instructions and replied, nervously, "I don't see why you should." I started to explain why we should when I saw an American at the top end of the gangplank. I shouted up to him whether we could come on board. "I don't see why you can't," he answered with a friendly wave.

We walked up the gangplank. The American who welcomed us was the first mate. "Twenty-five years," he told us, when I asked him how long he had been at sea. His weathered face confirmed it. "You guys from NBC?" He noticed the company logo on the camera. "I used to work there. In Chicago," he said. "At the Merchandise Mart, nineteenth floor?" I asked. "Right. I was an announcer."

I explained my background in Chicago and wondered how an NBC announcer in the glory days of radio, when an announcer was a star, ended up on a rusting freighter in Bombay. He met the question cheerfully. "When the war broke out in '41, I joined the navy, fell in love with the sea and the travel." He said he could not imagine going back to a studio with no windows to read somebody else's words into a microphone. I felt a kindred spirit, except I could travel the world and speak my own words into the microphone. Still, I did not know where the next anchorage would be. When I returned to the United States from Saigon, the only opening NBC had for a foreign correspondent was in Rio de Janeiro. As pleasant as Rio would have been, South America was (and unfortunately still is) largely a lost continent for American journalism. A television correspondent would get on the air two or three times a year if he was lucky. I turned down Rio and was sent to India for a month. Now that assignment was ending and I had no idea what would happen next.

The answer was waiting for me when I returned to New Delhi, waiting in an NBC envelope that had been sent from New York. There was no letter in it, only a one-page press release announcing that NBC News was starting a new weekly half hour program that would deal with the Vietnam War in depth. "Good idea," I thought. I read on and learned that I would be the anchorman. I was stunned. I didn't know whether to be elated or irritated. I had not known that the program was being planned. No one asked me about hosting it. Once it was decided, no one told me officially. There was just an anonymous press release that I was reading while sitting in the garden of the Imperial Hotel in New Delhi late at night. I was happy about the assignment but could not suppress a deep unease. If network television bestowed such jobs in this cavalier manner, no doubt it would take them away in the same fashion.

The *Vietnam Weekly Review* is a long-forgotten footnote in the annals of television news. It was unique in that it provided a coherent wrap-up of the Vietnam story every week, the sustained in-depth reporting television rarely undertakes today. Unfortunately, though perhaps inevitably, the program was relegated to what was then the television ghetto of Sunday afternoon. Professional sports leagues were only beginning to exploit the financial bonanza of network contracts as television discovered the audience-drawing appeal of the NFL, the NBA, and a seemingly endless array of golf tournaments that would soon fill up Sunday afternoons like high-rise condos on what had been a quiet residential street. Still, in 1966 there was room to slip in a modest program focused on the Vietnam War. Our small team of eight producers, writers, and production assistants was given a windowless office that reflected our lowly status in the hierarchy at NBC. We had few sponsors, but that was not surprising; the Vietnam War was as hard a sell for NBC as it was for Lyndon Johnson. In addition to featuring the latest combat footage arriving from Saigon, we produced stories on the impact of the war at home. There were reports on the growing protest movement, on the disproportionate number of blacks, measured against the total population, who were being sent to Vietnam, as well as the growing and ominous distrust that had opened between the government and a large segment of the public.

The *Vietnam Weekly Review,* whose name was as pedantic as the *Our Weekly Reader* of school days, was an introduction to the work of a television anchor. I soon learned the limitations and frustrations that go with the job, along with the perks and power. In the early weeks of the program I was able to draw on my Vietnam experience and provide personal perspective. But after two or three months, the erosion of time began to take hold. Week by week and then day by day I was losing touch with Vietnam. I was rewriting other journalists' reporting instead of providing fresh experience and direct expertise. This, of course, is what most anchor work is: you are "anchored" to your desk and studio far from any actual news event. You depend on wire service stories, newspapers, and telephone conversations with colleagues on the scene to get information. Intellectual capital is drawn down.

What was most satisfying about our weekly Vietnam program was that we were under no pressure to "dumb down" the news. Viewers were treated as adults interested in the events of their community and world. Five months after the program was launched, it was time to turn my job over to another NBC correspondent back from Saigon who could provide fresher personal experience. And there was an ideal job waiting. Europe again. Berlin.

SEPTEMBER 1966.

I woke up, pulled open the curtains of the bedroom window, and looked out on the past. That is how a day began in Berlin.

From the top floor of a postwar apartment building in the heart of the city, I could see the past clearly. A mile away, standing alone in an open field, was the Reichstag, Germany's old parliament, whose imposing presence seemed to keep other buildings from encroaching on its space. It was the stony equivalent of a tragic figure from a nineteenth-century novel. Once it had stood in the center of Berlin, which was the center of the German nation, which, in turn, dominated Europe—its politics, its economic strength, its culture. Now, twenty-one years after Hitler's and Germany's descent into fire, rubble, and ruinous defeat, it retained a proper facade but little more. Behind its back was the present: the wall of concrete slabs, barbed wire, watchtowers, and minefields built by the East Germans to divide Berlin, Germany, and Europe. The

Reichstag had been rebuilt after the destruction of war, but the makeover was not convincing. It was now a dowager parliament building in waiting, properly dressed and made up but having little to do while the West German government conducted its business elsewhere. Occasionally, government committees would come from Bonn to hold meetings in the Reichstag, but this was little more than the dutiful visits of children to their aging parents. The building had no purpose. Except to wait.

To the right of the former parliament was the Brandenburg Gate straddling the entrance to Unter den Linden, the broad avenue down which German armies, three times in seventy years, had marched off to war. To the south of the Brandenburg Gate was a vacant lot where Hitler's headquarters had stood, and next to it was the underground bunker where he died—a mound covered with scraggly grass and weeds surrounded by a fence to keep out the curious and those sympathetic toward the late *Führer.*

There are few places that impose its past on the present with the emotional force of Berlin. I would walk down a street or sit in a cafe when suddenly a shiver of recognition would strike. It was not so much the monstrous past intruding on the complacent present as the realization that the past was still alive. Anyone over forty-five had played some role, if only a passive one, as an adult under the Nazis. Hitler was dead and Nazism was buried. But people who had made that nightmare possible were chatting at the next table in a restaurant or elbowing their way by me on a crowded bus.

Young Germans, however, were growing up surprisingly undamaged by the sins of their parents' generation. I had met a number of them four years earlier when I had come to Berlin as a student. At that time we were nearing the end of the postwar era, that exceptional quarter-century walk in the sun during which the

United States dominated and helped rebuild Western Europe while assuming a mantle of moral authority that, we decided, suited us well. West Berliners could seek Old World refuge by looking down on the nouveau riche lack of sophistication they saw in Americans, but they understood it was the United States that now provided the only defense against the Soviet Union, whose army stood battle ready on the other side of the concrete wall that sliced through the city and the country and the continent.

On the western side of that wall American prestige had never been higher than it was in the winter of 1962 and the glorious spring that followed. The Cuban missile crisis continued to resonate among Berliners, who had felt particularly vulnerable during the showdown between John F. Kennedy and Nikita Khrushchev. The threat of the Soviets making a grab for isolated West Berlin, if the United States struck at Cuba, had seemed real and imminent. When that shadow of Armageddon passed, Americans and West Berliners basked in the glow of American power and Kennedy's personality. Then in June 1963 John F. Kennedy came to Berlin.

It was a warm, sunny day. Could it have been otherwise? From the moment Air Force One touched down at Tegel Airport, West Berlin television covered Kennedy's every move. I watched the black-and-white images in a room filled with German students in the dormitory where I lived. There was Kennedy sitting on the back of a convertible waving to the cheering crowds that packed both sides of the road as his motorcade headed toward the center of the city with Willy Brandt, the mayor of West Berlin, sitting on one side, and Chancellor Konrad Adenauer on the other. There was Kennedy inside the giant Siemens plant speaking to admiring workers. Next he was mounting the platform opposite the Brandenburg Gate to see the wall, the most important "photo opportunity" of the day, although the term had not yet been coined. The East Germans, though, had hung huge banners between the columns of the gate to block Kennedy's view into East Berlin and to prevent East Berliners, who were also watching West Berlin television, from rushing into Unter den Linden to wave to the American president.

At high noon the American hero rode into the large square in front of city hall to speak to the people of Berlin, on both sides of the wall. The Berliners in the square and those watching on television knew what he would say. They were accustomed to American officials praising their courage and reaffirming the American commitment to defend West Berlin. From Kennedy, though, they wanted something more. As much as they cheered him and needed his presence, they remembered that two years earlier he had done nothing when the Communists had built the wall, dividing their city and separating their families. Kennedy was aware of that too, aware that he had to make a commitment that went beyond the usual policy pronouncement. He had to make a personal commitment or what appeared to be one.

So he said, "Ich bin ein Berliner."

In the room in which I was watching the speech on television with young Germans the impact was electrifying. Kennedy's words swept across Berlin and around the world. The American president had told Berliners that he was one of them and by implication would stand with them against the Russians. But that is not all he said that day.

As an American student at the Free University, I had a front row seat when the president came to the campus to deliver a second speech. The sun was still shining; indeed, it had turned more golden in the late afternoon as Kennedy strode to an outdoor podium amid the cheers of students and faculty members. He did not repeat his "Ich bin ein Berliner" applause line. He did not talk so much about standing up to the Communists as dealing with them, negotiating with them. He talked about the wall; he talked about political and personal divisions and how they could be overcome only through dialogue. It was the vital importance of détente Kennedy was proposing, indeed urging. He had used the day brilliantly, mixing emotional theater with substantive politics. But the theater got the headlines.

NOW IT was autumn three years later.

At midnight on September 30, 1966, the lobby of the Hotel Gehrus in West Berlin was jammed with reporters and photographers. At that moment the gigantic gate of Spandau Prison swung open, and two cars sped out into the night. One carried Baldur von Shirach, the former head of the Hitler Youth. The other, Albert Speer, had been Hitler's architect and armaments minister. The two men had completed the twenty-year sentences imposed by the Nuremberg War Crimes Tribunal. While Shirach headed for the Hilton Hotel to spend his first night out of prison, Speer came to the Gehrus, a turn-of-the-century villa that had been converted into a discreet hotel favored by industrialists, actors, and orchestra conductors seeking quiet and avoiding publicity.

A barrage of flashbulbs erupted as Speer and his wife entered the lobby and made their way through the crowd. Suddenly the Third Reich had a face again in a neatly pressed dark suit under the glare of the television lights. There was an uneasy silence in the vaulted two-story-high hall, the only noise coming from the cameras performing their mechanical duty. The German reporters did not hurl questions as journalists usually do. What could they ask one of the principal figures of Nazism? "Herr Speer, are you sorry for what you did?"

The stiff silence was broken when Speer stopped on the stair-case leading up to the second-floor bedroom suite that had been reserved for him. He leaned over the railing and addressed the crowd below, in German: "I have something to tell you." A young German reporter standing in front of me, too young to remember Nazism but old enough to live with its legacy, turned his back sharply on Speer and muttered to no one in particular, "You have nothing to tell us." That night Speer made only a short state-ment—that he was happy to be free and that all he wanted to do was spend time with his family. In the years to come, however, he would have much to write and say about Hitler and Nazism.

Most of us can say with confidence that we would never be an Adolf Hitler or a Heinrich Himmler or a Hermann Goering. But an Albert Speer? All it took to be seduced was rampant ambition and an ability to close your eyes to what you did not want to see. Eleven years later I caught up with Speer. He had written a book on his experiences in the Third Reich, and I went to interview him for NBC's *Today.*

EVEN IF Albert Speer had not grown up in Heidelberg, it is where he probably would have settled when the gates of Spandau Prison closed behind him and he faced a world he did not know. More than any other West German city, Heidelberg remained untouched by time and Allied bombing patterns. On the hills rising behind the city stood the homes of the city's leading families. I drove up Wolfbrunnenweg, one of the roads climbing up from the city below. On this March morning a thick, immovable fog hung over the Neckar Valley. It was a German winter day from which color had been banished. Buildings, trees, and people all seemed to wear gray. Around a sharp turn the car came to a tall iron gate. On one side was a sign: A. Speer.

The Speer family was not true "old" Heidelberg. The elder Speer built the house in 1905, the year Albert was born. He had been free with his use of wood and gables to make a spacious gemütlich home, surrounded by wooded land, for his family. It was still that. Albert Speer had six children. One son was living with his family in a smaller house on the property, and tricycles and other toys lay scattered around the play yard. I had an uneasy feeling as I approached the main house, as if something was not right, or real. Albert Speer, Hitler's architect, armaments minister, and one of the most powerful figures in wartime Germany, was history, someone to read about, not a man who in a few seconds would open his door, smile, and invite you inside.

Albert Speer opened the door, smiled, and invited me inside. There was no difficulty establishing contact. Speer wanted to talk; indeed, I sensed he was driven to talk. At Nuremberg he admitted his guilt, but neither twenty years in Spandau Prison nor two lengthy books had eased his need to go over the past one more time. He was a man who stepped repeatedly into the backyard of his life to turn over the familiar soil, hoping to find something new, something to explain a life that had been sacrificed in such a grotesque manner to ambition. It was a self-analysis very much the product of Speer's well-ordered mind.

Speer's study was not well ordered, he acknowledged. Correspondence was piled high on his desk and worktables. One wall was lined with filing cabinets, some containing the bits and scraps of paper on which he wrote his Spandau diary. The papers were smuggled out of prison and edited into the book whose German, French, and English versions lay about, sent by the publishers for the author's signature. In his final years Speer became a very successful author. His memoirs sold over 200,000 copies in hard-back in the United States, and over a million in paperback. Speer spoke of this with a note of pride and then produced a sheet of figures he had worked out to prove he had not grown rich on his past. In addition to taxes, there were entries for contributions made to organizations in the United States and Germany, even money for his former guards at Spandau. A Speer expiation was itemized.

We walked into the living room. The furniture was old and new, and comfortable. In the corner stood a *Kacheloffen*, a tall German tile stove that reached to the ceiling and kept the room comfortably warm. Albert Speer looked very much at home and, although in his seventies, remarkably fit. He pointed out that twenty years in Spandau had some positive benefits. Yes, there were the depressions, the ferocious battles to keep intellectually alert and disciplined. Compared to that, maintaining physical fitness was easy. Speer worked in the garden and walked there daily. So did Hess, Shirach, and the other Nazi leaders who did not die in Hitler's bunker and escaped execution in Nuremberg. Speer, though, kept a record of how much he walked around the rectangular prison path and where he walked. His first goal was to cover the equivalent distance to Heidelberg.

"Like many prisoners I sometimes felt that once I reached my home in my mind I would be released." When Speer reached Heidelberg, he still had sixteen years to serve in Spandau. Sixteen years walking around the garden. So his mental journey continued southward through the Balkans, across Turkey and Asia Minor, and then north into China. As he kept track of his progress, Speer obtained books from the Berlin library to study the countries and people he would be passing through, their history, culture, and art. From China he continued through eastern Siberia. In early 1963 Speer reached the Bering Strait. He asked an

American guard who had been stationed in Alaska whether the strait froze in winter. He was told it did. "And so," said Speer, recalling his relief, "I walked across it."

Now Speer's mind was in Alaska walking down the West Coast to Seattle, San Francisco, and through Yosemite National Park. In his living room in Heidelberg Speer's eyes and voice came alive with the excitement of his adventure, his mental odyssey. When he was released from prison on September 30, 1966, he was, in his mind, approaching Mexico City.

Speer spoke easily in English. In Spandau Prison, he said, he had thought of writing Hitler's biography, indeed, thought that he, of those closest to Hitler, was best qualified to write it. "If history is to be a lesson to us," Speer said, warming to the subject of his former patron, "it is dangerous that this man is depicted incorrectly. He was not always in a rage, a carpet-biting megalomaniac. Hitler had charm and by showing charm the story becomes even more cruel." I asked Speer why he thought Hitler had charm, and he told of the first time Hitler invited him to lunch. Speer had been inspecting a newly constructed building where some plaster had fallen on his suit. Hitler said, "Oh, you are dirty" and had a servant bring one of Hitler's jackets for Speer. That was his charm, according to Speer, and to receive it from the most powerful man in Europe, when he was barely into his thirties, was more than a temptation; it was instant seduction.

Speer, I thought, was surprisingly relaxed as he spoke about Hitler. Yet his anecdotes revealed more about himself than the man he served so loyally. Perhaps that is why he never wrote Hitler's biography, but rather his own memoirs. The memory was not dimmed by time. The twenty years in prison were, he said, like suspended time when he thought back to 1945. It was an easy reach.

"I was pulled more to the man than to the Nazi Party." Speer was speaking carefully now as he approached the basic decision that forever changed his life. "Like many Germans, I suffered under the Versailles Treaty, or Diktat. My political philosophy was simple: Germany should be strong again. Hitler promised to do that." A simple explanation and a common one among Germans in the 1930s. What made Speer uncommon is that his talent came to Hitler's attention. By 1935 Hitler needed an architect to build the grandiose buildings that, like the ruins of Athens and Rome, would be permanent reminders of a third glorious civilization. When Hitler dangled the offer, Speer grabbed it. At age thirty he had the biggest contract an architect could dream of—architect of the Third Reich.

"Power is sweet and to go off power is, for a man in power, obviously something which is almost impossible," Speer observed. Once hooked by Hitler, Speer never left him. "I couldn't get away from him. He was like a magnet to me." It was a magnet that demanded unquestioned loyalty, which Speer was more than willing to provide. In 1942 Hitler asked Speer to become his minister of armaments to oversee the entire war production effort. Speer accepted, and his Faustian tale began a new chapter. He was now one of the most important wheels driving the German war machine.

Speer's pragmatic mind and his tunnel vision made it possible to ignore other things happening around him. "I must admit I was too careless with the Jewish question," Speer acknowledged to me and the camera, without showing the slightest awareness of the preposterousness of his understatement. He claimed he was never anti-Semitic and quickly added with pride (and no doubt much practice) that unlike other Nazi leaders he never included anti-Semitic references in his speeches. Yet Speer repeatedly heard Hitler rage in public and in private against the Jews, vowing to destroy them. Speer did nothing. "I must confess I never asked him about the Jews, and I did my job as if nothing were happening. I said it is not my thing." Speer offered his apology, as he offered it at the Nuremberg trials. Unlike the other defendants, he was clever to accept the guilt for what he and Nazi Germany did, but he offers no satisfying explanation for why he did it. Speer, the intellectual who claimed he held no hatred for the Jews, could only say, "It was not my thing."

An American psychologist who examined Speer after the war described him as a racehorse with blinkers. He was wearing the blinkers early one morning in Berlin when he saw a column of Jews being led quietly through the streets to a railroad station. "It was said they were going to the East," said Speer, "but of course, I should have known where they were really going." Did he ask what was to happen to them? Speer answered quietly, "No." There was a silence in the room. There was nothing more to say.

Albert Speer remained minister of armaments until the very end. It was partly loyalty to Hitler, partly the organizational challenge that he found exciting. Although the Third Reich was collapsing about him, he was able to keep war production flowing through the use of forced labor brought in from Germany's conquered lands. Five million slave laborers. Speer's blinkers could not hide them.

More than three decades later Speer showed no qualms about it. "Actually of the 5 million slave laborers, only 2 million were in my industries and were my responsibility." Speer in his precise way wanted to get the figures right. But not, as it turned out, to lessen any sense of guilt. There was no feeling of guilt, only the responsibility, the obsession, of getting the job done. I asked whether having 2 million slave laborers under his authority did not bother him. "Of course it did," Speer replied, "because the laborers could and did sabotage our work. We would have preferred to employ German women in the plants, as women were used in the United States. That was denied by Hitler, so we had to turn to forced labor." How were they treated? "I wanted them to be well fed and healthy because no work can be done by people who are starving." Speer's voice still carried the self-justifying tone of the supreme technocrat.

Albert Speer did not consider himself to be a friend of Hitler. "He had no friends, nor the capability to have friends. Even Eva Braun was only a mistress." If it was not friendship, there was something else that kept Speer close to Hitler, something more than loyalty. Speer called it the gift of fascination. Speer could and occasionally did ignore Hitler's orders, as when he refused to carry out a scorched earth policy in Germany at the end of the war. But he could not reject the man. Seven days before the end of the war, Speer, who was safely out of Berlin, flew into the capital and landed near the Brandenburg Gate next to Hitler's bunker. The Russian army was closing in rapidly and Speer knew that he might not get out, that Hitler might order him to stay in the bunker to die with him. It was more than the power of fascination that led Speer to do that. Was it a subconscious wish to die with the *Führer*? Speer would not say and probably did not know. He did know that of the ten years with Hitler that final moment in the bunker was most memorable. "He came out of one of the rooms and I said I wanted to say farewell to him. He was very cold. He just said good-by. It was done in such a cold manner that I thought it was strange that this man whom I'd venerated so long, and now knowing it was the last time we would see each other, had not a warm word for my family, not a warm word for me, just a good-by. I was so shocked. I just turned and left."

Albert Speer was silent as he sat in the comfortable armchair in front of the picture window looking out on the bare trees in his garden. He caressed a glass of old Armagnac in his hand as he thought of that last meeting with Hitler. Some people have sold their soul once. Speer did it twice. First, when he embraced Hitler and Nazism, and again when he abandoned his art, architecture, to head Germany's war industry. Speer was aware of both, aware that there was little left in life except a place in history, and even there as little more than an extensive footnote.

Today, nothing remains of Speer's creative work, which was destroyed by the war he helped to nourish as armaments minister. In his home in Heidelberg, Speer showed me the designs of buildings that were to have been built. They too say much about the man. At a time when the Bauhaus movement had finally pushed German architecture into the twentieth century, Speer was still updating the nineteenth century, complete with ponderous facades and neoclassical columns. "I was expressing Hitler's ideas and aims," Speer acknowledged. "The buildings expressed, and I expressed, the cruelty of Hitler."

Like most men in their seventies, Albert Speer enjoyed the basic pleasures best: good food, classical music (Richard Strauss and Anton Bruckner sat alongside the nineteenth-century romantics on his record shelf), and his grandchildren. If Speer had not joined Hitler, it is safe to say that he would have become a successful, if anonymous, architect and would have ended up exactly where he was on that winter day, sitting in his living room in Heidelberg sipping an old Armagnac. But he did meet Hitler. Would he do it again? "If I knew the consequences, no," said Speer flatly. "Not knowing the consequences?" Speer posed the question himself. "If I were asked again as a young man, and given all those powers again, the temptation would be very great. It would be hard to say no." Speer's answer was more than honest. It was human, which made it all the more frightening.

It was time to go. Speer opened the front door. I thanked him for his time and told him that his latest book should sell well in the United States. "I don't really see why it should," he said with what appeared to be genuine modesty. "Who is interested in these stories now?" I told him that many people were. Many books dealing with the Nazi period are published, and one reason they usually sell well is that Jews, who have an understandable interest in the period and its horrors, are big book buyers in America. Speer was not aware of this, and for the first time in our three-hour conversation he was caught off balance. He was at a loss for words. He did not realize that there was nothing that needed to be said about what was a simple fact of the publishing industry. His face, though, told me that he was searching for an appropriate response. Suddenly his eyes lit up. The well-ordered Speer mind had found the answer. "Well, you know, some of my best friends are Jews. I had a wonderful interview here the other day with Israeli television." Speer's face was open, his smile warm, and his handshake firm.

Outside on the lawn the toys of Albert Speer's grandchildren remained scattered about. The fog still covered the Neckar Valley.

Chapter 10

1968!

ONE OF THE more important pieces of advice I have received
in my journalistic wanderings came from a veteran network
news executive. "Garrick," he said, "anyone who pays for a vacation in this business is crazy."

Fortunately that advice came early, and in February 1968 I was
breathing in the alpine splendor of St. Moritz, Switzerland. The
flow of news in Europe was slow and unexciting. Aside from the
distant sounds of war in Vietnam and the American version of a
cultural revolution in the United States, 1968 appeared to offer little work to foreign correspondents living in Europe. Yet, within a
few weeks, any sense of calm and false complacency would be torn
by a chain of events that would extend from Saigon to Memphis to
Los Angeles to Prague. It was 1968, after all, the most challenging
year television news had faced. It began quietly there in St. Moritz.

The story, or at least the excuse for going to Switzerland, was that Club Med, the French purveyor of bargain basement vacations, was invading the winter Valhalla of the super rich. Club Med had bought two hotels on the outskirts of St. Moritz and each week brought in a chartered train from Paris packed with skiers seeking an ambiance of luxury and glamour at an affordable price. A Saturday morning on the station platform vibrated with the distinctive cacophony of mass tourism, French style. People pushed to get off the train as parents passed suitcases and skis through the windows of their compartments to their children on the platform below. Two impatient teenagers squeezed through a window and dropped to the platform with a resilient spring in their feet. Tour guides struggled to herd the groups while grown-ups, still rumpled from the night's sleep in the narrow berths, tried to keep baggage and family intact. The inevitable breakdown in organization was heard in the frightened cries of a child lost in the milling confusion.

None of this was seen or heard in the private chalets and stately old hotels rising up the mountainside above the station. The inhabitants of these elevated heights arrived by Ferrari or at least Mercedes, and at best in their private jet. At 8:30 in the morning, while the train station reverberated with the excitement of arrival, a stately silence resonated through the broad corridors of the grand hotels. Shoes left on the hallway carpet outside the double-thick bedroom doors had been polished and returned, one of the small extra touches tradition and money still provided the guests, who slept, skied, dined, and danced to the daily and nocturnal rhythm of the St. Moritz elite. By 10:00 A.M. some stirring could be detected as the guests began to don their designer ski suits in time to make at least one or two runs on the slopes before lunch at a private club on the mountain. The old guard, which didn't ski, held forth in the curling rinks, their English accents and personal gravitas as quiet and weighty as the heavy stones that glided with a whisper across the manicured ice.

Late in the afternoon, in the Kulm Hotel, was the daily tea dance. A small combo performed a medley of fox-trots with a restraint that moved only a few guests to step on to the small parquet dance floor but did allow quiet tête-à-tête conversations over freshly cut cucumber and smoked salmon sandwiches. Restraint and discretion were also the words I heard when I asked the hotel manager for permission to film the tea dance. "Of course you may," he replied. "But please ask each couple before you take their picture," he added. His knowing eyes announced his next line: "Some of the gentlemen here may not be with their wives."

Life in St. Moritz in February 1968 seemed inviolate. On a television in the hotel bar Charles de Gaulle, a figure of self-styled grandeur and unquestioned authority, was opening the Winter Olympics in Grenoble. Outside, in the narrow streets and snow-covered lanes of St. Moritz, Farah Diba passed in the well-dressed ski crowd. Her husband, the Shah of Iran, was the undisputed leader of the St. Moritz set. A few in the fraternity of bankers and business magnates were aware that inflation rates were beginning to rise in the United States, where the government was not taxing its people enough to pay for the war in Vietnam. "Bad economics," they said, but "politics is politics." Conversation turned briefly to Czechoslovakia. Wasn't it exciting, how Alexander Dubcek was throwing the old Stalinists out of power! Could a human face be grafted onto communism? And so the chitchat continued at the bar and over dinner. Who could have imagined that within a few days Vietcong commandos would enter Saigon, penetrate to the very center of the U.S. embassy grounds, and destroy an American presidency? Who would have predicted that by May stable France would be paralyzed by strikes and demonstrations, and the French monarch-president, like Louis XVI, would be forced to flee Paris? And who could have conceived that by June, in the United States, Martin Luther King and Robert F. Kennedy would no longer be vibrant figures but memories? By August, the Red Army had wiped away the human face of Czechoslovak communism, while the anger and agony of a divided America erupted inside and outside the Democratic convention in Chicago. But that lay so far in the future, all of seven months.

FEBRUARY 24. It is night, and it is dark. I am lying on the earthen floor of an underground bunker. I am trying to sleep. So are the other men of the U.S. Army's First Division. We will sleep here, safe from the danger of North Vietnamese artillery shells. In the dark, I think of St. Moritz on the morning I left, just a few days ago. The snow was so soft and deep, the sky a rich blue, so perfect, so peaceful. I ask myself, "Why am I here?" There is the comfort of a good answer: the Tet offensive, big story! Okay. How do I feel about being here? Not in the stale air of the bunker, where bodies are packed together in sleep, but back in Vietnam after an absence of two and a half years. There is an uncomfortable answer: I feel vulnerable. Three years ago, as a twenty-five-year-old, I knew something unpleasant could happen to a person in a war, including a journalist. But I didn't think it would happen to me. Now that false faith in youthful immortality is gone.

One week later I am walking along a small irrigation canal in the Mekong Delta. With me are an NBC cameraman and sound technician. Marching ahead of and behind us is a column of soldiers of the U.S. Ninth Infantry Division. The sun, straight overhead, beats down. It is hot and sticky. We have been on patrol since before sunrise but have not found the Vietcong, or they have chosen not to find us. I look at the soldiers, their shirts soaked in sweat and their helmets heavy and hot on their heads, and recognize a truth—the most demanding, thankless, unrewarding, and boring job is that of combat soldier. That the work is unremitting tedium interrupted by the occasional horrors of war is an old cliché. But within the cliché is the paradox. The combat soldier, the "grunt," cannot afford to allow the tedium to numb his mind. His life depends on a superhuman effort to remain alert. So do the lives of others. And now our alertness is about to be put to the test.

We have halted along the banks of the canal. I hear the "cracks" as the sniper opens fire. I do not think. The neuro-wiring between the ear and the legs, a survival mechanism that bypasses the slower, rational, decisionmaking part of the brain, kicks in, and I drop. Everyone is flat on the ground. Somewhere, from deep inside me, I hear a voice saying "Move!" Suddenly I am diving over other prone forms into the muddy canal water four wonderfully protected feet beneath the bank. Here it is safer. As the sniping continues, I shout at the cameraman to jump in with me. He looks at the water up to my neck, thinks of my six feet six inches, and shouts, "I can't, it's too deep. We'll lose the camera."

"It's all right," I yell back amid the earsplitting din as the American soldiers return fire, "I'm on my knees." He and the soundman, who is attached to the camera by an electronic umbilical cord, jump into the water with a shout of relief.

The sniper is hiding in an earthen bunker only forty yards away. We think he is alone. We can't see him but he can see us, or at least any American helmet that rises above the banks of the canal. Helicopter strikes are ordered in, and within ten minutes their rockets are tearing up the earth ahead of us. The sniper has stopped shooting. Is he dead? Most likely he has escaped through

a hidden tunnel. The patrol begins moving again, and we head for
the protection of a tree line, where we will set up defensive positions for the night. We have our story, our brief bang-bang. It will
soon be too dark to film. We want to get out and get back to
Saigon.

As we wait for the supply helicopters to arrive, a young
American officer, a captain, is carried in on a litter. He is in pain
as four soldiers lay him down on the edge of the field where the
medevac helicopter will land. The officer has been shot through
the stomach. We wait twenty minutes and then another forty-five
minutes, and then we wait some more. This is not good. The captain has grown quieter. He wants water. His men huddled around
him know that with a stomach wound he cannot be allowed any.
A sergeant pulls a handkerchief out of his shirt pocket. It looks
eerily out of place. Somehow, it has stayed clean and white and
carefully folded, unsoiled by the messiness of war. The sergeant
spreads some water from his canteen on the handkerchief and
lightly presses the moisture on the lips of the captain, who is slipping into shock. The men follow the procedure they learned in
basic training and have practiced so often in Vietnam. They keep
the wounded man's legs raised slightly. One soldier holds his left
hand and speaks quietly to him. He tries to get the captain to
answer, to talk about his home and family. He tells him that help
is coming.

The captain's replies are becoming softer and his silences
longer, and dusk is settling over the delta. On the field radio come
assurances that a helicopter is on its way. We are all listening for
that faint sound, the first distant staccato beats of the helicopter's
rotor. For Americans in Vietnam, it will forever be the theme
music of the war. You strain to hear it. Sometimes you imagine
you hear it but it's not there; it is only an aural mirage. Yet like the

104

mirage of a desert oasis you want it to be real, for the helicopter means rescue, release, escape from the war. The helicopter will sweep in and lift you out of the mud and danger and transport you to your civilized, imported, prefabricated, air-conditioned world where Elvis or Mozart is on the tape player—the world in which you belong. For the captain, that big mechanical bird with the beating wings means life. But the day is fading.

The helicopter is overhead now, about 1,000 feet up, out of range of Vietcong ground fire, searching for the smoke grenades that we are setting off to mark our position. The colored smoke, though, blends into the dimming twilight and the tree line. The pilot can't see it. The radio operator tries to "talk" him to the landing zone. In ten minutes it will be night and the helicopter will return to base. The captain will die. More smoke grenades are ignited and finally we are seen. The helicopter races in. There is no red cross on its side, there is no medic on board, but it is rescue. The captain, on his litter, is placed on the floor of the helicopter between the two door gunners. I climb on with the cameraman and soundman. I am asked to put my helmet under the captain's knees to keep his legs up. He is unconscious. He is breathing very slowly. It is twenty minutes to the field hospital.

We take off. We are tense. The helicopter is a naked, exposed target until it rises above the range of ground fire. At 1,000 feet we have ascended to a world of invulnerability. The door gunner next to me takes his hands off his .30-caliber machine gun and lights a cigarette. We stare at the last rays of sun spreading across the flat delta plain, absorbing the intense and infinite beauty and peacefulness of the moment. He offers a smile of shared relief, of having survived another day. I smile back at him, then we look down at the captain. He is dead. The door gunner shakes his head, takes another puff on his cigarette, and looks at the captain's face, filled with peace. Then he turns and loses himself in the contemplation of the setting sun.

THE GRILL ROOM of the Crillon Hotel in Paris is packed. The wine is flowing and the conversation is animated. It is May 1968; the eve of the first session of the Paris Peace Talks on Vietnam, and the American press and television hordes have descended on the City of Light. Outside in the Place de la Concorde there is little traffic, for the French are going through the preliminary motions of a revolution. Across the Seine, in the Latin Quarter, students and police mount their nocturnal confrontations under a shroud of tear gas in what will be filed in French history under the benign heading of the "events of May." Strange, how culture defines action, even in street demonstrations. The students don't attack the French police, but rather, in the time-honored tradition of Parisian uprisings, they build barricades as each side digs deeper into its resistance to the other.

Four weeks have passed since that day in the muddy canal, and the helicopter lifting off above the Mekong Delta with a dying soldier. The French maître d'hôtel is passing out the large menu. A small arrangement of freshly cut flowers stands in a shallow vase on the white linen tablecloth. Each place is equipped with a fully arranged arsenal of cutlery with which to attack the delights of French cuisine. The matching napkins are folded and sharply creased, and they remind me of the sergeant's carefully folded handkerchief back in the Mekong Delta.

Several hundred American reporters, technicians, picture takers and executives are in Paris, loaded with technical gadgetry and expense accounts to provide massive coverage of the event at hand, America's desired exit from war. Our presence is like the arrival of a circus in town. It has prompted local press comment and debates over whether the enormous logistical effort by the networks should be viewed with awe as the powerful lion of technology or dismissed as a sideshow curiosity—a fat lady noted for her physical size rather than mental acuity. But, like the traveling circus, we have become part of the local landscape. NBC and other news organizations have pitched their tents at the Crillon Hotel, which in addition to its old world luxury and its prime location on the Place de la Concorde, is the headquarters of the American negotiating team. That gave the Crillon's Grill Room a leg up on its competitors as the journalistic meeting place. Just around the corner, Maxim's restaurant, with its Michelin stars and Belle Epoque decor, is a constant lure, particularly as Maxim's has sent a card to each of the accredited American journalists welcoming us to Paris and offering a 25 percent discount on all meals at the restaurant for the duration of the negotiations. Poor Maxim's knows a lot about public relations and obviously a lot about French cuisine, but little about the ability of diplomats to sit and talk forever. The peace conference will run for nearly five years. And so will the war, which is being waged on more than one front.

SHORTLY BEFORE the deluge of 1968 broke upon us, our NBC office in Berlin was contacted by an East German film agency with an offer they thought we could not and would not refuse. They were right. The offer was seven and a half hours of filmed interviews with eleven American prisoners of war in North Vietnam, plus silent film of life in a POW camp filmed by an East German documentary film team. It was the first time that pictures of the prisoners, or interviews had been offered by the Communists. Once again we faced the delicate and potentially explosive test of drawing a line between legitimate reporting and abetting propagandists, not to mention the enemy. And again there was competitive pressure. If we did not buy the film, CBS News certainly would. So the negotiations began.

Our office was headed by a Berlin-born naturalized American, Gary Stindt. Five years earlier he had displayed journalistic flair by sending a camera team into a tunnel as it was being secretly dug beneath the Berlin Wall into the eastern side of the city. The camera team filmed the dramatic escape of East Berlin families, adults and children, to the West and freedom. The documentary film won the Emmy award that year as the best television program in any category in the United States, the only occasion in which a news program has scaled such critical heights.

Not surprisingly, it was no longer advisable for Stindt to show his face or passport in East Berlin, and when there was work to do on the Communist side of the wall I shuttled back and forth through the crossing point at Checkpoint Charlie. There was no telephone link between the divided sides of the city, but one morning a message came clattering in over our telex machine. It was an invitation to come to an editing room of the East German film company to view some of the material that was being offered, a seven-minute film of a prisoner of war camp near Hanoi.

The two producers of the film knew that they possessed a world scoop as they sat me down at the editing table in the small room, dimmed the light, and started the film. I looked intently at the illuminated screen in front of me as the black-and-white images began moving, silently. The pictures showed the Americans pilots in pajama-type outfits walking slowly about an outdoor garden area and then in their quarters. I felt I was peering into a forbidden world, one that no outsider was allowed to enter, certainly no other American. I was also looking carefully to see if the scenes had been staged, whether the Americans were cooperating with the cameraman or performing under duress. There was a sequence of prisoners decorating a Christmas tree with paper chains. The next scene showed four prisoners playing cards, the next an American reading a letter from home and then writing a letter. Finally came the food, a table covered with large quantities of rice and meat that the pilots ate with spoons. The performance, I felt, was too perfect, and throughout it there were telltale signs, deliberate signals that shouted out in their silence that what I was seeing was not the truth. A handwritten card on the Christmas tree said "Merry Christmas Day." An American would say "Merry Christmas," not "Merry Christmas Day."

Throughout the brief film, the faces of the prisoners remained impassive but their hands did not. One American sat on the edge of a bed. On the screen his face was immobile, void of any emotion as it stared at the lens in close-up. Slowly, the camera began to pan down to the floor. As it did, the prisoner leaned slightly forward, rested his forearms on his knees, with his hands loosely clenched, except for the middle finger of his right hand. It hung straight down. The East German hovering behind me leaned over and asked, with a betraying note of worry in his voice, "Does that mean anything?" "It doesn't mean anything to me," I replied, knowing that giving someone "the finger" had not yet entered the physical vocabulary of East Germans. A few seconds later I watched another prisoner turn his back to the camera as if he did not want to be filmed. He scratched the back of his neck and as he did, he quickly extended his middle finger upward and then withdrew it.

As I drove back through Checkpoint Charlie, I knew that we

were on the inside track to getting the film, but also that at some point we would have an unsightly bidding war with CBS News. The East German producers had given me the names of the American POWs they had interviewed. As I went down the list, one name leapt off the page, Colonel Robbie Risner. I had interviewed Risner sitting in his fighter-bomber at the Da Nang air base in January 1965. Perhaps, I thought, this would be worth more than money. I sent a telex to the East Germans that we had the Risner interview. I could imagine the wheels turning in the producers' heads. A response came almost immediately; yes, they wanted the interview as part of the deal. Risner, it turned out, was not just one of the pilots interviewed; they wanted to make him the centerpiece of their program.

We reached a tentative agreement; NBC would provide a copy of my Risner interview and a fee of $15,000 in exchange for the seven minutes of prison scenes I had viewed. The long interviews with the American POWs would not be available until after a documentary program, to be called *Pilots in Pajamas*, was shown in East Germany. We agreed to sign the contract in West Berlin a few days later. But when the East German producers (who had the rare authorization to visit the West) arrived at Kranzlers Cafe on the Kurfürstendamm, they were upset. That morning the *New York Times* had published a story claiming that the Communists were selling propaganda film of American prisoners and demanding half a million dollars for it. The article quoted an NBC News denial that we had bought any film, which at the time was still correct. I suspected that CBS had planted the story in order to smoke us out, to see whether we had already purchased the film and if we had, to embarrass us. The East Germans were worried because they thought that the NBC denial meant we had changed our mind and would not go through with the agreement. They also hinted that they were having trouble with the North Vietnamese, whose propaganda interest was in having the film shown in the West. Now the comrades in Hanoi were also motivated by the prospect of earning a share of the money. For us, the dilemma was not only the widely publicized, but fictitious, half million dollar figure. CBS would know, from the NBC denial, that we did not yet have the film in our possession.

We plied the East Germans with tea and rich German cake and agreed to meet again that evening. An hour later we were in our office when the telex sputtered to life. Slowly it printed out the inevitable. When the East Germans returned to their office, they found an offer from CBS that was considerably higher than ours. Would we care to make a counteroffer? The clacking of the telex gave way to the quiet hum of its motor as the operator on the other side of the Berlin Wall waited for our response. Gary Stindt and I called a top new executive at NBC in New York, and the decision was made not to get sucked into a bidding war over what could, and would, be seen by many back home as propaganda material. We activated our end of the telex and sent back a curt message: we would see them as planned at seven that evening in the bar of the Kempinski Hotel.

They were on time. We settled into a corner table away from the cocktail hour piano. The room was filled with prosperous businessmen and stylishly dressed women, not the proper setting, I thought, for making deals for a film about fellow Americans in captivity. Yet I had no doubt that the film was journalistically valid. It showed Americans who had not been seen and confirmed that they were alive. We would state that the scenes were apparently staged and that we could not and should not take them at face value. But there was still the CBS counteroffer. As a white-jacketed waiter served us drinks and the pianist broke into Johann

Strauss waltzes, we told the East Germans that we had reached our limit, $15,000. Our offer was final, I said. If they preferred CBS, they should take their money. The East German producer asked whether my interview with Colonel Risner was in Berlin ready to be handed over. It was, I replied, in our office across the street. He nodded, paused, and then pulled out a copy of the contract from his pocket and signed it on the spot. The film was ours. And the American POWs in the "Hanoi Hilton" would soon be on American television screens, on NBC.

PRAGUE, JULY 1968.

The gentle Valtava River winds quietly through Prague, dividing the city without separating it. On one side, up on a hill, the Hradcany Castle, the home of kings past, sits shrouded in the morning mist dominating the city below with the weight and self-assurance that was the special gift of Gothic architects.

On the opposite bank of the river, you step into the old town. It is a rarity, a genuinely old town; the facades of houses and larger buildings carry the grime of centuries. The residents of the old town conduct their daily shopping in the traditional central European fashion, moving from shop to shop, searching for what is available in the stores and filling their net shopping bags as they make up that evening's dinner menu. As they head home, umbrellas shelter raincoats, which protect sweaters, which keep out the chill of this wet, disappointing summer. But there is no protection from the tension, which is palpable. Their hopes and fears for the immediate future have turned their well-ordered, predictable Czech lives into a stomach-roiling roller coaster ride of manic and depressive proportions.

Is it 1968? Or is it 1938, when another crisis cast its shadow over Czechoslovakia and Europe? On a Sunday in late July, I walk down from the Hradcany hill after a long lunch with Czech journalists. It has not been a happy gathering. For a week now, the Soviet Union has been escalating its war of nerves against Czechoslovak leaders, who have been moving their brand of socialism away from the orthodoxy of Marx and Lenin and away from the unrelenting control of the Kremlin. The polemical attacks and slightly veiled threats hurled at the leadership of Alexander Dubcek are echoed and amplified by the Polish and East German chorus anxious to propel the drama to its fated conclusion. We live with constant rumors of imminent invasion.

When I reach the Valtava, and the baroque Charles Bridge, I pause and soak up the peaceful scene. The sun is making one of its rare guest appearances in the city. The bridge, closed to traffic, is filled with families strolling and young children playing, from one end to the other. Students sit on benches talking and gesticulating rapidly. We are all savoring the fragile pleasure of a peaceful Sunday afternoon. We know that by next Sunday it may all be gone; the Red Army could be occupying the country, its tanks blocking this exquisite bridge.

Alexander Dubcek and his fellow leaders have been summoned to a showdown meeting with Leonid Brezhnev and the entire Soviet Politburo. It is to take place this week at the railroad station at Cierna, a tiny town on the Czech side of the border with the Soviet Union. It is a small stage for such high drama: the first time the entire Soviet Politburo has traveled outside the Soviet Union. It will be an inquisition conducted by the cardinals of the Marxist-Leninist Church. Like inquisitions of the past, the choice it offers the heretics is to recant or face the 1968 version of death at the stake. Hundreds of thousands of Czechs and Slovaks have signed petitions and sent letters to Dubcek urging him not to give in to the Soviet pressure. The mood is a Central European version of "Give me liberty or give me death." It will be Dubcek and his petitions versus the Russians and their tanks.

Now, on a Sunday afternoon on the Charles Bridge, I indulge in what I suspect everyone else is doing: fixing the moment in our minds. The chips have been played, the tiny shining ball is bouncing around the spinning wheel, and the course of events to follow is no longer under anyone's control. Europe lived through this on the eve of World War I and again in 1938 and 1939. Americans tasted it, briefly, during the Cuban missile crisis. Since then, the management of political conflict has become an honored and rather successful craft called crisis management. Ultimatums and deadlines are no longer supposed to be the stuff of diplomacy. Armies no longer mobilize along borders. But here it is happening again; armies are mobilizing. The mind is concentrated.

Foreign journalists have not been allowed to travel to Cierna. Like everyone else we now sit by the radio waiting for the latest bulletin. If Dubcek is reported to be smiling when he comes out of a session, national spirits rise. But as the talks continue into a second and third day, spirits sink. The Russians must be browbeating poor Alexander, the Czechs say. Finally, the Russians take their train back to Moscow. Dubcek returns to Prague and announces an extraordinary event.

There are rare moments that a journalist cannot search for but can only be fortunate to recognize when they occur, the moment when a big, complex story is reduced to a single illustrative incident, when history becomes anecdote. It happened on August 3, 1968, on a hillside outside Bratislava. The hill overlooked the Danube and the capital of Slovakia, whose people had long felt slighted by their belief that the wider world saw them living in the political shadow of Prague. Like most self-images, and self-fulfilling prophecies, it was largely true, since that is the way the Slovaks saw themselves.

This second-city complex was brought home to foreign journalists by friendly Slovaks eager to correct our adjectives. It was not the "Czech" crisis, we were told, but the Czechoslovak (or better yet Czecho-Slovak). The Russians were sensitive to the delicate ethnic balance in the nation, and at the end of World War II they erected a memorial on the hill in Bratislava to the memory of the Soviet liberation of Slovakia from the Nazis. In its monumental size and in the heroic pose of the Soviet soldier on top, it conceded little to other works of socialist realism that had been churned out by sculptors and architects since the war. From the base of the memorial, a walk ran about eighty yards to the top of broad steps, which then descended a similar distance to a road below, where a motorcade of black limousines, on this hot, sunny day, was pulling to a stop. The configuration of the hill made for a purposefully long climb and then a final, dramatic approach to the memorial. The architect and landscapers wanted to give those who came to honor the war dead a sense of pilgrimage.

The agreement that Alexander Dubcek and the Soviet leaders had reached in the small railroad station in Cierna was to call an urgent summit meeting of the Communist leaders of Eastern Europe to resolve the crisis. Now those leaders who had come to Bratislava were stepping out of their limousines. They were about two dozen, dressed in conservative business suits of a far superior cut and quality than normally spied on the streets of Bratislava or Moscow. Without any orders or discussion, they formed a phalanx three rows deep and began moving up the steps. When they looked upward, they beheld a shocking sight: one they had never seen in their Marxist-Leninist world, one that must have filled their authoritarian hearts with disdain and fear. For looming above them was a human wall of Western TV cameramen and still photographers spread out across the top of the steps, furiously taking pictures of the scene below. What we were witnessing as we looked down was more than a photo op. It was a Communist gathering of unprecedented dimension—the presidents, prime ministers, and party general secretaries of six countries. Never before had Western journalists been this close to them and never had we been allowed to operate so freely in the presence of so much Communist power. There was a babble of voices in English, French, German, and Italian among the photographers as they jostled for position, hoping that the next click of their camera would be next week's cover on *Time* or *Paris Match.*

I was in the throng, standing next to my cameraman, whose zoom lens was pulling the distant figures into close-up. "I've got Brezhnev," he said. "And there is Kosygin [the Soviet prime minister] and Podgorny [the president] and Suslov." Even Michail Suslov, the secretive and doctrinaire defender of the Communist faith who rarely left the Soviet Union, had come to Bratislava! Incredulity mounted as we saw the picture that was moving toward us with an unwavering gait. There was Ulbricht from East Germany, Gomulka from Poland, Kadar and Zhivkov from Hungary and Bulgaria, and, amid them, Alexander Dubcek of Czechoslovakia. What, I wondered, were these Communist leaders thinking as they moved steadily, if slowly, up the steps? In front of them, seemingly as impenetrable as the Berlin Wall they had built, was their greatest nightmare come to life—an uncontrollable free press at work, journalists who showed no fear, little respect, and no intention of stepping aside. The local authorities had failed to organize security or press arrangements, and the scene was quickly taking on the dynamics of a Central European

Battle of Bunker Hill. The forces of oppression, arrayed shoulder to shoulder, their exposed chests protected only by the medals they had awarded themselves, moved resolutely forward to take the hill that their orthodoxy taught them was rightfully theirs. On the summit was our ragtag, undisciplined army of rebels who had long seen the whites of their targets' eyes through their zoom and telephoto lenses and were now defending that inalienable right of photographers everywhere for "just one more shot, please."

Suddenly there was no space left between the advancing leaders and the horde of journalists. Led by the bulky Leonid Brezhnev, the Communists broke through the journalists' ranks. We had lost our first line of defense, but we knew how to conduct guerrilla warfare on the run. What followed, I suspect, caused lasting trauma among the comrades as they tried to maintain their composure. This was not easy given that they and the photographers and camera teams were now helplessly intermingled as journalists pushed and shoved each other to get the better close-up picture. One cameraman spun around in the moving crowd, banging his camera into the head of the Communist leader of Hungary. The party leader of Bulgaria nearly tripped over a television camera cable. I was knocked off balance by a photographer and, in turn, bumped into the humorless Walter Ulbricht from East Berlin, who clearly was not amused. The Communist leaders proceeded around the memorial as Brezhnev, in the lead, pointed out the litany of battles inscribed on the sides, the horrendously costly route, paid in lives, that the Red Army had followed from near defeat by the Germans to victory in 1945.

The issue facing Brezhnev and his acolytes that day, though, was not the sacrifice of Soviet lives. It was how to maintain control over a small country that wanted to practice the Marxist faith in its own way, or even abandon it. Amid the circuslike scene of

Communist dictators and Western journalists stumbling around the war memorial, Brezhnev and the others clearly did not have much confidence in Alexander Dubcek. He had promised that he would control his press. Now they saw that he could not even control a gaggle of reporters and Western paparazzi. Czechoslovakia's fate may have been sealed that day. Seventeen days later, led by their tanks, a quarter million Soviet and Warsaw Pact troops invaded the country.

Chapter 11

ONCE IN A LIFETIME

Aᴼᴛᴇʀ ᴄᴏᴠᴇʀɪɴɢ the Soviet invasion, I left the sorrow of Prague and returned to Berlin. It was time to get away—away from news, away from the still vivid memory of Vietnam at Tet and France in near revolution, and away from the gray, wet summer of northern Europe. I headed south to Spain to look for the sun and visit friends, and I decided to drive instead of fly. And why not? For all its turmoil and upheavals, 1968 was still a time when one American dollar bought four German marks, when four thousand dollars could, and had, purchased a Mercedes 230-SL roadster with only 15,000 miles on the odometer. I headed through East Germany to Munich, where I spent the first night.

The next morning my route continued south through the lake country of Bavaria. The top of my roadster was down, the sun was rising warmly, and the wind on my face added to the sense of exhilaration that I felt. Ahead loomed the dramatic profile of the Alps, more formidable and enduring than any wall built by the emperors of Rome or the Communist masters in East Berlin. Now, on this beautiful day in early October, the rugged mountains were more a gateway than a barrier. The Mercedes accelerated up the mountain highway into Austria, the road twisting and switching back constantly as it struggled for altitude. At the top of the pass I stopped at an inn with a panoramic view of the surrounding peaks covered with eternal snow. Beauty and majesty were everywhere. And there was peace. In eight months, from the Mekong Delta to Paris to the hope and tragedy of the Czechs and Slovaks, 1968 had been a year of unimaginable intensity—violence, death, passion, and dreams destroyed. Looking out on the stillness of the Alps, I realized that never again was there likely be such a series of crises and dramas around the world, one piling up against the next in so little time. And if there were, it was not likely that I would be able to experience them all. Or if I did, I would not be tasting them with the freshness of youth.

I headed down the other side of the pass, drove for several hours through the Austrian Tirol, and then cut over into the southeastern corner of Switzerland. That evening, as the last sunlight was retreating from the valley, I reached St. Moritz. In February the village had resonated with skiers and the international set and, for a couple of days, an NBC News team observing the social rituals and an afternoon tea dance in one of the grand old hotels. Now it was the end of the summer season. Only one hotel was still open, and it was to close the next day for vacation. The only other guests in the nearly empty dining room belonged to a small group of off-season English tourists.

Two days and an overnight boat ride from Barcelona brought me to the island of Majorca. Ahead lay a month free for the sea and the sun, and long siestas in the afternoon heat. Or so I thought. Within a week, a telegram summoned me to meetings in New York with my bosses. I was happy living in Berlin and traveling to cover stories anywhere in the world. In New York, though, I discovered that correspondent jobs were opening up in London and Paris. London was the top European post, but Paris was a part of life waiting to happen. The executives told me I was qualified for either job but not yet senior enough (which I took to mean old enough) for London. That left Paris, if I wanted it. I didn't want it yet; perhaps a year in the future, I said. A year in the future, I was told, the job wouldn't be there.

I arrived in Paris on a Sunday in December in the belief, or hope, that I would have a better chance of surviving the reputed madness of French drivers if I were to slip into their capital on a weekend rather than a workday. I had given up my apartment (rented, furnished) in Berlin, and what I could not fit into the trunk of the car I had shipped to Paris. As I crossed the border, I turned the radio dial from a German station to a French one, and tuned in to a new lightness of being. It was in a language that hovered in the air—words spoken and words sung, beautiful sounds joined together in elegant, flowing lines, which in turn expressed thoughts with an enthusiasm, an élan so different from what I had left behind in Germany.

A few weeks earlier, on a visit, I had found an apartment (rented, furnished). I discovered quickly, and happily, that I am not one of those Americans who have to choose sides when dealing with the French; I am neither Francophile nor Francophobe. I developed a proper live-and-let-live relationship with neighbors, the food merchants in the local marketplace, and above all with the building concierge, an elderly woman who in the best tradition of her profession knew everything going on in her domain, including the discreet fact that the charming little hotel across the street with the high-priced rooms was more than a quiet retreat for tourists. It was, I learned later, a well-known hideaway for French husbands and their mistresses who were ready to rent the rooms by the hour.

The NBC News bureau was located on the Champs Elysées. From my small corner office I looked up the avenue to the Arc de Triomphe. On the narrow balcony outside, I could film my on-camera standups with a Paris picture postcard backdrop. Below, in a side street, there was a busy bistro where long lunches could be enjoyed. The Bordeaux red was cheap, the oysters and vegetables fresh, the crusts on the tarts divine, and cholesterol an unused word in either everyday French or English. And in a Europe recovering from the traumas of 1968, the news work was not too demanding.

If geography is destiny, then I suppose Paris is the right place to meet your wife. It happened in the spring of 1970, and not under the best of circumstances. One morning I received a phone call from Gertje Rommeswinkel. The name sounded Dutch. Her accent in English had an indefinable European lilt, but she was born and raised in Berlin, had gone to university in Paris, and made her career there as an account executive at a major public relations company. I knew of Gertje from my Berlin years, where I was told I should get in touch with her as soon as I arrived in Paris. There had been a few failed attempts on the telephone to contact each other, and then mutual silence. My silence came from the belief that she was about to be married. Her silence came from the fact that, yes, she had been involved with a man, but she had not married him. The misunderstanding came to light with a phone call from her one fine spring day. At first it was all business. Gertje was flying to New York with some of her top management people to learn how the Americans, then as now the perceived masters of

image and message, handled public relations and political lobby-
ing. She was looking for business contacts and we agreed to have
lunch the next day. Consulting my *Michelin Guide*, I found a
restaurant near her office and called back to confirm the time and
place. I thought I had made a good choice with L'Escargot, a two-
star restaurant—good but not pretentious. Three stars would have
been overdoing it, but no stars in a restaurant I didn't know could
be risky. One or two stars seemed the right answer. Voilà!

Voilà indeed. The next morning as I was shaving and only half
listening to the radio, the announcer finished his newscast with an
item on the new *Michelin Guide* that was to be published that day.
He rattled off the winners and losers among the culinary land-
marks. And there it was. The venerable L'Escargot had lost a star
and went down from two to one. I looked in the mirror and asked,
"What do you do now, Garrick?" Change restaurants? No, that
would show that I put too much on "star" status. Tough it out and
stick with the one star? Why not, I thought. How often does a person have the chance to enter a French restaurant for the first meal
following the loss of a Michelin star, and the prestige that disappeared with it? It might be fun, I thought.

It wasn't fun, at first. If restaurants hold wakes, this was one of
them. L'Escargot was only partly filled. The elderly waiters stood
patiently along the side of the main dining room wondering, no
doubt, how many of their not-so-faithful clients would desert
them. The maître d', though, smiled and welcomed me, a total
stranger, and an American at that, as if I were a steady customer.
He whisked me to the table, and then I saw why he was smiling.
There was Gertje, gorgeous, illuminating the surroundings. We
shook hands. As I sat down next to her on the banquette, I asked
myself silently why I had waited so long. Gertje, it was clear, did
not have the same reaction. At our second luncheon date she

brought along a girlfriend she thought I might be interested in meeting. Love and marriage came slowly. The first, over a year of dating and time spent together. The second, three years after that first lunch. But then there had been career changes.

In December 1970 I received a call from NBC in New York. Reuven Frank, the producer who created the *Huntley-Brinkley Report* and was now the president of NBC News, put it directly. "We would like you to come back to New York for a couple of weeks and help to anchor *NBC Nightly News.*" My heart skipped a beat or two as the news sank in. In television, at the time, it was the equivalent of a bishop being summoned to the Vatican to sit in for the pope. Except NBC News had three popes. Following Chet Huntley's retirement, NBC had been unable to settle on a successor to work with David Brinkley. The solution was, as it so often is, or was, in television, a compromise. There would be three anchors, Brinkley, John Chancellor, and Frank McGee, all three rotating on a seven-day basis. One day viewers would see David and John, the next day Frank and David, and perhaps the next John and Frank, and so on until viewers were totally confused, not to mention the anchors. It didn't make sense and it couldn't work, although no one at NBC was prepared to acknowledge that at the time. Meanwhile, Frank McGee was undergoing surgery, and there was a hole in the rotating anchor trinity. "Will you come?" asked Reuven. "Of course," I replied. Who wouldn't?

There may be some television viewers who think that what occurs behind the cameras and comes through the screen is the result of careful planning, meticulous preparation, and precise execution. Sometimes it happens, but I have never counted on it. The first day I anchored *Nightly News,* I came into the newsroom in the morning, carefully read every newspaper I could get my hands dirty on, went through the copy from the news wires, and braced myself for my debut. The producers thought that I should wait until after the first commercial break in the program before I would be let loose on the nation. David Brinkley would handle the top stories in the opening segment. I wrote my copy then rewrote it with a fervor of the novice back in Brussels auditioning for a job. In fact, I was, all over again. Not this job perhaps, but for the added recognition of being a broadcaster as well as a seasoned correspondent. As I worked on my script, I hoped there would be some rehearsal time, or lighting checks—an opportunity to become comfortable with the studio and the operation of *Nightly News.* I was told that wasn't necessary; I should just get to the studio by 6:25 for the 6:30 broadcast.

At 6:25 P.M. I walked into the studio, makeup in place and tie straight, and sat down on the stool behind the desk. The floor director, the man who gives visual cues when the camera comes on, walked over and said in a laconic voice, "There are only three things you need to know." He pointed to the one and only camera facing the desk. "That's your camera." He gestured at a television monitor standing next to the camera. "And that is where David Brinkley will appear." Then he motioned to the telephone on the desk. "This is your link to the control room in case anything goes wrong. Good luck."

I survived the broadcast and several more that followed, and then I went to Chicago to spend Christmas with my parents. When I returned to New York on my way back to Paris, I was asked whether I would stay on and host NBC's monthly magazine program, *First Tuesday,* in January. I sensed something was in play. Something was. Management was looking for a new permanent host of the monthly two-hour program. I was one contender; another was a young anchor at the NBC station in Los Angeles named Tom Brokaw. I commuted between Paris and New York as each of us did a few of the programs. That spring I got the call that I was to be the regular host, which history will record was the only time I, or anyone else, ever beat Brokaw out of any job. After two and a half years in France it was time to make another move, back to the United States.

My possessions were still few, although I noticed that they now filled a couple of good-sized crates when the movers came to my small apartment in Paris's Latin Quarter. There was the bric-a-brac of the journalistic life—old press cards, photos for a scrapbook one day, souvenirs from Vietnam to Africa, scripts that had been beaten out on a portable typewriter in more hotel rooms than I could remember. The next day I would fly to New York in about eight hours, but it would take longer than that to get back in touch with American life. Nine years was a long time to be away.

Chapter 12

HOME AGAIN

EACH OF US has moving images of news events engraved in our memory, from the 1937 black-and-white newsreel film of the *Hindenburg* gently approaching the zeppelin mooring station in Lakehurst, New Jersey, only to erupt in flames, to the grainy, fleeting, color pictures of John F. Kennedy in a motorcade in Dallas as the Zapruder film captured and preserved the final instant of Camelot. A scene that sticks in my mind, though, is rarely mentioned or remembered in the short history of television news. Perhaps this is because it contained no violence, caused no headlines to be written, and affected no one on planet earth. Yet hundreds of millions of people watched the event around the world. And we were fascinated.

It was barely six weeks after my return to the United States from Paris, and I watched the scene unfold from an NBC studio in

Houston, where I was taking part in the live coverage of the *Apollo 15* mission to the moon. On August 3, 1971, at 167 hours, 22 minutes, and 6 seconds into the journey, the mission commander, David Scott, stood in front of a television camera holding a feather in one hand and a hammer in the other. Working out of their lunar module (the *Falcon*), he and Jim Irwin had completed their explorations near an area of the moon known as the Hadley Rille. In their four-wheel-drive vehicle, they had driven seventeen miles across the dusty surface and for the first time were sending back color television pictures to earth. Since Neil Armstrong had pressed man's first footprints on the moon two years earlier, the Apollo program had faced no difficulty in seizing imaginations and viewers. The astronauts had thought up ingenious ways to demonstrate what the moon's weaker gravity meant. Some had jumped and bounced across the surface like a kangaroo in a space suit and helmet. Alan Shepherd brought a golf club and teed off with a drive that would make anyone lined up at a country club bar take notice. But David Scott went a step farther. He understood that he had a unique opportunity, and an enormous audience, to test a scientific hypothesis that could not be proven on earth: Galileo's assertion that in a gravity field void of atmosphere, two objects of different weights will fall to the surface simultaneously.

And now David Scott was standing there on the moon, facing us, and speaking to us through a television camera. On the screen was the running time of the *Apollo* mission.

167 hrs, 22 mins, 06 secs:

Scott: Well, in my left hand I have a feather; in my right hand, a hammer. And I guess one of the reasons we got here today was because of a gentleman named Galileo, a long time ago, who made a rather significant discovery about falling objects in gravity fields.

And we thought where would be a better place to confirm his findings than on the moon.

The camera, operated via a very long remote control from Mission Control in Houston, zoomed in on the feather and hammer and then pulled out to show the experiment.

167 hrs, 22 mins, 28 secs:

Scott: And so we thought we'd try it here for you. The feather happens to be, appropriately, a falcon feather for our *Falcon*. And I'll drop the two of them here, and, hopefully, they'll hit the ground at the same time.

Scott held the feather and hammer between his thumbs and forefingers, the feather in his left hand and the hammer in his right. He lifted his elbows up and out to the side and released the objects. The feather and the hammer floated gently down, landing on the surface at the same time.

167 hrs, 22 mins, 43 secs:

Scott: How about that!

How about it! Watching David Scott, we were seeing where television could take us (literally out of our world), what it could show us, and how it could stimulate our imaginations. But back on earth, the gravitational field in which commercial television operated, and prospered, was growing stronger. In the summer of 1971 network television was still the master of all that its electronic eye surveyed in broadcasting, with the emphasis on "broad." The business of television, more than ever, was about attracting mass audiences with programs of wide appeal. The idea of "narrow"-casting to niche audiences was at most a distant concept that claimed little time or nervous energy from network executives comfortable in their carpeted offices, corporate identities, and predictable rhythms of a television world. This was all the more remarkable in that almost everything else in the country seemed to be going through dramatic upheaval. The war in Vietnam was still a nightly visitor in living rooms, though by now it had become an unwelcome guest who had overstayed his welcome on the screen and in the nation's preoccupations. Rock music, drug use, the political and cultural rebellion of the young, and the new movements of feminism and the environment had redrawn the older and more comfortable portrait of the nation. Richard Nixon was in the White House and civil rights had been achieved in law and were beginning to be attained in the behavior of white America. In the economy, the long post–World War II boom now faced inflation, and soon stagflation. Living and income standards would begin to plateau in the 1970s, but who knew it then? And who at the networks knew that their years, our years, were numbered?

In addition to reporting on the Apollo program, in 1971–1972 I was hosting the NBC monthly magazine show and began anchoring the Saturday and Sunday night editions of *Nightly News.* NBC had abandoned the revolving door of three anchors on the weekday news: John Chancellor now sat at the desk alone, with David Brinkley offering his commentaries. Frank McGee had moved on to become host of *Today.* Life at NBC seemed settled, the future undisturbed. Walter Cronkite and CBS News still enjoyed their dominant positions, but that did not cause many sleepless nights at NBC. And while ABC was beginning to stir as a competitor in news, the idea that it would one day lead the network news race was to think the ... well, one didn't think of it.

On several occasions I attended lunches and meetings with top management. The small gatherings were held in private executive dining rooms where the decor was polished mahogany, the suits dark, and the voices well modulated. No one ever mentioned it aloud, but we all shared the silent understanding that we were living through a unique, privileged, and highly lucrative period of the television business. For two decades two major networks, and now a third, a growing ABC, had been granted a near monopoly on the right to broadcast and the right to sell advertising time with no competition to speak of; indeed a right, as critics happily pointed out, akin to printing money. And like all rights or power believed to descend from heaven, or the limited channel space on television sets, there had developed among those at the networks an inability to see this beneficent era ending. Cable television, VCRs, movie rental shops, the Internet, and someone named Ted Turner lay too far in the future to shake network complacency. We in the news divisions realized that we benefited from this good fortune but accepted it as the natural and indeed just order of things. Still, the cost of running and subsidizing a money-guzzling news operation was rising, and changes were appearing on the nightly news screen. The most dramatic change, though, had little to do with money and everything to do with the power of words and political pressure.

It is safe to say that Richard M. Nixon was never a fan of network news; likewise, most of those working in network news, or elsewhere in mainstream journalism, were never fans of our thirty-seventh president. The animus ran back to the late 1940s and young Congressman Nixon's red-baiting, which defeated opponents and destroyed careers as it advanced his own political fortunes. Nixon's effective use of television in his Checkers speech in 1952, which preserved his position with Dwight Eisenhower on the Republican ticket, also pushed many journalistic noses further out of joint. The rational, analytical journalistic temperament recognized the potential for a person to manipulate television for personal gain, and it did not like it when it saw it. Another reason for unease among broadcast journalists was that the future vice president (and eventually president) demonstrated in his half hour talk how a public figure could use television to vault over the heads of journalists and communicate directly with the public. That, of course, is precisely what any elected official, particularly a president of the United States, wanted to do. And he did not want to be criticized or critiqued immediately after he did it.

If the tensions between Richard Nixon and network news organizations had deep roots, a public test of strength was perhaps inevitable once Nixon entered the White House. Of all the slights and unfair (in his eyes) attacks he might feel, none was more offensive than the analysis and comments offered by network journalists immediately following a presidential speech to the nation. The networks argued that offering this instant analysis was part of their journalistic duty to provide context and perspective for what had just been said in the Oval Office. From the perspective of the Nixon White House, however, the instant analysis was all too often a platform to attack the president. When Nixon appealed to the "silent majority" in November 1969 (one year after his election) and some television commentators criticized his speech, the White House chose confrontation. Speechwriter Pat Buchanan drew up a speech attacking the network policy and its journalists and submitted it to the president, who added his own words to toughen it up. Vice President Spiro Agnew, who had also felt the sting of the media, was chosen to be the vehicle of the counterattack. At a meeting of Republicans in Des Moines on November 13, 1969, Agnew derided what he described as "this little group of men who not only enjoy a right of instant rebuttal to every presidential address, but, more importantly, wield a free hand in selecting, presenting, and interpreting the great issues of our nation." A week later, Agnew gave a second Buchanan speech in which he attacked the *New York Times* and the *Washington Post.* Later Agnew speeches written by William Safire would refer to "elite" East Coast journalists as "nattering nabobs of negativism." The speeches (if not the alliteration) touched a nerve in the "silent majority." They also raised the blood pressure at the networks, and not only because of the concern over the White House campaign to turn public opinion against network news. From the White House Office of Telecommunications Policy came rumblings that the Nixon administration might begin to look more closely at the licenses of local television stations, a move that would prompt their owners to put pressure on the networks to behave more kindly toward Nixon. If the networks did not bend compliantly, the pressure was felt. And there were many at the networks who recognized some truth in the criticism directed at them.

Throughout the 1960s, network journalists had been so busy covering the agitation, and the news, of antiwar demonstrations, civil rights marches, urban riots, and counterculture rebellion that they devoted little attention to people or events that did not make news—people who happened to make up the majority of the nation and the viewing public of network news. The valid journalistic reason for this was the familiar one: normal life is not news, an uneventful event is not worth reporting. If the networks would not concede anything to Nixon's charges of political bias, they could bend to the charge of social bias and neglect. Soon after the Spiro Agnew speech, NBC News dispatched Jack Perkins and Tom Pettit, veteran correspondents with sharp eyes and fine writing styles, to the Midwest to begin a series of reports on how people and communities were reacting to events happening around them, events they mostly saw only on television. At CBS, Charles

Kuralt was already "on the road," showing the popularity of grass-roots reporting. Kuralt's work had been seen within the networks as valuable features, not as news. In the 1970s, though, slice-of-life reporting would become a central ingredient of reports on domestic issues in the United States. It was the beginning of the drift away from straight, factual news reporting and a move to something that was more "user friendly" or "accessible," to use the new jargon. Although Nixon and Agnew may have lit the firecracker under the networks, the change would have come anyway, for the power of the White House criticism coincided with another major development in network news: we were running out of news. Or what we thought was news.

If, in the 1960s, the news on television was the reporting of events, in the 1970s, it was increasingly about how to attract viewers and a mass audience. It did not happen all at once, and it happened in local news sooner than at the networks. No one was immune to the forces that were taking the drama out of news. As the Vietnam War wound down, as university campuses grew quieter and street demonstrations rarer, news was losing its punch. News was becoming stories that were important but lacked visual drama. Inflation affected everyone, but how often could we lead a newscast with scenes of a supermarket and interviews with housewives complaining that the cost of chopped steak had gone up. One night on the Saturday news, I opened the program saying, "Good evening, I don't know what you are having for dinner tonight, but President Nixon is having chicken." The White House, in an effort to ease concerns over inflation, had announced the presidential menu for that evening. When I wrote those words for the program, they felt strange; it was a clear attempt to "relate" to, or empathize with, the viewers. That has long since become standard operating procedure in television news but was unknown at the networks, where anchors and reporters felt more comfortable talking at their viewers than communing with them. New ways of attracting and holding viewers while informing them were needed. Even the biggest stories of the 1970s—Watergate, the oil embargoes, and the rocketing cost of energy—offered television little advantage over print media. Indeed, the fall from grace and office of Richard Nixon was almost entirely a print story until the impeachment proceedings before the House Judiciary Committee eventually played to television's strength: its ability to cover a live, dramatic event.

As news on television changed, a new breed of producer began to take charge of newscasts, both local and network. If the individual stories were no longer as compelling as they had been, these producers argued, the news program itself could be made more compelling to attract an audience. Stories could be reduced in length, removing complicated detail and subtle nuance. More stories could be packed into the half hour program. "The show really moved" became a high compliment among producers. There was also the search for emotion. If it was no longer easily served up by the stories of the 1960s, television journalists would simply have to look harder for it. Reports on inflation or the early downsizing in the steel and auto industries of rust belt America featured individuals who could be the "person next door." One junior producer who had recently joined NBC News commented in the newsroom that anchors should not be distant authority figures or even experts on the news, but rather the kind of person a viewer would meet in the neighborhood bowling alley, rolling a strike in the next lane. Empathy was in.

One night the *NBC Nightly News* led with a relatively minor plane crash that offered flames on film, if not much significance. There had been no other story that demanded pride of place at the beginning of the program, and after the sign-off the program staff gathered to discuss the decision. The regular executive producer of the program was on vacation, and the young producer who had filled in for him and had made the call to lead with the plane crash said, "Well, what do we want to do on television? Inform? Yes. But we also want to make the viewer cry." On a printed page, the comment may appear cold and cynical. But on the television screen the decision held an undeniable logic for that medium. Compared to the decline of traditional news values at local stations, network programs would hold the journalistic line with considerable valor for many years. But the tide was flowing out.

In 1972 foreign news was far from my mind or my news beat as I reconnected with the rhythms of American life, reporting on the presidential campaign from the primaries through election night. Further lessons about television news came at the two party national conventions held in Miami that summer. The Democrats, who met first, lived up to their reputation for poor organization and high entertainment, with raucous floor fights over the party platform. Chicago 1968 was still in the air as George McGovern activists fought the rear guard actions of Richard J. Daley and other party veterans who were trying to hold on to their power and what had been their party. The evening sessions ran past midnight (and once past sunrise) before the gavel sent us, exhausted but elated, to breakfast and then to bed.

The Democratic gathering was a major test for NBC News, which had comfortably crushed the competition in the convention ratings since 1956, when Chet Huntley and David Brinkley had made their television debut as a team. Now Huntley was retired and an untested convention anchor, John Chancellor, sat next to Brinkley in the booth suspended under the rafters, hanging vertiginously over the convention floor. The veteran NBC floor reporters who had covered previous conventions had dispersed to other jobs. NBC News had to field a new team of rookies. I was tapped, as were Catherine Mackin, Tom Pettit, and Douglas Kiker. We were all relatively young, but experienced, reporters; above all we were enthusiastic. We knew we were going up against not only CBS News but CBS News at the peak of its performance and nightly popularity. Up in the CBS anchor booth we could see the back of Walter Cronkite's head as he faced the camera and the nation in what, over a period of twenty years, had become a television ritual: the political process in action, live, with lights, bands, balloons, oratory, ambitions, and egos on display from coast to coast. On the crowded convention floor we offered tight smiles to our competitors, the big-name CBS floor reporters. There was Roger Mudd patrolling one side of the floor. And there were Dan Rather and Mike Wallace, whose young *60 Minutes* program was still struggling to find an audience. But with all the reporter firepower CBS executives had assembled on the convention battlefield, they made two tactical mistakes. First, each CBS reporter was confined to a particular area of the floor. We speculated that this was to keep the television stars from colliding as they pursued a story. The consequence of this was that Rather or Mudd or Wallace could not pursue a story from one state delegation to another if it meant moving out of their preserve. The producer in the control room had to call on another reporter to pick up the thread of the story, which meant the thread and the story could be lost. Meanwhile, we NBC reporters could careen around the floor like bumper cars in an amusement park going wherever the news pulled us. CBS's second mistake was also serious. Up in the anchor booth, Walter Cronkite talked at great length and interviewed his guests at great length while much of the heated action on the floor went uncovered. One night I passed Mike Wallace on the convention floor, standing idly with his microphone hanging uselessly from his hand. I asked how CBS coverage was going. "The usual," he replied in clear frustration. "Walter is up there talking with Teddy White about the history of American politics. They are up to 1936!"

Perhaps what was happening on the floor was not history, but it was exciting politics and compelling television. When the Democratic convention ended on its fourth night, with George McGovern giving his acceptance speech long after the bulk of the prime time audience had gone to bed, NBC threw a big party at a Miami Beach hotel. Following the appropriate decompression, John Chancellor sat down with the four floor reporters and pulled out a piece of paper with some numbers written on it. The NBC audience research department had tabulated the ratings for the week in the major cities. They showed what the national ratings would confirm later. We had beaten CBS News. We had beaten Cronkite, Mudd, Rather, Wallace, all of them. "We did it!" a relieved Chancellor said. "You guys did it, we did it together." It had been our reporting and our enthusiasm. An anchor sitting in an isolation box removed from the action, no matter how talented and prestigious he might be, could not do it alone anymore.

The Republican convention, which followed in the same convention hall, also brought a ratings victory to NBC. But everything else was different. Unlike the Democrats, the Republican organizers turned their convention into a made-for-prime-time television show. There was no contest over Richard Nixon's nomination for a second term and no fuel for floor fights over the party platform. That helped the "producers" of the convention write a script that would be strictly adhered to, a script made for a TelePrompTer and the Republican supporters watching at home. Journalists might bridle at the antiseptic taste of it, but the Republicans, better than the Democrats, understood where television and politics were headed, and they were taking voters with them. The party films prepared for the convention delegates and shown on television were slicker and more emotional than those produced by the Democrats. Where Democrats spoke in a style and at a length fit for the age of declamation, the Republicans had mastered the art of what would come to signify (and stigmatize) the medium, politics, and much of American discourse: the sound bite.

In the 1960s sound bites were the work of producers and film editors who cut down a speech or an interview to a few punchy phrases that might run thirty seconds or longer. By the 1970s, savvy users of television had learned the trick and the skill of providing their own sound bites—prethought and often practiced short statements of no more than fifteen seconds, which they knew would slide easily into the television news format. Television news reporters and producers were not unhappy with that; it made our job easier. Still, it was uncomfortable evidence of television's power that the medium could change the way people actually spoke, could persuade them to acquiesce and learn this new media language. Today we see a similar process as a new language, or at least a new vocabulary and manner of writing, emerges on the Internet. The medium is not only the message, as Marshall McLuhan proclaimed; it also bends and defines the language.

In May 1973 Gertje and I married in a small ceremony in Chicago. That was not to be the only change in our lives. Earlier that year there had been a management shift at NBC News. The NBC magazine show I had been hosting went off the air, a fate that would await so many other magazine programs on the network for two decades until *Dateline* broke the losing streak and established itself as one of the network's most successful programs. More significant, though, was the decision to bring in two anchors from Los Angeles, Tom Brokaw and Tom Snyder, to take over the weekend newscasts. The message was clear. The network was looking for not only a new generation of news anchors but a different type, those who were raised in local news and had spent most of their careers in a studio. It had less to do with journalistic experience and talent than the kind of broadcast experience and talent and personality the network news division felt was needed to attract viewers in the future. John Chancellor would continue, with distinction, in the anchor chair for another decade. But it would not be an easy tenure. Within NBC, voices began to be heard, usually indirectly, that Chancellor was not the model for what television news was becoming. Certainly he was not likely to be the person the viewer would meet at the bowling alley or the local McDonald's. But then neither was Walter Cronkite. The difference was that CBS was a solid number one in the nightly news ratings, whereas NBC was a respectable but, alas, solid number two. The gap in the ratings, though minor, helped feed a widening gulf between the cultures at the two networks. While CBS was able to continue its hard news approach, due to Cronkite's popularity and journalistic philosophy, the second-place status of the *NBC Nightly News* allowed strange ideas to germinate in the executive suites and occasionally filter down to the newsroom floor. One proposal was that the news division should put Tom Snyder on the *Nightly News* as Chancellor's coanchor, as if Snyder's Los Angeles glitz and intense personality could possibly work with Chancellor's solid news credentials. The president of NBC News, Richard Wald, a veteran newspaper journalist and editor, fought that off. But the pressures would continue.

Initially, Snyder was touted as the newsman of the future. If he was not given a seat on the weekday *Nightly News*, he was propelled into specials, magazine programs, and other high-profile positions. Snyder's problem was not talent but focus; he appeared to be forever lured by the attractions of show business. He could not decide in his early years at the network whether he wanted to be John Chancellor or an entertainer, a "star." In the end, though enjoying some success as an interviewer, he was neither. Tom Brokaw, however, was much more focused. From the beginning he knew what he wanted and had the talent, both on and off the air, to get there. Those traits were noted at CBS, where the changes occurring at NBC News were followed with some interest, if little sense of threat. An acquaintance at CBS described a meeting he attended in the office of Frank Stanton, the long-serving and much-respected president of the company, when the subject of NBC's decision to promote Snyder and Brokaw came up. Snyder, the executives concluded, would not make it (or want to make it) in news. Brokaw, though, was a different matter. One CBS executive who had known Tom in Los Angeles observed, "His greatest strength is that he will never make a mistake. His greatest weakness," he continued, "is that he will never make a mistake." If it was an insightful assessment of Brokaw, it was also one of the state of television as the 1960s receded and the 1970s shaped their own television persona. Not taking chances was the model for success. Eventually, caution would become a trap for the networks in their own culture of conformity. But again, we are getting ahead of our story.

NBC executives did not have to spell out what the Snyder/ Brokaw move would mean for me. It was time to move again. There was a new offer and opportunity on the table: London, the top job for a foreign correspondent. The timing was right. Gertje and I were starting married life together. She was European, I loved Europe, and London it would be.

Chapter 13

FOREIGN
CORRESPONDENT

A N EARLY MEMORY of England.

It was a warm night. I came out of a theater in London's West End where a young and ferociously talented Vanessa Redgrave was playing in *The Seagull*: British theater at its finest. The route to my hotel led through Soho, then the trendy quarter for restaurants, jazz clubs, and sex shows. The street was narrow, the sidewalk crowded, and the one-way traffic was backed up at least half a block. A couple of motorists had begun to honk impatiently, although London manners discouraged such an undisciplined breach of reserve. Ahead was the cause of the blockage: a large Rolls-Royce had pulled up onto the edge of the sidewalk. The chauffeur had tried, but failed, to leave space for traffic to maneuver around the car. In the back of the Rolls an elderly man was speaking animatedly through the rolled-down door window with a much younger man on the sidewalk. They were in front of steps that led down to a basement sex show. The manager of the club had the requisite white shirt open halfway down his chest and a gold chain hanging around his neck. A small crowd had gathered to watch the unfolding scene. Walking by without breaking stride, I heard the sex club manager say to the gentleman (for no doubt he truly was one), "Don't worry, sir, it has all been arranged. You won't be seen."

Most Americans have a weak spot for the British. We are fascinated by the monarchy, dazzled by Harrods, entertained by the upstairs-downstairs class structure when it comes via a BBC television series (or witnessed late at night on a Soho street), envious of the genteel way of life that seems to be so (and here comes the inevitable word) ... "civilized." To a visitor from the United States, Britain is familiar and comfortable. It is only when Americans live in Britain that we discover, to our surprise, that it is a foreign country, as different from the United States in temperament, manners, and mores as Sweden or Germany, and more interesting for that.

London was to be home for six years. One of my predecessors at NBC had possessed the wisdom to purchase a long lease on one of the magnificent John Nash terrace houses that surround Regent's Park, like a precious necklace, in the heart of the city. After living in a one-bedroom Manhattan apartment, we now had four floors plus a basement. We learned a law of physics, or perhaps just living, that a married couple will expand its lifestyle to fill the space available. It took about a week.

Britain, though, was not a happy realm. The nation had liquidated its empire, was living on the emotional capital of its past, and could not make up its mind about its future. The British did not really want to be "European," part of the growing economic community across the channel, but glumly accepted their fate, knowing they had little choice. The "special relationship" with the United States was still evoked, but you could hear the quotation marks hanging in the air like a nostalgic artifact in a relationship that was no longer what it used to be but that neither partner wanted to throw away. They had gone through so much together.

The hard fact for Britain was that it was no longer a world power but just a big island, or isles, in the North Sea. Margaret Thatcher was still a political lady-in-waiting, and Tony Blair a university student. The economy and standard of living were in decline, unions and management were locked in mortal combat, and the conflict between Catholics and Protestants in Northern Ireland seemed to be a tragedy beyond faith or resolution. If London itself no longer commanded the attention of foreign journalists, it was still a center for news organizations. NBC's bureau was headquarters for our offices in Europe (Paris, Berlin, Rome, and Moscow) and the Middle East (Tel Aviv and Cairo). For a network correspondent it was a place to travel from, rather than work in.

A few weeks after our arrival, I received a message from New York that I should fly to Vienna to cover a meeting of OPEC that was taking place that weekend. "What's OPEC?" I asked in blissful ignorance. Oil prices were not yet an issue, and the Organization of Petroleum Exporting Countries was not an organization that attracted much attention. I quickly read up on OPEC and learned that the Vienna meeting was important because some of the member countries wanted to raise the price of a barrel of oil from $3 to more than $4. Could one, I thought half jokingly, imagine the implications of that, the outrage that would reverberate from oil-guzzling lands? It was clearly not the most earthshaking story of the moment, but off I went to Vienna.

The night manager of the Intercontinental Hotel offered a full measure of Viennese charm as he explained why he had not held my reserved room. Since more OPEC delegates than expected had arrived, and since it was close to midnight, all the regular rooms were taken. However, it seemed an arrangement could be made. There was a small suite, part of the larger presidential suite that the representatives from Saudi Arabia were occupying, if I cared to take it. I did, and the next morning I discovered that my door faced the main entrance to the presidential suite itself. And there, immaculately dressed in a dark blue suit and highly polished shoes, was someone who certainly looked very important. Knowing nothing about oil or OPEC, I introduced myself. The gentleman replied in a soft voice with his name, "Yamani." In my ignorance but playing the unashamed reporter, I asked, "What do you do?" He offered a tight smile and said, "I am in oil." Sheik Zaki Yamani, Saudi Arabia's oil minister, was not yet a household name, but then oil was not yet a world-class story. We were to continue to live in that wonderful world for a few more hours.

October 6, 1973, should, I believe, be inscribed in our collective memory, although few, I would wager, can pin it to its single earth-shaking event. Early that morning (it was Yom Kippur), the Egyptian army crossed the Suez Canal, blasted its way through the defensive sand barriers with high-powered water cannons, and surprised the Israeli defenders. The threat to Israel was even more critical on the northern front as the Syrian army launched its offensive and nearly overran Israeli defensive positions protecting populous settlements. In Vienna the OPEC meeting recessed quickly as the oil diplomats raced back to their hotels. Suddenly Sheik Yamani was accessible and talkative. When I heard a knock on my door, it was Yamani, asking whether I had any news on how the war was progressing. I could only offer the same fragmentary reports he was hearing on the radio. "Can't you get more information from Riyadh or Jeddah?" I asked. "No, the phone calls are not getting through," he said, frustrated.

Later that afternoon Yamani invited me into the living room of his suite. We chatted for about half an hour, passing the time, waiting for more news from the Middle East. I have no recollection at all of what we talked about, and yet that afternoon was a humbling lesson. The war would change the lives of everyone; October 6 was the dividing line between pre-1973 economic stability and post-1973 oil shock uncertainty. When the OPEC meeting resumed, several weeks after the war ended, oil prices, pushed mainly by Muslim nations, would begin to rise. Within a year they would reach $12 a barrel and would continue to climb far beyond the level that had been contemplated in Vienna. Overnight, the oil producers, especially the Saudis, seemed to have their hands on the financial throat of the world, and Yamani was an enigmatic and compelling world figure. And there I was that Saturday afternoon—in a hotel suite in Vienna with the one man who knew what was coming. How often are we at the center of some great event but totally oblivious to what is really happening around us? Talk about missing the story! There is one detail, however, that I did not miss and have not forgotten. It was the book Yamani was reading to pass the time that fateful day. It lay there in front of us on the coffee table: the best-seller *I'm OK, You're OK.*

THREE WEEKS LATER.

The northern Sinai was as flat as a billiard table. And so it has been since the waters of a larger Mediterranean retreated from the land two and a half million years ago, leaving little behind. Here and there sand dunes and small hills broke the monotony of the desert plane that receded into a distant, hazy horizon. How distant, was hard to tell. Reference points are few in the desert.

We knew where we were. Behind us were the Mitla and Gidi Passes, which rose out of the desert floor to form a natural defensive position against an army advancing from the west. But the Egyptian army was not advancing. In Cairo, Anwar Sadat was happy with what he had achieved: sending his forces across the Suez Canal and onto the land that Egypt had lost in war six years earlier. Sadat and his generals were not about to tempt fate and risk defeat by moving their troops beyond the protection of the Egyptian antiaircraft missile defenses along the canal. The Israelis were holding the desert passes and had sent their armored phalanxes forward to engage the Egyptians. There had been fierce and bloody battles, the largest tank battles since World War II. But the Israeli army had not made a serious effort to break through and destroy the Egyptians. General Ariel Sharon, who was eager to do so, was held on a straining leash by his superiors, who had to defeat the Syrians in the north first before turning their full attention and armored strength to the southern front.

The day after the war broke out, the morning after my conversation with Sheik Yamani in Vienna, I flew to London and a short stopover at Heathrow Airport. There was no time to go home. Gertje came to the airport with my Vietnam combat fatigues and boots. We had a quick airport dinner before I boarded a special El Al flight filled with Israeli reservists returning home to defend their land and their families. Tel Aviv was under blackout when we landed and I drove into the city. Along the sea front, the Hilton Hotel loomed in darkness. Its windows too were dark. The only light in the lobby came from candles; the only public room with electric light was the windowless bar. The hotel was empty except for journalists and a few determined friends of Israel: violinists Isaac Stern and Pinchas Zuckerman, conductor Zubin Mehta, and later Danny Kaye.

NBC already had reporters covering the fighting in the north. I turned to cover the Sinai, where the war would have to end. The problem was that we saw little of the war as we traveled with our military escorts on the few roads in the Sinai. The Israeli military press officers knew how to handle us. They did not allow us to remain overnight in the desert; too dangerous they said. Every morning we would leave the Hilton in Tel Aviv long before sunrise, carrying blankets and pillows to make ourselves comfortable in tourist taxis usually used for nothing more demanding than a trip to the Sea of Galilee. After hours of bureaucratic and military checks and delays we would reach the Sinai headquarters around midday. There the Israelis would provide a briefing, tell us little, and not allow us to drive any closer to the front line. They knew we would have to leave by midafternoon to return to Tel Aviv in time to develop the film, edit it, and prepare our report, as meager as it was, for the satellite broadcast to New York. Day after day this mind-numbing, unproductive routine continued.

One day, after yet another of the eternal drives into the Sinai, we made the perfunctory stop for the routine Israeli briefing. After lunch NBC cameraman Jim Nickless, a veteran of Vietnam and other war coverage, got into the car with our driver and sound technician. Our Israeli escort was not to be found. We looked for him, though not very hard or long, and realized we had time to explore on our own.

We headed west toward Tasa, the Israeli forward command post, located, we were told, on a hill from which we could see the Israeli and Egyptian tank positions in the distance. We could get some real war pictures or at least an interview with someone with firsthand news of what was happening at the front. We reached Tasa in the midafternoon. It was nothing more than a crossroads in the sand. The east-west road we were on was intersected by a north-south, two-lane blacktop road the Israelis had built to run parallel to the Suez Canal, a military road that did not appear on most maps. There was no one around as we approached the intersection. Only an occasional jeep or truck passed by in the vast emptiness of the desert. The place could not have seemed more desolate or a news story more improbable.

"What are we going to find here?" I wondered aloud.

"Don't worry," Jim said, his experienced eye taking in an important detail. "Something is going on. Do you see that fellow directing traffic at the intersection?"

"Sure," I replied. "So what?"

"He is a lieutenant colonel," Jim said. "When the Israelis have a lieutenant colonel directing traffic in the middle of the desert, something is about to happen."

He was right.

We drove on a half mile, found the forward command post, and filmed an interview with one of the commanders. He offered no clue of what was about to happen, nor did the lieutenant colonel at the desert intersection as we waved good-by and headed back to Tel Aviv. Then, suddenly, everything happened. Ahead, the narrow desert road was filled with vehicles racing toward us at high speed. First came Israeli tanks, followed by smaller armored vehicles with bulldozers mounted on their front to clear away enemy obstacles. In the wake of their billowing exhaust rolled endless columns of more tanks, some pulling what looked like giant oil drums behind them. These were the floating supports for bridges, and behind them came the bridges themselves on the backs of giant trucks. We pulled off onto the shoulder of the road to avoid being run over by the convoys as they raced toward the west and the Suez Canal. The counteroffensive, the crossing of the canal, was under way. We filmed from inside the car, hoping that we would not be noticed or stopped by the Israelis. To the side of the road, where an hour earlier we had seen only desolation and sand dunes, there were now large gaps that had been opened in the dunes where the invasion force, the weapons and the men, had been hiding and waiting.

There is nothing in journalism to compare with the elation of having the big one, the "scoop," of being on top of the story and knowing that it is yours and yours alone. News of the canal crossing would not even be announced until it was safely completed, which would be at least another day. Our elation, though, was tempered as we drove back across the Sinai. The Israeli censors in Tel Aviv would check every frame of our film. Question: does a scoop exist if you cannot report it and show it?

That night when the film came out of the processing lab, the censor, an Israeli army lieutenant, walked into our editing room. We showed him, with a mixture of excitement and trepidation, what we had shot that afternoon. The tanks, the pontoon bridges, the invasion force raced by at high speed on the small TV screen. The young officer watched and said with a note of professional admiration, "Great story you have there." And then after a short pause, "Too bad no one is going to see it."

And no one ever did.

GENEVA, DECEMBER 1973.

It was a cold winter day along the banks of Lac Leman. Around its western tip curls the city of Geneva, the home of discreet bankers, reliable watchmakers, and diplomats who earlier this century had discovered that Switzerland's neutrality, and Geneva's comforts, offered an agreeable setting for a new industry: peacemaking. At least that was the idea, and the impressive old League of Nations building down on the waterfront was a reminder of one failed attempt to make it work. Now the United Nations occupied the premises, and the U.N. was presiding over the latest peace conference to come to town.

We were six weeks from the Sinai desert and the cease-fire that ended the fighting. Christmas was three days off as Arabs, Israelis, Americans, and representatives of other nations gathered to see whether the outcome of the war could provide an opening to a settlement of the conflict that divided and defined the Middle East. The answer was no, or at least not then and there. Little was accomplished in Geneva, and the conference became a footnote, a Trivial Pursuit question about Middle East peace efforts.

But there is a footnote to that footnote.

One evening during the conference Peter Jennings, who had covered the Middle East extensively for ABC News, and I took an Egyptian official to dinner. Tahsin Bashir was an experienced diplomat, a suave propagandist, and a good contact. He was also President Anwar Sadat's press adviser. Over a meal in the old town on the hill above the city center, the Egyptian complained about the one-sided coverage of the war. "Egypt had a great victory in crossing the canal," he said, "and yet the picture the world saw was all from the Israeli side." Jennings and I pointed out that all the coverage came from the Israeli side for the simple reason that it was the only side that allowed reporters to work, even if under military censorship. Bashir backed off, nodding his understanding. He knew that Egyptian press policy during a war was to round up all the foreign correspondents in Cairo and ship them out of the country, or at least confine them to the Hilton Hotel along the Nile, where little information got in and no stories got out. It was an effective tactic when Arab governments wanted to hide their failures in war—a telling self-indictment of their insecurity and insularity. But now Egypt was claiming a military success. Thanks to American political pressure, Sadat had rescued a large part of his army and was claiming that Egypt had at least fought Israel to a draw. At the dinner table Bashir was making the same argument. Jennings and I spelled out his dilemma: if Sadat and Egypt wanted news coverage they would have to open the door to international journalists and, above all, to television cameras. This would demand more than a change in policy; it would require a basic change in attitude toward the outside world.

After dessert the three of us went back to the Intercontinental Hotel, the well-appointed camping ground for the delegations, both diplomatic and journalistic. Jennings went off, and Bashir and I sat down in the lobby. "I have a question for you," he said as a waiter brought us two cups of coffee. "What I want to know, Garrick, is how do television satellites work?" I was surprised by the question. It was so distant from the language of diplomats and political leaders of foreign countries who still spoke, and perhaps thought, in the traditional, well-manicured language of international politics. Image making—the use and manipulation of television by leaders and their governments—is a well-honed skill in the United States. But no one had ever used it on a grand scale on the world stage to speak directly to the people of another country in an attempt to influence the policy of their government. The Iranians under Ayatollah Khomeini would learn how to "use" television six years later, and demonstrate the muscle of the satellite picture, when they seized the American embassy and held hostages in it. In the 1980s Mikhail Gorbachev would know how to play and speak to an international television audience to win support and trust for his attempted reforms in the crumbling Soviet Union. Pope John Paul II would take to the world stage and its cameras with the ease of the actor he once was. But the first leader to use television to mold public opinion in another country was Anwar Sadat. His target was the United States, the American people. And now his press adviser and image maker was asking about satellites.

"We want to get our message out," Bashir said. "What do we have to do?" I told him again that the first step was the open door. Bashir said, "That will happen." I explained that we needed dependable film processing labs (this was before videotape was used overseas), telephones that worked, and airport customs officials who would not seize our equipment and demand extortionate sums of money for its release. And finally Egypt needed to plug into the television era with a state-of-the-art ground station to send these pictures up to the satellite and back down to the United States, and into American homes.

I didn't mean to nag, but here was an opportunity to expand our coverage in the Middle East. Oil prices were shooting up. We in the West needed to understand more about the Arab world. Bashir did not need a selling job. "You will see some changes," he said as we finished our coffee, "and you will see them soon."

Seven months later, when President Nixon visited Cairo in the terminal weeks of his presidency, a ground station was in place in Cairo, and we were able to report live to the *Today* program back home. Shortly after that, Sadat began giving interviews. An Arab leader few Americans knew anything about became part of the television landscape, a familiar presence in American homes. As viewers grew more comfortable with the man, they began to listen to his ideas. It was a brilliant use of television, all the more impressive because there was nothing in Sadat's background that would have molded him for his new public role. Nothing that was apparent to me, that is, until it was my time to interview him three years later.

WE SAT in a large reception room in one of his several residences, twenty minutes outside Cairo along the Nile. It was the week between Christmas and New Year 1976. Two months had passed since I had requested an interview with Sadat, and now the approval had finally come through. That morning I had been picked up at my hotel by a government chauffeur and driven to the interview site. It was a large villa, comfortable but neither overly imposing nor ornate. We set up our cameras and lights in a large reception room and then waited.

Sadat entered alone. He was what I expected, slightly under six feet, pipe in hand, relaxed, intelligent—a person who put you at ease. He seemed to be in no rush. I was wearing a dark London-made banker's suit, which I considered appropriate dress for interviewing a head of state. Sadat was wearing an attractive light gray suit. We shook hands. He looked me up and down, and a concerned expression came over his face. "Ah, pinstripes," he said. "I must change."

I assured him it was not necessary, since the light suit would show up well on the television screen.

"I must change," he said again, turned, and walked up a broad staircase. In fifteen minutes he was back down, wearing his best banker's blue.

We spoke on camera for half an hour. Sadat was anxious to talk. The negotiations with Israel to return the Sinai to Egypt were stuck, the peace process needed a push, and Sadat was pushing hard. About half of what he said, I felt, was sincere, a quarter was propaganda that he didn't expect anyone to really believe, and the remaining quarter was the language of a rug trader who has cornered you in a back alley of an Arab market. There was plenty of "my friend" and "I am trying to help you" as he gave his sales pitch to Americans gathered around the breakfast table watching the *Today* program.

Recently, while rummaging through a carton of old journalistic odds and ends, I came upon an audiocassette of that interview in the villa beside the Nile in 1976. As I played the tape, the distinctive Sadat voice came alive in my study. More than twenty years later, while listening to the interview, I was struck by two things. One was how little the substance we were talking about has changed; Sadat emphasized the need for the creation of a Palestinian state, of some sort, as the "crux and core" of peace in the Middle East. The second reminder on the audiotape was how Sadat spoke, slowly and haltingly. His English was clear but never totally under his control, never as good as he thought it was or wished it to be. He had certain stock phrases regarding Middle East politics committed to memory. At other times he would launch himself onto a train of thought in which his English was equal to the verbal task at the beginning of the argument but often ended up, like a car skidding out of control, in a semantic ditch at the end. In the 1970s that was not such a serious problem. Television correspondents and producers vied to get a Sadat interview and didn't hesitate a moment to put this leader of a foreign country, with his accent and jerky syntax, on breakfast-time television, where attention spans are notoriously short and distracted. Foreign news was important, Sadat was important, and the *Today* program faced no serious competition from CBS or ABC.

Today cutthroat competition among a host of morning programs would prevent even the most journalistically committed of producers from clearing ten minutes of airtime for the contemporary equivalent of an Anwar Sadat with a less-than-excellent command of English. Sadat required the viewer to pay close attention to what he was saying. Moreover, he did not speak in sound bites but needed time to express his thoughts. He was given that time and Americans listened, and opinion was informed and influenced. Sadat came to be seen as a man of peace. Eventually, that led to a meeting at Camp David and a peace agreement between Egypt and Israel. Television, and its ability to communicate a specific personality, as well as his ideas, played an important role in laying the groundwork for the peace. Could it play the same role today? Of course it could. Would it today? Would it grant the time to a slow-speaking foreign leader dealing with complex issues? To have to pose the question, unfortunately, is to answer it.

Chapter 14

ONE TO REMEMBER

W HAT IS THE most exciting, memorable, tragic, moving, interesting, or dangerous story a reporter has covered? It is a bit like asking an opera tenor to choose his favorite aria or a football player to recall his most memorable touchdown. Still, in anyone's life a short list emerges of memorable moments and events. South Vietnam 1964–1965, and the American descent into that pit of mistakes and ruin, is high on my list. So too is the hope and tragedy of Czechoslovakia in 1968, as is the fall of the Berlin Wall twenty-one years later. For pure, sustained human drama, though, coupled with a burning awareness of epochal historic change, the collapse and fall of South Vietnam in 1975 is hard to match. I kept a diary.

MARCH 26

I am back in the Caravelle Hotel. The mattresses are still rock hard, the air conditioning is still on permanent high, and behind the reception desk are the same faces that greeted me when I first arrived in Saigon many years ago. And a memory comes alive.

It is from late 1964. I am standing at the reception desk when an American businessman arrives after a long flight from New York. It has taken more than twenty-four hours. He is tired and jet lagged, and he wants nothing more than a room, a shower, and a long sleep.

"My name is ...," he offers his name in a peremptory tone to the receptionist, "and you have a reservation for me."

The hotel employee looks down his list in vain. "I am sorry," he says. "We don't have a reservation for you." The American grows concerned; decent hotel rooms in Saigon are hard to find. "Yes, you have my reservation, just look again," he insists and spells out his name. Again, the Vietnamese receptionist says he is sorry, but there is no reservation. The fatigue of jet lag begins to slide into open irritation as the American insists that his office in New York had confirmed the reservation and that is that. The receptionist begins to dig in and takes up a defensive position behind an impassive facial facade and icy demeanor. I listen as the conversation escalates. "You have my reservation!" "No, we do not!" "Yes, you do!" "No, we do not!" Finally, the American gives in and asks plaintively, "Well, what am I going to do? I need a room."

"Oh, you need a room?" the receptionist replies quickly. "We have a room available." The American's mounting anger now gives way to bafflement mixed with irritation. "Why are we having this argument? Why didn't you give me the room in the first place?" "But you didn't ask me for a room," the receptionist replies with what he considers to be immaculate logic. "You said we had your reservation. We don't have your reservation. But if you want a room, you've got a room. Here, fill out this form."

If an epitaph is ever written for the American-Vietnamese

effort to work and prevail together, it might read, "Here lies the result of a tragic misunderstanding!"

Outside the hotel's swinging glass doors, the tragedy is unfolding. The South Vietnamese army is collapsing. Its units are breaking and fleeing from the central highlands to the cities along the coast. The government does not govern beyond Saigon and a few other cities. American combat troops are long gone, and appeals for help from Washington are not being answered. Americans are watching on television, watching transfixed as they see a decade's investment of lives—so many lives—bombs, and billions of dollars come to end. An end like this.

MARCH 27

I fly north to Da Nang this morning on a commercial flight, one of the last going into the city, which is now surrounded by the North Vietnamese army. Da Nang, normally a city of 500,000, has been flooded with another 500,000 refugees coming from Hue, to the north, or from the coastal provinces to the south. One million people desperate and trapped. It is chaos on the precipice of anarchy.

At the airport our veteran Saigon cameraman, Vo Huynh, a soundman, and I learn we have only two hours before catching a press charter flight back to Saigon. It may be the last flight out of Da Nang. We hitchhike to the main gate of what was a gigantic American air base and then into town, looking for the man who for years has rented us a jeep. When we reach his home, he is gone. So is his jeep. Everywhere we turn, the streets are jammed with trucks, cars, and small buses, which in turn are filled with people trying to get out of Da Nang. But get out to where? Some try to enter the air base, hearing rumors of evacuation flights. Others flee across the river to the broad, golden beach on the South China Sea, hoping a ship may pick them up and take them south. One million people ready to panic.

It is not a visible panic, yet, but desperation is there, internalized; you see it in the eyes and on the faces. There are no smiles or friendly waves as in the past. Human expression has turned sullen and is turning now to anger—anger at what has happened to them, anger that their government has offered no warning or protection. But then there is no sign of government or leadership in Da Nang; no organization is to be seen, no authority exercised. A strange feeling, that: most of us go through life without ever experiencing the true nakedness, the terror of being stripped of all security, of any recourse to authority, of law and justice. Walking through Da Nang and the tense crowds, I feel as if I am walking on ground that had been covered with a thin layer of gunpowder. One spark from any source would ignite … ignite what? When one million individuals become a mob, what does the mob do? Whom or what does it turn against?

Americans are vulnerable. What if the anger turns against us? Not for any rational reason, but for irrational revenge. Revenge for what? It doesn't really matter. Revenge because we were here for so many years, conspicuous defenders. Now we are conspicuous and defenseless. Among the civilian refugees roam soldiers who have deserted or become separated from their units. They too are angry. They are also armed and subject to no discipline. They could easily shoot someone, anyone. No one would arrest them because there is no one to arrest them.

We move quickly. We film at the U.S. Consulate, where armed and nervous marine guards organize the evacuation of the last Americans in the city. We film in a makeshift marketplace where, amid the surrounding blur of confusion and vulnerability, two women calmly look through long rolls of fabric for clothing as if this were a normal shopping day, profiles in remarkable self-possession or deep denial.

When we return to the air base, our plane is waiting for us. It is a military version of the DC-3, and I discover that ABC and CBS are pulling out their Vietnamese employees in Da Nang, as well as their families. We have already evacuated our NBC staff. As we begin to load the plane, all human hell breaks loose. People begin running across the tarmac to the plane in a desperate attempt to get on the plane and out of the surrounded city. There is crying and screaming as a mother climbs up the loading ladder and into the plane, only to discover that her baby is still on the runway. We get them reunited as still more Vietnamese try to push their way onto the overcrowded plane. As the pilot starts the engines, we fight to raise the ladder from the grip of the people on the ground. A Vietnamese, safely on the plane, explains what has happened. Someone who knew about the flight has sold places on it; the extra passengers are posing as cousins, aunts, and nephews of network employees. One woman paid $100, all the money she had. Another paid $150. We are happy to take all we can accommodate and find it hard to look at the stricken faces of those left behind as the plane pulls away.

SAIGON, APRIL 4, 1975

This morning we flew down to Vung Tau, southeast of Saigon, along the South China Sea. When the French ruled Indochina, they turned Vung Tau into a seaside resort, an easy hour's drive from Saigon. You could go for the weekend or on a Sunday drive for a leisurely lunch and a swim. That was before the war, their (the

French) war and then ours. Sounds strange, doesn't it, "their war," "our war," as if the Vietnamese have not paid a far higher price. We Americans acknowledge that; we cannot deny it as the weekly casualties are announced. And yet we measure the cost of this war in American lives lost and maimed. The tribal instinct at work? No time to think about that now; too much is happening. We are watching a country collapse.

When Vo Huynh and I arrive at dockside in Vung Tau, an old military transport is pulling in. Its deck is covered, every square foot of it covered, with refugees coming down from up-country. They are about to pour ashore to add to the thousands of refugees who have already arrived. The once elegant colonial resort is being turned into a massive refugee camp. There is little preparation or food, and no idea among the few aid workers and the arriving refugees of what will happen next. Rice soup is ladled out, and I watch a crowd attack a jeep loaded with bread. The refugees, who have been on the move a week or two or three, bring little with them. Most carry just a bag or a suitcase or, in two instances, even a television set. Everyone has his priorities.

It is a moving story, but so are so many stories, every day, as we watch families and lives disintegrate. The eternal question reporters face is posed again: how will we make this day, this place, these people stand out? How will we get viewers back home to stop chewing their supper and watch what is happening in this small, lovely port? I start to scan the deck of the ship for someone we can focus our camera and story on, someone we can make come alive. And then I see her. A woman with three small children at her side and a baby in her arms is standing amid the pressing crowd next to the upper end of the gangplank that is being shoved into position. Her face is an unreadable mask hiding what she has been through. It is an elegant face, a compelling presence that leaps out. I turn to

Vo Huynh and say, "There is our subject shoot her!" There is a certainty I have about her. She is one of 5,000 people on this ship, yet she is apart from all the others.

She comes off the ship and the instant her feet touch ground she sits down, gathers her children around her, and begins to cry. Shake and cry. Her story pours out with the tears. She is from Quang Tri, the most northern province in South Vietnam. Her husband is an officer in the army headquarters there. Three weeks ago she fled with her children and elderly mother. Her husband stayed behind. She doesn't know where he is. Whether he is alive. They went south to Hue for several days but were forced to flee again, to Da Nang, by foot. They spent six days in the crucible that was Da Nang before they could escape to sea on a small fishing boat. The boat owner demanded that they turn over all their money before he would take them to larger boats waiting offshore. That was his promise. But the woman and children and mother did not end up on a boat. They were taken to a barge with no motor, no food, no water. For three days and three nights, along with a hundred others on the rusty vessel, they drifted at sea. Finally, they were spotted by a South Vietnamese navy ship and towed to Cam Ranh Bay, a large military port. It had become the dumping point for refugees from the north and the central highlands. By the time the woman (her name is Le Thi Kieu Liem) arrived there, Cam Ranh itself was no safe haven as the North Vietnamese closed in. After twenty-four hours, they were put on another ship and evacuated again. But in the confusion at Cam Ranh, Le Thi Kieu Liem became separated from her mother. Now she doesn't know whether her mother has gotten out safely or whether she is now lost to her, missing in the disorder of the collapse, just as her husband is.

We talk with Le Thi Kieu Liem for about ten minutes as her

children surround her. Her tears have stopped now, but not her story. Or our story. We are making some final shots, following her as she picks up her bag, takes her children, seven, five, three, and four months, and starts walking down the dock, still dazed, shocked, lost. What future do she and the children have? No husband, no relatives at this end of Vietnam to support her. No work, nothing except the dead end of a refugee camp she can see being haphazardly erected in front of her. And then it happens. While we are walking with her and filming, Le Thi Kieu Liem suddenly shrieks and starts running. But running where? We are with her, pushing through the thick crowd of other refugees. And there on the dockside, in the crowd, is ... her mother. There are more tears, and embraces. A mother, daughter, and grandchildren have been reunited. And tonight on *NBC Nightly News* many millions of Americans will see it.

Or so I think when we return to Saigon this afternoon. I sit down in the bureau and begin to write my script. With the help of an interpreter I listen to an audiotape of the interview. When the story is finished and my narration recorded, we put the film, tapes, and script into a bag to be shipped late that afternoon to Hong Kong, where the film will be developed and edited and sent by satellite to New York. Then it is time to relax.

But no, there is never a time to relax, not these days, in Saigon. A call comes into the bureau from Tan Son Nhut airport on the edge of town. There has been a plane crash—a U.S. Air Force transport plane has gone down shortly after takeoff. Our camera crews race to the scene with a reporter who will cover that story. And then there is another call with more news. This was no routine military flight. The plane was filled with 228 Vietnamese orphans being flown to the United States. Many of them are dead, along with American civilians who were also being evacuated on the plane. This is the tragedy, the story that will shake American viewers; this is the lead of tonight's news. And rightly so. Will anyone hear Le Thi Kieu Liem's story now?

APRIL 11

The war is over. Saigon is surrounded. But there is still no official order for the Americans left in Vietnam to pull out. But everyone knows there will be an evacuation. And the Vietnamese know it. In hotels and restaurants guests are now told that American Express cards will no longer be accepted. American Express is closing down its office and getting out, just as the banks and other large American firms already have.

I am out in the street with a camera crew filming the signs of the American departure. One American I interview berates me, and the press, for defeatism. He came to Vietnam years ago as a construction engineer. South Vietnam is not going to fall, he assures us. There is no reason to bug out, he repeats adamantly. Two hours later we are filming at the U.S. Consulate and I see our defiant American in a line trying to arrange a visa to the United States for his Vietnamese girlfriend and her family. He acts a little sheepish when we discover him. Well, yes, he acknowledges now, perhaps it is time to prepare for the worst, you never know....

There is another drama occurring at the American embassy, upstairs in the ambassador's office. Graham Martin is the latest and certainly the last of Washington's proconsuls to be sent to Saigon. He fits the familiar profile of a particular generation of American diplomats, those in their fifties or sixties who rose to positions of influence in the Cold War. Their dress, voice, and demeanor are cut from the cloth and in the style of privileged backgrounds in the old South or Boston, even if they are from a small town in Colorado. Their eyes are steady and hard. If they wear glasses, they have colorless wire rims. They are the brokers of American diplomacy and power. They execute the foreign policy of today based on conceptions of the world formulated ten or twenty years ago. Their conceptions may have been correct then, but realities change, as they have now in Vietnam.

Graham Martin talks passionately about the importance of not abandoning South Vietnam. For Vietnam's sake certainly, but also for that of the United States. He likens the mood in America to the one after World War I and the opposition to the League of Nations, or Congress and public opinion keeping America out of the world's conflicts in the 1930s. Even if he is right, and I don't think he is, he is missing the point. Back home, 75 percent of the American people are opposed to more military aid for South Vietnam. Americans are washing their hands of Vietnam. But Graham Martin is not, yet. In the interview he offers the now worn argument that with just a little more perseverance we will one day be able to leave the South Vietnamese on their own, etc., etc. Then he says, "I have always believed in the importance of telling the American people the full truth." He says it with a riveting stare that defies contradiction. I sense what he really means is, "I don't believe that at all. But I say it because I still hope. I do not want to be remembered for going out like this, ending my career as the ambassador who pulled down the American flag over Saigon."

My instinct is correct. After the interview I talk with Martin for another quarter of an hour. Now we are on background, and there is a distinct change in the ambassador's tone. He is worried that someone in Washington will push the panic button and try to evacuate Americans suddenly. That, he worries, could set off a violent reaction here in Saigon. Even if the Communists do not attack, he asks, will the South Vietnamese watch passively as the mass evacuation of Americans gets under way? Will they allow us to go quietly? There is still one last act to write in this drama.

APRIL 17

Tonight I try to grasp what this story is. It is not just the collapse of the South Vietnamese resistance, the failure of the Saigon government, and the end of the American gamble here. It is not simply, and dramatically, a historic event of the first order. It may look that way on television screens in American homes. But here, close-up, what we are living and have been reporting for days and weeks is something few of us will ever experience—the collapse of structure and authority, which imposes order and law, regulates control and self-control, those qualities of life we see and don't see, values we take for granted ... until they are no longer there. And what do we do when these girders of civilized life come tumbling down? We think of the danger of chaos and even anarchy. But what is amazing, truly amazing, is how normal life appears to go on. When structure and control and personal security vanish, we cling to what is no longer there by willing it to be there. Habit becomes reassurance. Denial becomes a survival skill.

This morning, when I come to work at the NBC office, I run into the custodian of the building. I have known him since 1965, when I rented the office and my apartment. He is standing in the corridor, one side of which faces a back court open to the sky. In that sky a military transport plane, an old prop-driven veteran, is flying over Saigon. The custodian is peering up at it as I approach him. He turns to me with a hopeful face and says, "Those must be the B-52s coming back to defend us." I tell him quietly, no, the

B-52s will not be coming back. His face falls as he goes back to his work.

This afternoon I drive out to the Circle Sportif, the leading Saigon club built by and for the French, and in more recent years the oasis for the Vietnamese elite. I am looking for a businessman who has agreed to be interviewed about the end that is fast approaching. A waiter tells me I will find him on the tennis court. The businessman, dressed in his tennis whites, invites me for a drink. "Saigon is going to fall," he says with equanimity. "It is only a question of whether it is tomorrow or a week from tomorrow." I remark on how calmly he appears to be facing this prospect. He and his friends pause between their tennis games, moving through their customary daily rituals. "But you must understand," he explains, "when everything else is lost, and it is too late to get out or do anything about it, the only thing left is habit." He took a sip of his Pernod. "It is why I go to Mass when I have personal problems. It is habit, ritual as comfort."

Tonight we had the last supper. That is what someone called it as we left the home of an American official here. He had invited representatives from each of the American news bureaus to have dinner and to listen to the words of a senior CIA analyst at the embassy. They were blunt and urgent. The analyst confirmed what we suspected. The North Vietnamese could attack and take Saigon whenever they wanted.

We talked about evacuation. There are, as we thought, no embassy plans. No one believes it could accomplish anything more than getting the Americans out. What about the Vietnamese who have worked for the United States—civilian employees, government officials, and intelligence agents? They would be the first to be marked for retribution by the Communists. The United States would do its best, we were told, but there can be no promises. The North Vietnamese could shell Saigon's Tan Son Nhut airport, halting an evacuation if they didn't want Vietnamese to get out, which in turn would stop any evacuation of Americans. One had to be realistic. The CIA official said it was time for the news bureaus to begin their evacuation. It was no longer possible to cover stories outside of Saigon, so we wouldn't need so many people. We already have our evacuation plan worked out at the NBC bureau.

APRIL 18

I write this on the Cathay Pacific flight to Hong Kong. The flight attendant has passed out hot towels following a good meal. Through the window I see Hong Kong in the last light of an early evening in April. We are on our final approach. The music system in the plane is pumping out soothing Muzak—Burt Bacharach's raindrops are falling on my head. Two hours from a collapsing city and crumpling lives in Saigon to a vibrant, prospering Hong Kong, where the lights in the streets and homes are just coming on.

Chapter 15

DATELINES

V. S. NAIPAUL, writer, traveler, and literary journalist, calls it the "anxiety of arrival." It is the feeling that envelopes a reporter upon arriving in a strange country or city, where the language is unfamiliar, local contacts unknown, and the story unclear. Unlike the tourist, who faces no deadline, the pressure of work and of producing a story clings to you like your shadow as you walk around town in the hope that soaking in the local geography, seeing the faces of the people, and hearing, if not always understanding, the voices in the marketplace will begin to establish your bearings. In the less prosperous parts of the world, in the era before cell phones, the "anxiety of arrival" was aggravated when the local phone system didn't work or when the one name given to you as a reliable source turned out to be away on a trip. And if you were working in a country ruled by a dictator or a gov-

ernment bureaucracy that justified its existence by joyfully plac-
ing obstacles in the way of a reporter's assignment, the anxiety
was quickly supplanted by pure frustration.

With time and experience reporters penetrate these barriers
and get the job done—get the story out to viewers or readers. I
suspect most of my colleagues have asked themselves more than
once, and particularly when the frustration factor reaches critical mass, why they keep doing it. Is it to get "the story" and
inform the public back home? Or is it for the glamour, the adventure, and the challenge? The answer is usually an imprecise "all
of the above." On occasion, usually late at night after a tiring day
or over a lengthy dinner in some distant place, foreign correspondents may indulge in a little self-revelation and acknowledge that the initial attraction tends to fade. The glamour goes
first, although it may linger on in the eyes of family and friends
back home. The sense of adventure lasts longer, one hopes forever, but it is not always enough to sustain a career or fulfill a life.
The self-testing never disappears in the active reporter, nor
should that most basic human need: to ask and to know. What
permeates all of these drives and gives them that extra push, is
the pure joy of seeing so much of the world and its people. It is
intoxicating. But sooner or later foreign correspondents, particularly television correspondents, who leap from country to country, have to confront a sensitive question: has the traveling itself
become addictive? When do we begin to mistake movement for
action? The day comes (or more likely it is a night far from home)
when a reporter recognizes having spent too much of life on
planes and in hotel rooms, racing from one crisis story to the
next. In London in the 1970s (as my wife still reminds me) I was
away from home, in some years, as much as 75 percent of the
time; the inevitable result of the jet plane, satellite communica-

171

tion, and a large network's appetite, at the time, for international news.

MARCH 14, 1978.

It is a Monday morning in London. I am in the office planning future stories but will go home early; today is Gertje's birthday, and we plan to celebrate.

At 11:00 A.M. comes the bulletin. In Holland, South Moluccans, immigrants from the former Dutch colonies in Southeast Asia, have been venting their nationalist grievances against the government by hijacking trains, seizing buildings, and holding hostages. Now they have struck again. I race home, scribble a note of apology to Gertje, and tell her there is a bottle of champagne chilling in the refrigerator. Just how she is to celebrate her birthday alone with the champagne, I am at a loss to explain and don't have the time to figure out. I pack an overnight bag and race to the airport, where a chartered executive jet is warming up to fly me, a camera crew, an editor, and a producer to Groningen, Holland. Forty-five minutes later, we land. Rented cars with drivers take us to the town of Assen in the north of the country, where police have surrounded the building in which the Moluccans are holding sixty-one hostages. As the standoff continues, we prepare our report for *Nightly News*. It is midnight before we finish the satellite transmission and check into the local hotel. I begin to worry that I have made a mistake in bringing only an overnight bag; the Moluccans' last siege lasted nineteen days. But good fortune prevails. The next day Dutch marines storm the building with guns blazing, free the hostages, and capture the three members of the Moluccan "suicide squad," who raise their hands shouting, plaintively, "Don't shoot." We wrap up the story that night, and I make a reservation for a flight back to London the next morning. Gertje and I will celebrate her birthday two days late; the champagne, she assures me on the phone, is still chilled.

Three A.M. and the phone in the room jars me awake. The New York news desk is on the line. The Israelis have just invaded southern Lebanon. At noon I am at the Amsterdam airport to take the first flight to Tel Aviv. I arrive at 8:00 P.M. and drive immediately to Jerusalem, where Prime Minister Menachem Begin is in the middle of a news conference. As I walk into the room, he is saying Israel will not give up the land north of the Lebanese border until there is an agreement that prevents the Palestinians from using it to launch attacks against Israel. I drive back to Tel Aviv (another hour) for the satellite broadcast to *Nightly News*. At 1:30 A.M. there is time for a one-hour nap, and then we prepare for a late-night special in the United States, dawn in Israel.

At 8:00 A.M. I crawl into my bed after instructing the hotel operator that I am not to be awakened. At 11:15 A.M. I am awakened. "It is an emergency," the operator says with an apologetic voice. "New York is on the line." The news is now in Italy, where Italian Prime Minister Aldo Moro has been kidnapped by terrorists. The 2:00 P.M. flight from Tel Aviv to Rome is full, and there is no other commercial flight that will get me there by evening. NBC decides to charter a small plane to Cyprus, where an executive jet can pick me up and take me to Rome. However, the Israeli military has closed the airspace going into Cyprus because of the invasion of southern Lebanon (which is now yesterday's story). I take a flight to Athens, where a chartered executive jet can fly me on to Rome. But the charter plane has mechanical trouble, and there is no other flight or charter available. At 10:00 P.M. another charter jet is located and finally arrives in Athens and we take off.

We will arrive too late to make the *Nightly News* broadcast, so I relax, sip a soft drink, and read a book as I sit alone in the back of the Lear. What all this is costing NBC is only a fleeting thought. It is well after midnight (yet again) when I arrive at the Hotel Hassler in the heart of Rome.

The next day, Friday, I drive with our Rome camera crew to the site of Moro's kidnapping. There is not much to see apart from some flowers left in the street in memory of the bodyguards who were killed. That night we send in our story, although there is little new to report.

On Saturday morning, I walk out of the hotel, down the Spanish Steps, and into the bustling Via Condotti filled with shoppers. There is a touch of spring in the air. I buy an extra birthday present for Gertje, in addition to the one still waiting at home. As I stroll about the city, before the flight to London, I add up the week. In five days I have reported from three countries on two continents. Is this good journalism or is it madness? Or is it just television news in its golden years?

When I arrive home, Gertje is at the door but the birthday champagne is not in the refrigerator. "I drank it," she says with a shrug, and a smile.

Chapter 16

A STORY OF NEGLECT

W HEN THE STORM struck, the small boat was barely
halfway across the river. It was a warm tropical downpour
that quickly began to come through the frayed canvas cover under
which we huddled. The boat, no more than twenty feet long, was
ferrying Africans and their goods across the broad Niger River.
Ahead on the far bank lay Biafra, the eastern state of Nigeria that
had declared its independence from the rest of the country and
now faced political isolation and the imminent prospect of war.

It was not an easy story to get to. When Biafra announced its
secession in 1967, I flew with an NBC camera team to Lagos, the
capital of the now diminished African nation. Nigeria was one of
the models of postcolonial Africa—the most populous country on
the continent with the tantalizing prospect of vast oil revenues to
fuel growth and eventual prosperity. That much of those oil

reserves happened to lie off Biafra's coastline was a detail that did not go unnoticed by the Ibos who lived in what would briefly be known as Biafra or by Nigeria's leaders in Lagos.

The morning after our arrival, we hired a car with driver, shoved our dozen cases of camera equipment into the trunk and onto the roof, and headed east on the two-hundred-mile drive to the Niger River, Biafra, and its capital, Enugu. After about an hour and a half, the highway dwindled to an unpaved road. Two hours later, as the four of us in the car had exhausted conversation and were bouncing along in communal silence, we were jolted by a sharp bang that occurred as we raced over but did not quite clear a rock in the road. For a minute or two the car continued to behave. Then it began to lose speed. A grimace spread across our driver's face as he pushed the accelerator to the floor with no discernible response. None of us said anything as the driver coasted the car to the side of the road, where it came to a halt. There was no help or village in sight. We got out, unloaded our baggage and lined it up on the other side of the road, and waited for a bus that, our driver assured us, would come along in an hour or two to take us back to Lagos.

To fill the idle time, which now loomed large, we unpacked our short wave radio, raised its antennas, and began turning the dial in search of the news on the Voice of America or the BBC World Service. When we found it, the news catapulted us out of our tropical torpor. In the Middle East war had broken out (a war that was to last only six days, which is all the time it took Israel to push Egypt out of the Sinai desert, Syria off the Golan Heights, and Jordan out of the West Bank and the eastern half of Jerusalem). Sitting on our suitcases and camera boxes on a roadside in the middle of Nigeria, waiting for a bus, we felt painfully lost, out of it. Of all the envy-creating, anxiety-raising pressures a foreign correspondent faces, missing out on the big story ranks near the top. And there were few stories bigger than the one we were now in no position to cover.

We reached Lagos late that night, after seven hours in a bus with maximum heat and minimum suspension. I sent a telex to New York suggesting to our producers that we forget Biafra and get ourselves to the Middle East and the war as quickly as possible. The next morning the reply was waiting at the hotel's front desk in the abbreviated language of cables priced by the word: "no need you Middle East, proceed Enugu interview Odumegwu Ojukwu," the leader of what was now inevitably referred to in the predictable language of journalism as "breakaway Biafra."

We tried again. This time we flew halfway to the Niger in an old DC-3. When we landed, we looked for a driver with a car large enough to carry us and our equipment for the remainder of the trip. The terms of trade were not in our favor when we found only one available car, a taxi. I looked hard at the driver and said, "Twenty-five dollars a day plus fuel," which I had been told was a fair rate. He laughed, looked at the three of us and our equipment, read the urgency in our demeanor, and replied, "One hundred fifty dollars a day." The negotiation did not last long. He had the car, the only one, and we didn't. "One hundred dollars," I said. "OK," he replied with a satisfied shrug, "load up your things; it is two hours to the river." And so it was. Except when we arrived at the Niger the long steel bridge across it was closed. Nigerian soldiers in camouflage uniforms had stopped traffic and were issuing the order of the day: no one was going into Biafra and no one was coming out.

Actually, that wasn't quite true. Our driver turned the car around and headed up the western side of the river. About a mile north of the impassable bridge we found a thriving riverside market filled with food stalls and racks of colorful clothing, as well as old records of the 78 and 33 rpm era. The threat of war cast no shadow over the market, which attracted buyers, sellers, and traders from both side of the river—Nigerians and Biafrans immersed in their daily rhythms and personal concerns.

Our driver was clearly disappointed that his lucrative job was ending after one day. I paid him off and then hired, for about $10, one of the many small ferries crossing the Niger. That is when the tropical squall hit us. It was heavy but brief and the last drops were falling as we reached the Biafran side. There was no landing or dock, only a steep and now muddy six foot high embankment we had to climb, slip down, and climb again as we struggled to carry our equipment up to a road. After we had collected our gear and tried to clean the mud off ourselves, we looked around with some satisfaction. We had made it: we were in Biafra. It was not the Middle East, but it was a story and we felt proud; we were probably the first foreign journalists to be there. Still, a question nagged at us. Would anyone be interested in our scoop?

We began looking, once again, for that basic necessity of the television news team—wheels, a car to take us to Enugu. Within a minute our luck seemed to change for the better as we saw a car approaching, a four-wheel-drive Land Rover, and a second van behind it with plenty of space for us and the equipment. It seemed ideal; the driver was even wearing a uniform. It was not ideal. The uniform was that of a police sergeant. "Good afternoon, gentlemen," he intoned in the crisp, practiced language of British-trained policemen everywhere. "Who are you, and where have you come from?" He asked for our passports. We were now, after all, in independent Biafra and national sovereignty had to be duly exercised. I explained that we were with NBC News.

"You are from the Nigerian Broadcasting Corporation?" the policeman shot at me with a hostile look.

"No, the National Broadcasting Company," I replied, "from America, the land of Abraham Lincoln."

I hoped I was not laying it on too thick, but I was afraid the policeman might order us to get back on the boat and get out of Biafra. I quickly told him our story, that we had come from a great distance, at great cost and effort, to be the first to tell the story of independent Biafra to the world. To do that we needed to get to Enugu and interview his leader, Odumegwu Ojukwu. Would the police sergeant please help us in this important mission? No. He would not let us go to Enugu.

"You have to have special permission to do that," he explained.

"Where do we get this permission?" I asked.

"I am not sure, but I will take you there," he assured us.

"Take us where?" I wanted to know.

"I will take you to where you may get the necessary permission, or may not."

It was clear that this was not going to be easy. The policeman escorted us to a local government building, where we were led into a large, empty assembly hall and told to wait. "The major will come and see you," we were told. "When will he come and see us?" I asked. It was already midafternoon and we wanted to be in Enugu by nightfall. "He will come when he comes," came the noncommittal reply. We waited for an hour and were repeatedly assured that the major was indeed coming.

It was about five in the afternoon when he finally appeared. He was an army officer, not a policeman, for this was now an "operational zone" with the military preparing for an attack from the Nigerian side. The major greeted us politely and checked our passports and press cards. NBC caught his eye and I launched again into what was becoming an incantation about NBC News, America, etc., etc., and our desire to tell Biafra's story, etc., etc., and who better to tell it than Odumegwu Ojukwu in Enugu, etc., etc.

The major pondered our request. Biafra, as a self-asserted independent nation, was only a few days old, and clearly there was nothing in the army manual to cover an unexpected and unprecedented case of three bedraggled and muddy television journalists showing up unannounced. Like any experienced bureaucrat, military or civilian, the major came up with a solution that would neither throw us out of the country nor get him into trouble: he referred us to a higher authority. He wrote out a pass allowing us to continue to Enugu and told us to check with the authorities there before we did any filming. He gave us our pass, shook hands, and told us where we could find a taxi for the last lap of our trip.

It was late at night when we arrived at the hotel, a comfortable, recently built, and resoundingly empty hotel. The lone receptionist on duty agreed to give us small suites at single room rates; the terms of trade were now working in our favor. At the bar off the lobby the only other hotel guest, a lonely European, was nursing a beer. He introduced himself as a fellow reporter working for Swiss radio. We shared a nightcap to a long day and as a lubricant for a deep sleep.

The next morning we came down for breakfast and were greeted by a policeman who was waiting for us at the front desk. We explained who we were and what we wanted to do and showed him the pass that had gotten us to Enugu. The policeman examined it closely and shook his head.

"This is permission to come here, not to work here." He was right, of course.

"Where do we get this permission?" I asked, with a note of impatience creeping into my voice.

"I will take you to the Foreign Ministry," he replied.

"You mean there is a Foreign Ministry?"

"Yes," he said with a proud smile, "it opened this morning."

As we drove through Enugu, we saw the signs of an infant nation acquiring its new identity. At a branch of the Bank of Nigeria workmen were putting up a new sign: Bank of Biafra. At the studios of the Nigerian Broadcasting Corporation (the dreaded NBC) a painter had whitewashed out "Nigerian" and was replacing it with "Biafra," a new BBC that, no doubt, would spread endless confusion on the airwaves in Africa.

At the edge of town we drove up to a one-story school building set in a shady grove of trees. The building had been commandeered by the new government and the students packed off to other classrooms. Here too a painter was at work on a sign announcing the new Ministry of Foreign Affairs. We walked up to a reception desk set on a wide verandah that extended around both sides of the former school. I presented our credentials and asked to see the director of the foreign press department. I was getting excited. Following our adventures and misadventures we were now one step from our goal, the interview, a world exclusive. The receptionist, a college-age girl, had no idea where the foreign press office was or who headed it. She asked for our patience and disappeared into one of the classrooms turned diplomatic office. A minute later she returned and motioned us to follow her. At the end of the verandah we turned a corner, walked across an open exercise yard, ducked under a volleyball net, and entered a second building. At the end of a corridor we came to a small office. There was no name on the door. There was no window for light. There was a desk, a few hard chairs, a pile of newspapers in the corner, and, hanging from the ceiling, a single lightbulb. Behind the desk sat a man in his mid-twenties dressed in dark trousers, a white shirt open at the collar, and an expression I took for boredom.

So, it had come to this, a scene familiar to foreign correspondents working in countries and cultures not yet plugged in to the ways and speed of the emerging information age: a single individual in a position of authority who was able to make your trip, your ordeal to even get to the story, a rewarding success or a bitter failure. There was, no doubt, a measure of latent neocolonial attitude in me, a visitor carrying his European culture like an insignia, as we exchanged pleasantries and I tried to size up the man sitting across from me. Did he grasp who we were and how we could be important for Biafra? Was he the kind of government official we would need to wine and dine a few times to win his support? Did he, sitting in this small room in the backyard of a school in what had been (and after a bloodythirsty war would again be) eastern Nigeria, understand what a mighty and wondrous thing an American television network was? I began to talk myself through the litany one last time. We were the American NBC, not the Nigerian one, we had come ... and so on. Then I rested my case.

There was a silence in the room as the director of the Foreign Press Office, his face still frozen in noncommitment, weighed what he had just heard and set me up for the fall. After a moment he spoke.

"This is for NBC, you say?"

"Yes," I replied quickly, "NBC, USA, not the Nigeri—"

"Yes, yes," he cut me short, and I could now see his growing impatience with my labored effort to plead our case. "I believe I understand you now," he continued with a twinkle developing in his eye and a slight smile on his lips. "Now tell me, Mr. Utley, this interview. Is it going to be on the *Today* show or the *Huntley-Brinkley Report*?" There was another silence in the room, an embarrassed silence from me. "You are familiar with our programs?" I asked. "Of course I am," the twenty-five-year-old director of the Foreign Press Office of the two-hour-old Ministry of Foreign Affairs replied. "I was a great fan of them in America. I have just returned from two years of graduate school at Princeton."

AMERICANS and Europeans, journalists included, have had a difficult time dealing with Africa. How much of it is attributable to racial attitudes among viewers, readers, reporters, and editors (however unacknowledged) and how much, among an older generation, is the result of identities scarred by the loss of empire and European domination is hard to measure. The unpleasant fact is that news coverage of the vast African continent south of the Sahara has been limited largely to racial conflict, genocide, and famine. All are important stories, and each has attracted the attention of Americans, particularly when television pictures have been able to show conflict in Soweto, famine in Sudan or Somalia, and the atrocities in Rwanda or Congo. But the attention has usually been fleeting. When the television camera moves on to the next hot spot, attention wanes.

On a few occasions network news divisions have attempted to bring a different Africa to the television screen. One of the earliest efforts came from ABC News in 1967, when ABC was still the smallest of the three networks and its news organization trailed far behind NBC and CBS in size, prestige, and audience. ABC felt it had little to lose when it devoted four hours of an entire prime-time evening to a documentary that explored the many dimensions of Africa, the land and its people. It was ABC's attempt to make its mark as a news heavyweight, and the months invested in sending camera crews and producers across the continent glowed on the screen. It was a landmark broadcast but roused little comment and found little resonance among the American public.

A more telling, and well-known, test of Africa's pulling power with viewers came in 1992, when Bryant Gumbel took NBC's *Today* program, which he was hosting, on a weeklong visit to Zimbabwe, Botswana, and other African nations. Since the 1960s, trips to foreign lands have been among the most popular audience-drawing features of *Today*. From London to the beaches of Rio de Janeiro to the Great Wall of China, the scenic video postcards served up to a breakfast-time audience have usually driven ratings above the normal weekly levels. Would a week in Africa perform as well? There were skeptics at NBC, but Gumbel felt a personal commitment and had the clout to take his show to Africa. Two million dollars were spent as forty-five producers and technicians prepared for the broadcasts with reports on the life, politics, and stunning scenery of the countries visited. There were reports on the role of women in Africa and on the problem of rapid population growth. Live interviews were arranged to create the familiar *Today* show mix of news and features. All of this was brought into American homes and breakfast nooks. It was impressive broadcasting and exceptional television journalism. But when the Nielsen ratings were tabulated, they showed that Africa week had brought the *Today* show its lowest ratings in years. Gumbel and NBC had done their job magnificently, and viewers had offered their response. More of them tuned into ABC's *Good Morning America*, which also went on the road that week: from the Grand Canyon to Las Vegas. With the exception of South Africa, where the story—racial conflict—was easy to understand, Africa was, and would sadly remain, a complicated, distant, and therefore "lost" continent for American journalists.

A Story of Neglect

BUT THEN it always has been for eyes and minds raised in a European culture. Stereotypes grow quickly and die slowly, if at all. They are too comforting for the public to abandon. Journalists understand this, though we do not like to acknowledge it and do try to fight it. And foreign correspondents have accepted another fact: no reporter for an American publication or television network has built a major career in Africa. Well, one did. H. M. Stanley was his name, of the *New York Herald.* But then his story was really about a European in Africa. And it was a while ago.

IN 1855, David Livingston, who had come to Africa for God and Queen, was halfway through his epic march across the continent from Luanda, in Angola, to Mozambique on the Indian Ocean. For much of his arduous trek he followed the Zambezi River, guided by members of the Mokololo tribe who spoke of a giant falls on the river that no white person had ever seen. The falls sounded like one of the great natural sights of Africa, and Livingston, the explorer as well as the missionary, was determined to be the first European to find it. His trek had already lasted fourteen months when, on the evening of November 15, 1855, he set up his camp on the banks of the Zambezi. In the distance, more than six miles away, he could hear the thundering roar of the falls.

The next morning, Livingston and his native guides set off in their canoes. Soon he could see the cloud of mist rising like white smoke over the falls in the distance. The canoes moved swiftly downstream as Livingston marveled at the giant palms lining the riverbanks. Later in the day he would write in his diary, with Victorian flourish, that "scenes so lovely must have been gazed upon by angels in their flight." Half a mile above the falls,

Livingston changed to a smaller canoe paddled by men who knew the Zambezi and its accelerating current and the danger of being swept over the falls. They steered down the middle of the river and landed on an island, which led to the edge of the watery precipice. Livingston "crept with awe" and looked down into the abyss more than one hundred yards below. To his left and right he saw a thundering sheet of water one mile wide, 47 million gallons of water a minute crashing into the chasm below. Slowly, he moved back from the edge. His excitement got the better of his Scottish missionary reserve, and he carved his initials into a baobab tree, "the only place I have indulged in this vanity" he would write in his diary that night.

As a true representative of his Victorian times, David Livingston did not hesitate to name the falls. The Africans who led him there called them Mosi-Oa-Tunya, the smoke that thunders. The forty-two-year-old Livingston, soon to become one of the most famous figures of his time, could name them only for his queen.

IN THE AUTUMN of 1976, 121 years after David Livingston leaned over the precipice and into the smoke that thunders, the afternoon sun cast its warmth over the terrace of the Victoria Falls Hotel. Built by European settlers to their colonial-era tastes, the public rooms had high ceilings from which fans turned quickly. On the broad terrace with its heavy wooden easy chairs and tables, freshly painted white, hotel guests sipped their afternoon tea, or early gin and tonic, and gazed out on the impressive view across the well-manicured lawn: the rising, billowing clouds of mist from the falls themselves.

Actually, there were very few guests, and the hotel was nearly empty. The reason was evident when I arrived by plane at the small airport a few miles away. I collected my baggage, boarded a bus, and watched with some apprehension as a white Rhodesian soldier mounted a jeep, locked and loaded a .30-caliber machine gun, and escorted us to the hotel. The Rhodesian side of the falls was a war zone, as was the entire country. The white population of barely 250,000 was making its last stand against nearly 6 million blacks who were demanding power. Black rule had swept over Africa except for its southern holdouts, most notably South Africa, but, just as defiantly, Rhodesia. Soon it would be known as Zimbabwe, but that day had not yet come. White Rhodesians still clung to the belief, rapidly becoming a delusion, that their colonial-era lives and privileged lifestyles could continue, that black Africans would "come to their senses" and realize how much better off they were than under the rule of their own people. Why, you only had to gaze across the falls at Zambia, which had once been Northern Rhodesia, I was told by the white Rhodesian honeymooners at the hotel. Look at what had happened to that country, they insisted, so rich in copper and other minerals, so well farmed by its big (white) landowners, and now so poor and corrupt and, well, hopeless. It was all so sad, the young couple kept repeating, as they tried to convince me, and themselves, of the justice of their fight and their confidence in their future.

As we looked out at the falls, my eye was drawn to the railroad bridge that spanned the deep gorge at a point where the two sides narrowed. Across on the Zambian side, a long train of freight cars was being pushed out onto the bridge, and then slowly across it, until the engine doing the pushing reached the middle of the gorge. The engine was then uncoupled and backed up into Zambia. A few minutes later, an engine on the Rhodesian side hooked onto the train and began pulling the cars off the bridge. It was a perfectly normal sight, except for one awkward fact: it was not supposed to be occurring. Rhodesia, after all, was an internationally boycotted, isolated, and ostracized pariah state. Nobody, with the exception of South Africa, recognized it or did business with it. So why were those freight cars moving across the bridge in both directions? Clearly, many people across the falls in black-ruled Africa were separating business from political rhetoric and doing business with Rhodesia and even South Africa, which is where the south-bound trains were headed. Always in need of concise visual metaphors, I found the bridge to be a useful prop to describe what separated and joined white and black Africa. Why the bridge exist-ed was clear: the Zambezi had to be crossed. Why it was built on what must be the most precarious site of the river was a question in need of an answer.

CECIL RHODES was getting impatient. "Everything in life is too short," he complained to a friend. "Life and fame and achieve-ment." It was 1897 and Rhodes had reason to feel that way. He was forty-four years old, he had wealth and power, and he had just suf-fered his third heart attack.

Rhodes never married. His passion was expanding the British Empire, and with it his own influence. Or perhaps it was the other way around. With his fortune built firmly on the diamonds and gold of South Africa, Rhodes looked north to the unmapped region David Livingston had passed through without leaving any notice-able trace. Rhodes moved ruthlessly; his mission was commerce, not Christ. His agents duped an African chief into signing a mis-leading agreement that gave Rhodes's company exclusive prospecting rights in the land he named, immodestly, after himself. Rhodes also pledged 1,000 rifles and a river gunboat in the deal but reneged on the gunboat. Rhodes's men moved in and took over. They were fortune hunters conquering their own frontier. Inevitably the African tribes rose up and tried to force the white man out. Inevitably the revolt was crushed, brutally.

If continental expansion was Rhodes's driving lust, railroads were his arms, their tentacles creeping up the African continent, claiming more and more land for himself and his queen. Rhodes began to dream of a rail line that would extend from Cape Town to Cairo. He ordered that the railroad he had built to Bulawayo, in central Rhodesia, swing west and then north to pass by Victoria Falls and from there continue due north. Rhodes knew the falls would be a magnet for visitors from around the world. The main obstacle, of course, was the wide Zambezi River. When his engineers walked into his office one day and unrolled their plans on a large table, they called for a bridge several miles above the falls, where the river was shallow and sluggish. Rhodes leaned over the maps and studied them silently for a minute. He jabbed his finger at a point just below the falls called the Boiling Pot. "This is where we will build." he announced. "I want the passengers on the train to see the full majesty of the sight. I want the spray to fall on the widows of the cars." Less than five years later, Rhodes was dead. The following year his rail line reached Victoria Falls.

The first train arrived on a fine morning in May 1903. Work crews and construction engineers poured into the tiny settlement, turning it into a roaring boomtown. Rhodes's railroad never reached Cairo, but he did get the bridge he wanted, and it was where he wanted it. The first problem was getting men and materials across to the other side of the Boiling Pot at the bottom of the falls, since the bridge was to be built from both sides simultaneously. The solution, it was decided, was a small, primitive cable car. A thin wire attached to a rocket was fired across the gorge. Halfway over it fizzled out and plummeted into the churning water below. A second rocket was successful, and a rope was pulled across, which in turn pulled a heavier cable. A boatswain's chair was attached for workers to make the harrowing high-wire crossing 335 feet above the bottom of the falls. It was strongly recommended that you not look down. With the cable in place, supplies could be pulled across and the work began. Steel plates were fastened onto foundations that had been poured at the foot of the two sides of the gorge by workers who had been lowered down with the wet concrete. Large girders were then lowered and added on, building the ends of the bridge straight up like towers flush against the sides of the opposing cliffs. At the top, large cables were run back into the cliff to hold each end of the bridge firmly in place.

The next step was to extend the bridge out from each side of the gorge. Large cranes lowered the steel beams and girders into position. As each section was completed, the cranes inched forward and repeated the process. Day by day the two arms of the bridge grew longer, as if they were reaching out to touch each other. On a nearby hill Africans gathered to watch the work, convinced the bridge would fall into the water. But the arms of the bridge kept moving closer, the space between them grew steadily smaller, and on March 31, 1905, it was time to place the final girder.

A hot afternoon sun beat down on the work teams as the heavy piece of steel was maneuvered into position over the small remaining opening. As the foreman waved hand signals to the crane operator behind him, the girder was slowly lowered. Suddenly, it stopped. It didn't fit. It was too wide for the opening that had been so carefully calculated and prepared. The engineers who had spent two years at Victoria Falls planning the bridge down to the last fraction of an inch checked their measurements. They were correct. But still the final piece did not fit. Then they looked up at the sun high over them and stopped worrying. Early the next morning the steel girder, which had contracted in the cool night air, was again lowered into the opening. It offered no resistance as it slipped smoothly into place.

Soon passenger trains began arriving from Cape Town and Johannesburg as pictures of Victoria Falls appeared on travel posters and the new illustrated magazines around the world. Each train delivered its load of elegant visitors, many with their own servants, who walked from the station across a road to the fashionable Victoria Falls Hotel, which was ready to receive them in comfort and in the style of the day. One dressed for dinner, one sipped tea from valuable china, one carried an umbrella for protection from the mist that fell like light rain. And then one went home to tell friends of the wonder one had seen.

IN THE AUTUMN of 1976, the railroad station was still standing behind the hotel. On the station wall were faded announcements for passengers requesting that tickets be purchased at least seven days in advance. Cancellations made less than twenty-four hours before departure could not be refunded. Over one of the empty benches in the waiting area was a large board with the headings "Trains North" and "Trains South." The two columns underneath were blank; the last passenger train had departed years ago. The only new sign was a large poster with green lettering announcing the required registration of all Europeans up to the age of fifty for military service. Failure to comply could mean two years in prison. It was signed by the director of security manpower. On the narrow gauge tracks in front of the station, a switch engine was jockeying freight cars and open gondolas from one track to another. In a small square room at one end of the station the white stationmaster sat at his desk working the crossword puzzle in the morning newspaper. I introduced myself and he invited me to sit down and chat. On the wall behind him was a travel poster showing two elephants bathing at a watering hole. In the corner stood a large safe, and on his desk two telephones. One had a normal rotary dial, while the other, larger phone had a handle to crank.

I asked about the freight traffic moving across the bridge and how that squared with Rhodesia's supposed isolation. "There is a simple reality," the stationmaster replied openly "They need our corn and other food products up north, and they also need to export their copper and zinc. This is where politics meets business." A few minutes later he turned the handle on the side of the large phone and began speaking to the stationmaster across the falls in Livingston, Zambia. The two men, the one white and the other black, had never met. In fact this one phone line was the only direct telephone link between Rhodesia and the neighbor with which it was doing so much business. The conversation was relaxed and businesslike as the two stationmasters discussed how many freight cars were waiting on each side to cross the bridge and which side should send the next train of thirty or forty cars across. "Doesn't politics ever interfere?" I asked. "Not really," came the reply. "Well, there was one incident recently..." and he went on to tell of the time that Secretary of State Henry Kissinger had visited Zambia. Government officials planned to bring him to see Victoria Falls from their side of the gorge. They understandably did not want him or the journalists accompanying him to see the active commerce passing across the bridge. Political illusions had to be maintained even if official policies were being flouted several times a day on the bridge and even if, as was no doubt the case, Henry Kissinger was fully aware of it. On the morning of the secretary of state's planned visit, a call came to the station in Victoria Falls with a special request: Could all train traffic be halted for the day? The Rhodesian stationmaster told me his response, with a chuckle: "I said of course, we'll take the day off. We Rhodesians are really British under the skin. We understand the importance of keeping up appearances."

BUT IT WAS becoming more difficult for whites to keep up the appearance of a normal life. In Salisbury, the capital, rush hour traffic still began at a little past four with steel streams of cars carrying the whites from their air-conditioned offices downtown to their homes in the suburbs, where a swimming pool, a sundowner drink, and a household staff of at least two or three blacks (gardener, cook, and maid) ensured that everything was ready for their employers to enjoy the good life. Unlike the whites in South Africa, the roots of the Rhodesian whites did not go back two or three hundred years. A few of the Rhodesians, a very few, could claim grandparents who had settled the country in the early part of the century. Most were second generation, or even first. After the end of World War II they had left damp, gray Britain, where milk and meat were still rationed, and had come to sunny Rhodesia. They left the mother country as middle or lower middle class and stepped off the plane in Salisbury as instant upper middle class. What a dream!

Elsewhere the dream was dimming. The jewels in the crown, India and Pakistan, were being granted independence. The British colonial tide was ebbing in the Middle East. But in Africa, and particularly in Rhodesia, the British settlers reassured themselves, there was no cause to worry. The Africans were not ready for independence, or so the white mantra went, nor were they able to organize an effective resistance when the winds of change finally did sweep across much of Africa in the late 1950s. When those winds reached Rhodesia in the mid-1960s, white Rhodesians simply declared their independence and said they would and could look after themselves, thank you very much.

Lady Jackie Wilson was looking after herself. Titles did not amount to much in Rhodesia, but Lady Wilson's husband had been the speaker of the Central Africa Federation Parliament of colonial days, which entitled his widow to carry the title from an era that was vanishing before her eyes. Journalists in Salisbury told us she was worth a visit. We drove east to the highlands along the border with Mozambique. I could see why whites did not want to abandon their lives and their homes. In the cool hill country of the Vumba Valley homes looked like baronial family estates set in the Scottish highlands, with views that unrolled for miles in front of the living room window. We drove along twisting roads and past the small Anglican church as we had been instructed. We had to be careful to look for Jackie Wilson's house. A wrong turn and we could end up in Mozambique, where the Portuguese colonialists had been driven out and a left-wing African government was giving aid and sanctuary to the black Rhodesian insurgents.

The view from Jackie Wilson's home was as commanding as the lady herself. There was a weathered face wearing no makeup and a gruff voice thickened from years of smoking; a cigarette smoldered in her left hand as we stood in the sun. She waved her hand in an arc toward the expansive view and then led us into her home. Inside the living room, there were few signs left of the good life. The sight lines to the valley were marred by protective metal screening on the windows and doors. Her house had already been attacked once, which was not surprising when she told us that the infiltration route for the insurgents passed up the hill just above her garden. Jackie and her seventeen-year-old son had two permanent houseguests, Rhodesian police who lived with them. Lady Jackie was such a well-known figure in Rhodesia that for her to abandon her home and move to the safety of Salisbury would have been a serious blow to the morale of whites holding out in the highlands. She was a woman who had become a symbol, with all the baggage that carries. At night she was a prisoner in her own home; she, her son, and the two policemen stayed indoors, with the doors barricaded and one policeman always awake. Like her white neighbors, they were linked to an emergency radio network connected to the nearest police station five miles away. In the middle of the night Jackie Wilson would listen to the radio traffic. If the attack was close to her home, she would get up, grab her rifle, and take up her position. If the incident was farther away, she would roll over and try to go back to sleep.

"The house is a mess," Jackie Wilson acknowledged. She and her husband had built it twenty-five years ago. Now it looked more like a place for messy communal living than a proper home. But how could it be otherwise with the two policemen constantly on guard inside, and the guerrillas lurking in the hills behind? The attack, another attack, would come. Jackie Wilson knew it. Her strong voice was infiltrated by a faltering bravado. Tension was already deeply etched, for life, in the face of her son. Jackie Wilson complained that the United States and Britain had ganged up on little Rhodesia, isolating it, squeezing it. Perhaps. But the white Rhodesians were engaged in that most futile of struggles, the attempt to defy history.

There was an honesty, a coming to terms in Jackie Wilson as she served tea, with brown toast and orange marmalade. She knew the stakes and the odds. As I was leaving, she seemed to relax for a moment, or perhaps she simply wanted to confide in someone. "It is strange staying on here, isn't it? In trying to keep my home, I may lose my life." She looked around the property. Not many miles north of where she stood, David Livingston had passed on the final leg of his God- and empire-driven trek across Africa that had marked the beginning of the European age in the heart of Africa. Now, a little more than a century later, Jackie Wilson's lawn was going to seed, and she clearly had lost her enthusiasm for tending the garden behind the kitchen door. "One more attack," she said, looking out at the valley below, "and I will probably be out of here." One month later, she was.

Chapter 17

FIREWORKS OVER RED SQUARE

V LADIMIR ILYICH LENIN is in an irascible mood. There he is in my Moscow hotel room. It is November 1917. Czarist rule has been destroyed, but all power has not yet fallen into the hands of the Soviets. Lenin paces the floor impatiently, hands clutched behind his back, shoulders hunched. "Will the masses never understand the glorious socialist future that awaits them if they will only seize it?" The actor playing Lenin in the television film spins on his heel and answers his own question. "Of course they will." The inevitability of dialectical materialism is a great comfort to the leader of the revolution. The moment of triumph is approaching.

It is November 1977, the eve of the sixtieth anniversary of the Soviet Revolution. Outside, army units and battalions of workers and students are preparing the celebration that will unfold in Red

Square. On television, the Soviet public is watching the official version of how it happened. It is an interesting interpretation of Lenin that has little in common with the austere, intimidating Lenin set in the monumental statues and revolutionary portraits of socialist realism. The actor playing Lenin on television fills him with physical and intellectual energy but does not play him as a heroic figure. Rather, Lenin is painted in the colors of dry humor and avuncular paternalism, worried about his children, the Russian people. Whether Lenin possessed these qualities is, of course, unimportant to the official who ordered up this interpretation of him. In any relationship between leaders and led there is a difference between what is and what is supposed to be, and television plays a major role in that distinction. It exists in a democratic society, but not nearly to the degree that we find it, or found it, under an authoritarian regime of the Cold War, where those with their fingers on the buttons of the television cameras and control rooms were answerable to neither the inherent rights of the people nor the dictates of audience ratings.

Next to the television set, where Lenin was still invoking the inevitability of revolution, the hotel window offered a panoramic view of Red Square and the Kremlin. Directly ahead the embalmed remains of the real Lenin lay in his mausoleum, behind which the floodlit picture postcard spires of St. Basil's Cathedral rose in the night. My eye was then pulled to the Kremlin itself, which stood under a thin layer of snow, like a large-scale model in the show window of an expensive children's toy store at Christmas time. Within its red brick walls, topped by pointed towers and turrets, a cluster of buildings were jammed together. Like the czars before them, the Soviet leaders ruled from behind these walls, presenting a forbidding, secretive face to the supplicants left outside. It was a role from which the leaders, defiant and dismissive, could not free themselves. Its only virtue was historical consistency.

In the middle of the Kremlin, however, my eye stumbled over an object tortuously out of place: the modern glass and concrete Palace of Congresses, the mammoth hall where party conferences and other Communist gatherings of importance were held. One might have thought that such a building, with its thousands of seats and an architectural style that grated against the age of czarist architecture, would have been built elsewhere in Moscow, perhaps along the banks of the river, where the building could have stood in its own space, and on its own terms; a sign to the people that the men in the Kremlin were ready to come out from behind their walls. At the time the building was planned, there were proposals to do just that. But in the end the Soviet leaders, the successors and heirs to the czars, bent under the weight of tradition and their insecurity. This showpiece of modern, and modernist, Russia was shoehorned into the Kremlin itself, and there, behind the walls, like wagons drawn into a circle, the Soviet leaders felt secure.

That evening I invited a colleague to dinner in the Hotel National, whose pre-revolutionary charm was locked in a long and inconclusive struggle with Soviet maintenance standards. When we walked into the dining room, about half the tables were occupied. We asked the head waiter for a table for two, anticipating the ritual that lay ahead. "Impossible," he said, pointing to his watch, "the restaurant is closed." Since it was only eight o'clock, that seemed unlikely. I leaned forward and said, "Of course we are paying in dollars." The waiter was transformed into the personification of solicitude and indicated we should follow him. He led us to the best table in the room at a window offering a splendid view of the Kremlin and Lenin's Tomb. The service was attentive, the food acceptable, and the vodka numbingly cold. When the bill came, it was written in dollars. However, we were only at the beginning of the transaction. The waiter suggested that perhaps I would prefer to pay with American cigarettes. He told us there was a hard currency store in the hotel, in the bar just down the corridor, where I could buy Marlboro cigarettes, several cartons in fact. We each understood how the system worked, this stirring of free market forces. For the holder of dollars, the dinner with caviar, wine, and vodka was cheap. For the holder of the other hard currency, Marlboros, the potential profit was even more substantial than accepting dollars. One carton, I imagined, went to the head waiter, a second was shared with the other workers in the dining room, and a third went to the kitchen staff to be smoked or sold at a marked-up price. The owner of the restaurant, the state, which bought the food and paid the salaries of the staff, received nothing. All of this was carried out in full view of the Kremlin and Lenin's Tomb, which added a touch of amusement to the evening. We settled our bill with the three cartons of Marlboros left under the table in a plain brown bag. The head waiter was all smiles as we strolled out.

It was just before dawn when I was awakened by the noise. A loudspeaker outside my hotel room was barking out numbers amid the rumble of diesel motors. I pulled open the curtains and looked down. A light snow was falling, and along the broad boulevard tanks and armored vehicles were being maneuvered into position, their metal treads grinding into the dark asphalt. The sixtieth anniversary of the Russian Revolution was upon us, the occasion for one of the world's great visual spectacles.

By 9:30 A.M., I was in the foreign press section of the stands that ran along the Kremlin Wall facing Red Square. To the right, at one end of the square, was St. Basil's Cathedral. Across the square was the GUM department store, its walls covered with revolutionary slogans. At 9:58 Leonid Brezhnev, the general secretary of the Communist Party, trailed by the other members of the

Politburo, mounted the steps of Lenin's mausoleum next to us. At 10:00 A.M. precisely, two gray convertibles raced in from opposite ends of the square. They stopped parallel to each other as the two generals in the cars exchanged salutes and barked out their orders. The spectacle had begun.

The military came first, thousands of troops marching into the square from the left and passing in front, their eyes riveted hard right toward the leaders standing above them. The army moved in a modified goose step, arms and hands held rigid, as if tied to their sides. The navy, in dark uniforms, swung their arms in sharp right angles across their chests, their white gloves flashing in precise synchronization. There was a special forces unit in blue berets. Even the border guards and police marched. Then came the main attraction, particularly for the Western military attachés in the crowd, with their cameras loaded and cocked. Large weapons began rumbling across the square. First came truck-mounted rocket launchers, antiaircraft missiles, and short-range ballistic missiles. Then the star of the revue appeared, as the new Soviet battle tank was shown for the first time in public. For half an hour the tools of war roared across Red Square, leaving behind a diesel cloud of blue-gray exhaust and the impressive image of military muscle.

Then Red Square filled quickly with tens of thousands of young Soviet citizens in blue, red, and white sports outfits. Next came formation marching with ranks of people in native costumes from the various Soviet republics. It was breathtaking theater. The effort and time that went into creating the show was incalculable, and there was more to come. An endless column of Soviet citizens spilled into the square, carrying flags and flowers, pushing and pulling floats, as a pulse-quickening movement of Tchaikovsky's Fifth Symphony roared out of the public address system. The music was accompanied by exhortations and slogans praising the heroic accomplishments of the Communist Party and system. If the leaders standing above on Lenin's mausoleum could run their country as efficiently as they organized this demonstration, they would have no worries.

In the end, though, as with all great propaganda spectacles, the occasion was empty for the very reason that it was so blatantly propagandistic. As I looked around, I saw Soviet television cameras everywhere, on all sides of the square and on rooftops above, more than twenty cameras; far more, I thought, than were needed to cover such an event. In the Soviet television age, however, the events in Red Square were intended mainly for the much larger audience watching at home. Across the vast land mass from the Baltic to the Pacific, television screens filled with seemingly endless columns of red flags, military might and loyal citizens paying the expected homage to their leaders, and to the Communist system.

That night Soviet television presented an edited version of the parade. Although the actual event was spectacular, it clearly was not spectacle enough. The reconstructed and improved version on prime-time television showed Red Square filled with people marching, carrying banners, and pulling a giant float bearing the likeness of First Secretary Leonid Brezhnev. In the parade the float had crossed the square only once, but in the hour-long television program that evening, the float appeared again and again, approximately every ten minutes. Now I understood why there had been so many television cameras around the square. The one float was shot from many different angles, stored on videotape, and then played back in the edited program in the evening. Each time the singular tribute to Brezhnev was shown from a different camera angle, giving Soviet viewers the impression of an endless stream of floats gliding across Red Square in praise of the Soviet leader. One reality had been edited into a new reality for the millions of viewers who no doubt believed what they were seeing.

A few minutes after the highlights of the reworked parade ended, Soviet television presented live coverage of a fireworks display over the Kremlin. From my hotel window I could see the square packed with Muscovites, but a low cloud cover brought disappointment. As the fireworks rocketed upward, they quickly vanished into the night mist and exploded, leaving a dull, diffused glow rather than the sharp brilliance of pyrotechnics. I turned away from the window to the television screen in the room and saw pictures of the scene below—the crowded square with searchlights playing against the Kremlin wall. I listened to the commentator describing the exciting climax to this historic day. To my astonishment, I also saw something that was not occurring outside: beautiful fireworks exploding in a rainbow of colors against a clear night sky. The visual sleight of hand was audacious. Moreover, the commentator added to this bit of Soviet realism with his vivid account of the filmed fireworks transmitted from the television control room as if they were the genuine, live event. The message was clear, if not exactly new. Once again, the reality presented to viewers was not what was, but what was supposed to be.

That sort of manipulation would not survive in the new information and media world. Even in the Soviet Union.

IF THERE ever has been any doubt that the force of history is, in large part, the force of technology, it could be laid to rest in the drama that was unfolding in the Soviet Union in the mid-1980s. That Soviet power was built on size rather than imagination no one inside or outside that vast continental empire doubted. But in the age of information technology, size alone, whether in Soviet industry or engineering, had lost its competitive edge. Looking back, we can perhaps glimpse the first telltale sign of that in the 1960s when President Kennedy challenged the Soviet Union to a race to the moon. We can imagine the scene in the Kremlin as the top scientists were summoned to report on how the Soviet Union would win that race. We can also imagine the shock in the Politburo when the scientists laid out the cold truth: the Soviet Union had the rocket power to reach the moon, but not the sophisticated computer power needed to put men on the lunar surface and bring them back safely to earth. That, however, was not what the Soviet political barons wanted to hear. They had grown up in a system in which success was a function of power, which, in turn, was the product of size—the size of a vast state-run steel mill, an overstaffed government ministry, or the number of divisions that could be mobilized to throw back an invading German army. Information technology was a foreign language. And its inherent imperative of a free flow of information made it an unwelcome concept to the Soviet leaders. If the implications were threatening, the reality was too visible to deny. Not only was the creaking controlled economy stagnating (as officials privately acknowledged to Western visitors), but the land of the grand Marxist-Leninist experiment was falling irretrievably behind the United States in the unending and unforgiving contest to build weapons of both mass and selected destruction. Enter Mikhail Gorbachev.

FOR MORE than a decade I had been traveling to the Soviet Union at least once a year. In the 1970s and early 1980s, a journalist's work was limited to what a sensitive and secretive Soviet official wanted us to see, and the frustration factor was high. With Gorbachev's arrival, though, doors began to open and Russians began to talk to foreigners, even on camera. It was a stirring time. And now, in 1986, I wanted to report on how information, and therefore power, was about to flow through a new type of box that, unlike a radio or television set, could not be easily controlled by the state: the computer. The key to unleashing its power, and its consequences, was Gorbachev.

Sitting in an editing room in our NBC Moscow office one afternoon, I watched a videotape of Gorbachev as he set out to change individual attitudes, as well as a sclerotic system. In one memorable scene he stood on the Nevsky Prospect, the main boulevard in Leningrad, debating with passersby. The familiar Russian fear of change and uncertainty was clearly heard in voices. Gorbachev responded sharply. "Each of us has to decide whether we are going to lag behind or move forward," he said, jabbing his finger for emphasis toward the crowd. "Each of us has been put on this earth for some purpose. I have decided why I am here, have you?" It was bracing stuff. On another tape, Gorbachev was visiting a microchip plant, one of the first Soviet attempts to catch up to the West in a field in which power grew in inverse proportion to the size. "We need a revolution, not evolution," Gorbachev preached to the assembled scientists and technicians. "Revolution can be achieved through technological progress." Gorbachev was a man in a hurry. He did not see how quickly and inevitably a revolution in one field, technology, would have its unraveling consequences on others, on Communist power and his own future.

A few days later, I arrived in what was arguably the heart of the coming Russian revolution. Akademgoradok is a unique community just outside the city of Novosibirsk, a privileged enclave for Soviet scientists and thinkers. The stores had more goods and shorter lines than the ones in normal communities. But the greatest privilege for those living, working, and above all thinking there was freedom from political dogma. For all the paranoid Kremlin fears of free speech and thought, Soviet leaders had long understood the necessity of allowing a small number of select and highly talented minds to think freely in order to develop a better hydrogen bomb or an improved way of teaching mathematics in schools. Now Gorbachev had ordered that computer theory be introduced into high schools and that training begin as soon as computers were available. It was to be Mikhail Gorbachev's great leap forward. It was to be Andrei Yershev's moment.

Andrei Yershev sat in his book-lined office. With his gray hair and sparkling eyes behind thin-framed glasses, he would have fit in as comfortably on an American college campus as he did here in his institute on the edge of Siberia. He wore a cardigan and had the air of a professor who had devoted his life and his mind to his work. Yershev was one of those Soviet thinkers who had received the special dispensation of free inquiry. Unlike many of his colleagues, though, the fruits of his thinking and writing had not seen the light of publication, let alone implementation, but lay unused in the filing cabinet next to his desk. For Andrei Yershev had been thinking the unthinkable in the Soviet Union. Unlike his scientific colleagues who worked at developing new weapons to kill people and destroy things, Yershev's "unthinkable" plan would kill no one. It would only destroy a political system. Yershev had drawn up a complete curriculum for computer education in the Soviet school system that involved freeing up the information flow. The implications had been too terrifying for Soviet leaders to accept. But now Mikhail Gorbachev had given the order to push ahead with computer education. Whatever number of years Yershev had had to wait, whatever frustration he had felt (and it must have been soul damaging), his reward was now at hand.

Yershev spoke English, slowly but precisely. "If the children become the bearers of new knowledge," he began, "they will make pressure, insistent pressure, as they learn more and demand more information." A critical question, though, continued to hang in the air: how could a free flow of information be tolerated in a society where information had been tightly regulated, not only by the Communists but also by the czars, who had kept printing presses under their personal control for 250 years after their introduction in Russia?

"Can the information age and Soviet society coexist?" I asked. "Certainly, and why not," Yershev replied. There were plenty of reasons why not, I thought. "What happens when young people use their personal computers at home?" I continued. "Kids love to hack, and the potential for individual empowerment is enormous." Andrei Yershev hesitated, squirmed a bit in his chair, and pondered the appropriate answer to this most basic of questions. Neither glasnost nor his writ for free inquiry was yet a mandate to dismantle Soviet control of information. Yet Yershev knew that was precisely where the computer age was driving him and his country. He tried to dodge the question. "Oh, there won't be computers in the home. First, we do not have enough of them and, second, the bandwidth on our telephone system couldn't handle it," he added, overstating the problem. "We see computers mainly as a means to increase efficiency of communication in our government ministries and state industries." His answer was a blend of political correctness and technological obfuscation. He was no longer speaking of the inevitable pressure for knowledge and expression from young people. But the young Soviet citizens and their pressure were just down the street from Professor Yershev's study. The local school already had computers up and running. During the noon lunch hour we found high school students playing a game of Star Wars that they had programmed themselves, in English. That was creative freedom. What Mikhail Gorbachev was looking for, and Andrei Yershev was providing, was something less: just enough information power and limited freedom to change the Soviet and Communist system, but not destroy it. It was too little too late.

That afternoon we videotaped the future. It was in a classroom where ten-year-olds had been introduced to the computer. The instructor had demonstrated how the young Russians could play with it, even draw a favorite figure by typing Xs line by line to create a portrait. It was the most basic of beginnings, but the children's imaginations had been allowed to run free as they huddled over the computer and chose their favorite image, which was then printed out on continuous roll paper, with its sprocket holes along the sides, and now was displayed prominently on the classroom wall in this Siberian school: the simple, distinctive, and international profile of Mickey Mouse, in all his digital glory.

Chapter 18

GLOBAL VILLAGERS

I N 1945, Arthur C. Clarke sat down in London and performed some calculations. He was interested in technology, space, and the future and how the three would affect the way we live. In time, Clarke popularized some of his speculations and calculations in *2001: A Space Odyssey*, a work that continues to resonate today, on both paper and celluloid. Another major contribution of his was based on a singular observation: an object placed into orbit 22,300 miles above the earth will rotate at the same speed as the earth and thus will maintain a fixed position over our globe. Clarke calculated that with three of these geosynchronous satellites it would be possible to transmit pictures and sound anywhere in the world. The implication of this was breathtaking; the popular reaction, lethargic.

Of course in 1945 mankind had not yet broken the gravitational tether that tied it to earth. Although the technology of television existed, it was not yet on the air or in the air. Those who were developing the box with the moving images were happy if their test pattern signal could reach the suburbs. The idea of programs bouncing off orbiting satellites was at best a distant theory; satellite television was an idea better left to the imaginative minds of science fiction writers.

But in the early 1960s Clarke's theory became fact. In July 1962 the first television satellite, Telstar I, was launched from Cape Canaveral. It was not geosynchronous. As it orbited the earth, the length of time Telstar I was in the line of sight between ground stations, and could therefore transmit pictures, was only fifteen minutes. The first demonstration for audiences in the United States and Europe came a few weeks later. The live, but brief, program from Europe featured quick reports from various cities, including an outdoor performance of *Tosca* in Rome. The program from the United States to Europe showed a herd of buffalo charging across a field and a Chicago Cubs game at Wrigley Field. The sportscaster expressed relief that he did not have to explain the infield fly rule to viewers across the Atlantic.

In 1963, the first geosynchronous satellite was launched and switched on. Satellite television was no longer a technological stunt; it was now a working tool for broadcast journalists and a reason for the decision to expand the evening network newscasts from fifteen minutes to half an hour. As more satellites were launched and ground stations built, today's news could be seen today.

How can the impact of satellites be measured? One way, I discovered in 1985, was to travel to the end of the television world or, as it turned out, its newest frontier, Belize. On trips to cover the leftist insurgencies in El Salvador and Nicaragua in the 1980s, the fastest connection from New York City was via Miami on a Taca

Airlines Boeing 737, with an intermediate stop in Belize City. I did not pay much attention to it on the first trip. We were jammed into seats that would have crushed a midget. The stop was blessedly brief, and I noticed that few people got on or off the plane.

On subsequent flights, as we flew over Belize City on our approach to the airport, I looked down and saw a town that seemed to be lost in time and place—a movie set town for a film version of a Joseph Conrad novel. When we landed, I noticed a 1940s-type airport building, short and squat (to call it a terminal would be an act of generosity). Visual contact whetted my journalistic appetite. Belize did not have a Marxist government or a leftist insurgency, or even a rapacious oligarchy, which is the grist of the daily news mill. On that scale its obscurity was not surprising, and an assignment there was something I stored in my futures file.

What finally galvanized action was yet another of those body-numbing flights. The ground crew in Miami had gone to great effort to erect a makeshift curtain behind the first two rows in the all–economy class cabin of the Boeing 737. It was an unusual gesture for a VIP, for in Central America cabinet ministers, generals, and wealthy landowners all rode in egalitarian discomfort. An airplane in that region of the world is one of the few places where social integration is fully achieved, not to mention the only place where people can congregate knowing that not one of them is allowed to carry a concealed gun. On this flight, though, class distinction had been imposed by the curtain, in front of which sat a delegation of British clergymen headed by none other than the archbishop of Canterbury. At Belize City he got off to be greeted by a welcoming committee of approximately a dozen people and a tropical downpour. I reasoned if the archbishop of Canterbury made the effort to come from London to visit Belize, an enterprising foreign correspondent could do the same. There must be a story there.

A few weeks later, I got off the plane in Belize, a country where most people lived just above sea level and a good number of them below the poverty level. Once there had been a thriving timber industry. The British had brought in labor from the Caribbean, workers to cut mahogany in the malarial rain forests of the backcountry. But as the forests were leveled and the mahogany trade moved elsewhere, there was little left to the economy. Farming was largely subsistence. A few tourists who shunned the beaten paths had discovered the offshore islands set in emerald waters, as well as the relics of ancient Indian civilizations onshore. Hollywood producers found a ready-made backdrop for movies such as *The Dogs of War* and *The Mosquito Coast.* In Belize City most of the simple clapboard houses stood on stilts awaiting the inevitable hurricane with a fragile fatalism. Belize, I also quickly discovered, is a land where news is mostly gossip. What served as newspapers were of the offset press variety, long on conjecture, misspellings, and rumor and short on facts and professionalism. There was only one radio station in the country, and it broadcast only part of the day, offering little if any news. What made Belize special, though, was the breathtaking, mind-bending fact that in 1985 it still had no television system. As Belize was one of the poorest nations in our world, its leaders had decided they couldn't afford television, and that was that.

Well, it was not quite that simple. Shortly after arriving, I heard the news sweeping the city: Chicago Cubs star Gary Matthews was coming to Belize on what appeared to be a state visit. The government of Belize had asked the Cubs to send one of its players to take part in a National Youth Week celebration. What lay behind the excitement, and Gary Matthews's visit, is precisely what Arthur Clarke had foreseen in 1945. Although there were no television stations in Belize, television was coming into the country.

Local entrepreneurs in various towns had set up receiving dishes aimed at the satellites hovering over North America. Through low-power transmitters or a primitive cable system they then distributed the programs to their communities. There was no government regulation. No one asked whether it was legal to take, or even steal, programs from the commercial stations in the United States. It was just done, and that too was that.

One of the most popular satellite stations or superstations that was being picked out of the airwaves was WGN in Chicago, which carried the Cubs games and made Belize a distant outpost of the Chicago Cubs fan club. Satellite television had destroyed distance. Belizeans lived and died with the fortunes of the Cubs. One local citizen who had resisted the tug of American baseball complained that he had never expected to wake up one morning to discover that his country had become a suburb of Chicago. But so it had.

To find out how this had happened and what it was leading to, I left the coast and headed into the interior of the country. The two-lane highway was paved most of the way, although I had to watch carefully for the potholes and make detours around bridges that had been washed out. After several hours I began to climb into the highlands and arrived at San Ignacio, the last town before the border with Guatemala. The air was cooler up here. The people were not the English-speaking Caribbean blacks of the coast but had Indian and Spanish features. English and Spanish were the operative languages.

Ainsley Leslie did not belong to any specific category. "I have a bit of everything in me," he said. What he clearly had was energy. You saw it in his strong forearms and barrel chest. You sensed it in his darting eyes and urgent voice. He was the village business magnate. For years, he had made his living driving his truck from San Ignacio through Mexico to Texas, where he would load up with refrigerators, radios, clothing, and whatever else the people in his town needed or wanted or he could persuade them to buy. It was a simple one-man, one-truck import business and a successful one. The people of San Ignacio, cut off from the mainstream of mass consumerism as well as communication, had only a limited idea of what they wanted. Their appetites had not been influenced by the guiding hand of modern marketing and advertising. Or television.

One day Ainsley Leslie heard that entrepreneurs along the coast were getting into the television business. Leslie thought it might be another profitable line for him. He reasoned that if he could provide television programming, people would buy television sets from him, a premise that sixty years earlier had inspired David Sarnoff, the legendary builder of RCA, to create the National Broadcasting Company to give consumers a reason to buy RCA radios and, later, television sets. Needless to say, there was a slight difference in scale between the corporate colossus to the north and Ainsley Leslie in San Ignacio. The population in and around the town was scarcely more than a thousand souls. But the spirit in Leslie was the same as in Sarnoff, and so was the inescapable driving force of the new technology. A brother who was the mathematics teacher in the local school helped Leslie get on the air. The brothers first bought the electronic equipment needed for a satellite dish and an instruction manual on how to aim it at the television way stations 22,300 miles above them. Money and material were tight, so Leslie decided to build the frame of the dish out of local products, wood, and mosquito netting. It was not much to look at, standing there in his backyard amid the laundry, the dogs, and the cats, but when he flipped the switch and powered up the dish, his television set came to life. It was, to be certain, a poor signal—images were blurred and the colors were bizarre—but there on the screen was unmistakably a television picture. Life in San Ignacio would never be the same again.

Unfortunately, a lot of rain falls in the highlands of Belize. Inevitably it warped the wood of the satellite dish, and with it the picture. Leslie, though, was not discouraged. Confident that his idea would work, he invested in a proper metal dish in his backyard, and then three more on a hillside above his house. He bought a low-power transmitter with a range of about ten miles, and he was in business. There were no more warped pictures or blurred colors. Ainsley Leslie's television empire was transmitting four channels of broadcasting, twenty-four hours a day: two channels in English, two in Spanish. All were taken from satellite systems based in and over North America. And he wasn't paying one cent for them.

Leslie was his own programmer, picking his menu from the electronic smorgasbord served up by the satellites. His *TV Guide* was a monthly publication the size of a telephone book of a good-sized city, which listed all the programs being transmitted around the world. There were the network morning shows, sports, the Nashville Network, Johnny Carson, cartoons for the kids, all cascading down like a tropical waterfall into the outstretched arms of Leslie's satellite dishes, which stood incongruously next to the ruins of ancient Mayan civilizations. There was, however, a problem. This twenty-four-hour, four-channel operation was serving a market of only a few hundred television sets in the village and the farmlands around it. The viewers were too few and too poor to support advertising or even pay a monthly subscription fee. But Leslie did not give up. He hired a man in a red T-shirt who walked around the village and visited the neighboring dirt farms, with hat in hand, asking viewers to contribute to the expansion of the television age. Ainsley Leslie was not making money on television, but, as the television king of San Ignacio, he was having fun and discovering the instant social status conferred on the person who brings entertainment and information into people's homes.

And what had life become in San Ignacio? The local movie theater had closed, since it couldn't compete. Some critics in Belize lost no time worrying that the image of American television and America itself would subvert Belize's cultural identity. A former government minister complained to me bitterly that "people ask why can't our streets be paved the way they are in *Dynasty*?" Then he got to the heart of his complaint: "Television is a direct invasion, more dangerous than an army." Hyperbole, perhaps, but within it was an essential truth. The people who produce television shows in the United States and the companies that sponsor them did not know they were being seen in San Ignacio, and probably would not care if they did. What, after all, is a market of a few hundred impoverished television owners? But the programs, and above all the commercials, created a demand for products that did not exist in Belize or in people's minds before the satellite brought them into their homes. Now viewers were asking merchants, including Leslie, for Mr. T's breakfast cereals and Sears lawnmowers. The public and the marketplace were being served. By the mid-1980s satellite television in Belize was exercising its predicted influence. There, as elsewhere, it was also fulfilling the inescapable law of unintended consequences.

ONE EVENING, in a hotel room in São Paulo, Brazil, I had just taken a shower and was getting ready for dinner when I noticed a printed message on the television screen. It was not for me in São Paulo but for someone in the Philippines. Among the many channels offered to hotel guests, and the one I was tuned to, was the satellite channel of the American Armed Forces Radio and Tele-vision Service, which transmits programs to American military installations overseas. A printed message on the screen was brief and to the point: "Attention Subic Bay and Clarke AFB, do not broadcast network evening news until you have checked your messages." I felt the voyeur. Here I was getting ready for dinner in Brazil while reading what was intended to be a closed circuit mes-sage from Washington to the two large U.S. military bases in the Philippines. But I knew what was happening.

A year earlier I had experienced another example of the unin-tended consequences of satellites. It occurred in the low, one-story building that straddles the border of the DMZ between North and South Korea. The building was used by the United States during the cease-fire negotiations that ended the Korean War in 1953. Today the American members of the International Commission still meet on the site as they try to defuse the unending tension and hostility between North and South Korea.

As I entered the office used by the Americans one morning, the television set was tuned in to the *NBC Nightly News* from New York, where it was the evening of the previous day. Tom Brokaw was introducing a report I had prepared two days earlier. The pro-gram was being transmitted to U.S. military installations around the world. But in Korea, the marvel of technology was colliding with the reality of local politics and creating a catch-22 of the satellite age. The Defense Department has a policy that American servicemen and -women overseas should have the same access to news and entertainment that they would have at home, and satel-lites provided that.

But the United States also had what was called a "sensitivity agreement" with the South Korean government, which, put simply, meant that no reports critical of the military dictatorship there at the time would be shown. To do so would be to interfere in the internal affairs of Korea, particularly since the American programs were broadcast on an open channel that anyone could watch, and many Koreans did watch. The result was that when the *Nightly News* carried a report on the political situation in South Korea that might antagonize the "sensitive feelings" of the host regime, the U.S. Army did not broadcast it in Korea. However, to eliminate the story while showing the rest of the program would have been censorship, and that was unacceptable to American principles. Another way had to be found around, or through, the conundrum.

The solution was to cancel the entire newscast when it carried a political report on South Korea, cancellation somehow being distinct from censorship. Here was the delicious paradox of the new technology: satellite television was being used by the Defense Department to inform American servicemen and -women of what was happening in the world, and indeed in the country they were assigned to defend. But they were not allowed to see reports about political struggles for freedom in the very country in which they were living and for which they were prepared to give their lives.

IN BELIZE the satellite paradox was human rather than political. Early one evening, as dusk was settling over San Ignacio, I drove out of town to a small farming community. The homes were simple, built of rough-hewn wood. There was no running water, no electricity. As darkness came lanterns were lit, and from one home came the unmistakable sound of a television that was being powered by an automobile battery. The light from the TV screen was the only illumination in the small living room. One of the family members inside the house was a young schoolteacher, Manuel Medina. We talked about what television was doing to his community. Unlike some self-appointed social commentators, he told me how happy he was with this new companion, television. Children who watched it were speaking a better English and a Spanish with a richer vocabulary than was normally heard in San Ignacio. Television, he said, was educating him and expanding his horizon far beyond the borders of his community, or even his country. "Now I can see the world," Manuel said, enthusiastically. "Right here in my own home."

"Would you like to see it in person?" I asked.

"Sure," he replied. "I'd like to go to the United States and get a job there."

Here was another consequence of satellite television. The American programs spanning the world and penetrating the most remote villages constitute one big commercial for American culture and society. For millions of immigrants, or immigrants-in-waiting, the United States itself had become the ultimate consumer product. Today, the dramatic increase in immigration, legal and illegal, is no doubt caused by the human drive for opportunity and prosperity. There is no way we can precisely quantify how much television adds to it. But the impact, I imagine, must be significant as it whets the appetite and holds up the brass ring of the American dreamland, where the streets may not be paved with gold but are paved. For much of the world that alone is enough.

The growing role and impact of global television led me inevitably back to the source: Arthur Clarke himself. Several days after leaving Belize, I spoke with Clarke via satellite. He was in Sri Lanka, where he had made his home. I was in NBC's Studio 3K in midtown Manhattan. We were using two satellites as we chatted. The first was between Sri Lanka and England, where the television signal was taken down and converted to American standards. The picture was then thrown back up those 22,300 miles to a transatlantic satellite, came down again in Maine, and was fed into our New York control room.

In our interview, Clarke raised two main points. The first was that anyone (or any government) who tried to stop the free flow of information would be swept aside by the force of technology. (This was before Tiananmen Square, the opening of the Berlin Wall, or the collapse of communism in Eastern Europe and the Soviet Union.)

Clarke's second assertion will take longer to realize if, indeed, it ever is. He argued that because of the pervasive, all-encompassing reach of television, people will become more tolerant of other people's points of view. The global village, he said, will become a global family. The phrase tripped off his tongue with the ex cathedra confidence of one who is already standing in the future and waiting for the rest of us to catch up. He saw television as both the umbilical cord and the pacifier of a global family.

It sounded reassuring, but an essential element of the premise, I felt, was missing. The television flow was overwhelmingly in one direction, from the United States and a few other industrialized nations to the rest of the world. In Belize viewers can plug in to American life in their homes, but Americans have been far less willing to switch on to other cultures in our homes or in our minds. True, other countries may not have the commercially attractive programs or the financial base or in some cases, such as Belize, the technical resources to broadcast to the world. Even if the language barriers are overcome, as they are with dubbed versions of American programs in non–English speaking countries, the current of American entertainment and information is so strong that it is difficult, if not impossible, for another culture or perspective to swim upstream against it. And it is almost impossible to reach the headwaters of our ethnocentric psyche.

Will time and satellites eventually alter this flow? Will the Internet accomplish it more quickly? Perhaps. In the meantime, what we are creating today is a global family in which a self-styled parent with an American accent does most of the talking and little of the listening. The parent's message may have merit, but it is a monologue and not a dialog. In the United States it is difficult and perhaps impossible to fully grasp what is happening because we do not see it, because it is happening elsewhere. It is the creation of a new American empire, one built not on the power of gunboats and colonial viceroys or maps colored in red by schoolchildren. This empire has no borders. Its power lies in its images, myths, dreams, suggestions, hopes, and fragments of information, each one possessing little influence singly but adding up collectively to that new empire without shape or borders, as intangible as it is powerful.

One night in San Ignacio, as a half-moon was rising slowly over the village, I walked along a dirt road. Around me were the soft night sounds of the subtropics—the crickets in the fields, the idle conversation of villagers talking over the events of the day. As I approached a simple house I could see, through an open window, the reflected glimmer of a television screen. As I passed the house, something made me stop. From within, I heard the familiar brassy beat of a television theme song. The music gave way to an announcer's voice reciting the names of the guests who were shortly to appear on the flickering television screen here in the highlands of Belize—names that would excite the studio audience and television viewers in bed across the United States and perhaps now in San Ignacio as well. I gazed up at the moon, that natural satellite that pulls the tides and attracts our imagination as no human technology can or ever will. The night sounds were now drowned out by the excited television voice that spilled out of the house and spread across the land where the Mayan civilization had once flourished. I breathed in the warm, humid air and waited for the inevitable cry of another great civilization that I knew so well. And then it came, as it always did, piercing through the stillness of the night.

"Here's ... Johnny."

Chapter 19

THE RULES CHANGE

O F C O U R S E Johnny Carson is no longer on the television
screen. Nor is the network era he represented. His thirty
years on television paralleled the beginning, rise, and gradual but
steady decline of the networks and of their newscasts as the central and formative source of television news.

When did we first notice it? Notice the ground slipping under
our feet, the audience beginning to erode? We were the passengers
on the *Titanic* after it struck the iceberg. The network, we reassured ourselves, might take on a little water, but that was no reason to worry, let alone race to the lifeboats. Still, alarm bells were
ringing for those who knew how to listen for them. In 1986, shortly after GE bought RCA (and with it NBC), a Wall Street analyst
asked me, "Are you ready for the revolution?" I replied that television and particularly television news were always changing; that

was the nature of our chosen professional beast. "No," he countered bluntly, "I am not talking about little changes. This is GE that has bought you. Your life will never be the same."

The first change made by the new owners was innocuous and yet revealing. One morning I opened a package that had arrived on my desk. Inside was a supply of stationery with the NBC logo on it. It looked fine but felt flimsy and cheap; the paper was tissue thin and curled up at the corners. I walked over to a cubicle where the person in charge of the office operation was seated. I showed him the new stationery and asked what kind of an impression it would make on someone receiving it. Was our news coverage going to become as thin as the paper? "Perhaps," he replied with a sigh. "They are sending us a message, and we'd better get used to it."

We were not alone. Corporate pressure was being tightened on all the network news divisions. In 1986, Larry Tisch, who had no business experience in broadcasting, bought control and was personally running CBS. CapCities, which had a large local television and publishing business, was the new owner of ABC. News divisions were no longer seen or treated as privileged sanctuaries where accountability to spending and profits would be dismissed with the wave of a benevolent hand. CNN was a growing competitor. Macs and PCs were becoming the new home altars and hearths for the information age.

Budget tightening and layoffs at the news divisions brought protests from journalists and critics of television. At CBS, there were complaints that more than jobs were being sacrificed to the bottom line; the distinguished and successful news tradition that led back to the glory days of Edward R. Murrow and then Walter Cronkite was being abandoned, and the public would be much the poorer for it. The cries from the heart and conscience were deeply felt. Journalists, whatever their personal career ambitions, possess a deep sense of calling to our craft. In the late 1980s there was still a sense of loyalty to a company, particularly among more senior employees. True, we had reported on the "downsizing" and "restructuring" of the steel and automobile industries with journalistic thoroughness (and detachment), but it was hard to accept that the same forces could, or would be allowed to, enter newsrooms. News, after all, was more than a business, wasn't it? While that question was debated in public and private, our future was being defined not only by the competitive pressures of computers and cable television but also by a singular event that would change news and what was judged to be news.

AT MIDDAY on November 9, 1989, I was in the large, windowless NBC newsroom in New York. In East Germany, power was rapidly slipping from the hands of the comrades who had ruled since the end of World War II. Tom Brokaw was in Berlin anchoring his *Nightly News,* and I was prepared to follow the next day for our weekend programs. Suddenly, without warning, a bulletin flashed on our computer screen. In East Berlin a senior Communist official had just announced at a news conference that East Germans would be allowed through the wall to visit the West. The decision had clearly been made in haste, and no details were given as to when and where the wall would be opened or whether East Germans would have to obtain special visas to breathe the air and see the forbidden land to the west.

We interrupted a network soap opera and went on the air to break the news, the first American network to do so. Brokaw was at the news conference, and after it ended he interviewed the official who had made the announcement. In the past it would have taken a reporter up to an hour to pass through the East German security checks and delays to get through the Berlin Wall to report live on the air. However, this was 1989; the cellular phone age had arrived. Tom simply dialed the telephone number of the New York studio and gave his live report of what was happening in East Berlin, where it was early evening. At the same moment, East Germans were getting the news fed back to them from television and radio in the western part of the city. Late that evening the instantaneous flow of information had turned into a human flood as East Berliners marched past stunned border guards, their automatic weapons hanging limply at their side, through the wall and into freedom. At the Brandenburg Gate Berliners from both sides climbed onto the wall and, using hammers, chisels, and their bare hands, began to take it apart.

This was the dramatic background for the *Nightly News* that night, as well as a network special report later in the evening. Other shocks were being felt throughout Eastern Europe. In Bulgaria, hard-line leader Todor Zhivkov had been pushed from power that same day. Czechoslovakia and Romania would soon have their revolutions—one peaceful, the other bloody.

I arrived in Berlin on Saturday morning. Our live broadcast position for the weekend programs was in front of the Brandenburg Gate, not far from my old apartment where as a young correspondent I had opened the curtains each morning, looked out on the wall, and wondered whether the bleak landscape of a divided city would ever change. Now it had with stunning swiftness and finality. I felt the historic pulse of the moment and wondered where the East Germans would head as they came through the wall that had imprisoned them for twenty-eight years. Would they choose to visit the museums, see the parks, or go to a Hollywood movie? No, they would not. Late that afternoon I walked over to the

Kurfürstendamm, the main shopping street in West Berlin, with its elegant boutiques, restaurants, and cafes. It had become a pedestrian mall, packed solid with East Germans, shoulder to shoulder, from the shop windows on one side of the broad avenue to the display windows on the other. The East Germans were interested in one thing that day: they wanted to see the fruits of the Western capitalist system. For twenty-eight years they had watched television commercials and programs from the West. Now they could see for themselves what was in the store windows and finally within their reach. The museums, the theater, the movies could all come later. On this Saturday afternoon, freedom meant, before it meant anything else, the bounty of the consumer society.

IN THE New York news bureau of CNN hangs a long rectangular chart tracking the audience ratings of major events since 1985. As a twenty-four-hour news channel that the public turns to when major stories occur, the chart is about as good an indicator as we have of what news attracts American viewers and what does not. Across most of the chart the line shows little change, reflecting the several hundred thousand homes tuned to CNN when no major news story commands attention. But when a big story does break, the line spikes, soars straight up, and then plunges back down once the heat of the moment has passed.

The first story on the chart to spike was the U.S.–British attack on Libya and Colonel Khadafy in 1986. Other news grabbers have included the *Challenger* tragedy and the Gulf War, as well as the O.J. Simpson freeway chase and trial, Princess Diana's death, and, in Washington, the political scandal and impeachment ordeal of

1998–1999. The soaring and plunging audience ratings of a twenty-four-hour news channel are about as accurate a measure we have of what news, and what kinds of news, turn viewers on, or at least move them to turn on CNN.

As I looked at the succession of dramatic events on the chart, I searched for November 1989 and the opening of the Berlin Wall. Guess what! There was hardly a ratings blip from American viewers. The mass public seemed barely interested. And there would be only a slightly greater interest three years later when the hammer and sickle were hauled down over the Kremlin and the Soviet Union ceased to exist. We can offer any number of theories why this was so, why there was such apparent indifference in the face of such monumental events. In the case of the Berlin Wall crumbling before our eyes, there was no threat to the lives or well-being of viewers in the United States. Nor was there a human tragedy to tug at viewers' emotions. Indeed, the sight of East Germans walking joyously through the wall and the sound of West Germans picking away at it to save a concrete piece of history merely confirmed that the world was becoming a safer place, which in turn allowed the American viewer to focus on other, more immediate concerns.

Whatever reasons or explanations we come up with, we cannot deny the facts on that CNN chart.

Chapter 20

THE NEW NEWS

I N NETWORK NEWSROOMS the story is told of a young reporter who had received his first overseas assignment. This was
before CNN, before the end of the East-West conflict, and before
the networks' lost dominance of the television news marketplace.
The elated reporter met with the producer of the evening half hour
newscast and asked what kind of stories he was looking for from
abroad. The producer replied, "Oh, about a minute thirty."

It is no longer a joke. The frequency of foreign correspondents'
reports, even of one minute and thirty seconds' duration, has been
in sharp decline. Television producers, like newspaper and newsmagazine editors, no longer fudge the issue. They openly acknowledge where their priorities lie in a highly competitive environment. The three networks will still make a significant effort and
financial investment to cover a few major stories and crises that

possess irresistible drama or command clear interest. What viewers rarely see anymore are foreign correspondents' reports on conditions and issues in other societies: elections and social and economic trends, which over time form a mosaic of the rapidly changing world in which the United States plays a unique and leading role.

Moreover, in recent years international issues involving the United States have been reported with increasing frequency from Washington by network correspondents based at the White House, State Department, or the Pentagon, where they are able to integrate video footage from overseas into their Washington-based reports, thereby imposing a clearly defined American angle on the story rather than a foreign one. The result is to reduce an international perspective to near invisibility, and the foreign correspondent to an occasional walk-on role.

Those who monitor this trend tell the story in cold numbers. In 1989, the year of Tiananmen Square, the opening of the Berlin Wall, and the collapse of much of the Communist world, the network evening newscasts carried a total of 4,332 minutes of reports from their busy foreign correspondents. In 1992, the year after the intensive coverage of the Gulf War, the number of minutes had declined to 2,521. In 1999 the balance sheet showed a total of 1,799 minutes of overseas-based reporting, 687 minutes on CBS, 654 minutes on ABC, and only 457 minutes on NBC. The absence of foreign reporting has not hurt NBC News; indeed, its formula for a softer, more domestically oriented news diet appears to have helped the network's ratings.

We may be dismayed by this defiant gesture of indifference to the world we live in, but we should not be surprised. A constant theme of the American experience has been a deep sense of self-containment and self-sufficiency, which has rarely been challenged and then only in cases of a direct threat to U.S. interests.

The Cold War conflict between "West" and "East" had the symmetry and the easy-to-follow plotline of a contest between "Good" and "Evil." It was the global environment Americans lived in and accepted as a defining structure of their era. As long as nuclear missiles were aimed at American communities, the question of international security had personal impact. Journalists quickly discovered that almost any story we could link to a Soviet or Communist threat, no matter how distant or tenuous, could be sold to our editors and to the public.

The passing of the Cold War era left many institutions adrift, searching, and at times grasping, for a new role and reason for existing. Television news was no exception. With the loss of foreign stories that could be presented as part of an overall threat to American security, newscasts have lost a dramatic element in an increasingly competitive medium that thrives, and perhaps depends, on conflict and sensation to attract and hold the attention of a mass audience. Former external threats, such as Soviet missiles, have been replaced by domestic ones, such as the drug dealer on the street corner. The importance of these themes—crime, poverty, education, health care, and the other items on the domestic agenda—is beyond question. But the consequences of this shift in emphasis form a paradox: broad viewer interest in world affairs is declining just as the United States is rising to new levels of influence as the only political and military power with a worldwide reach, just as U.S. business needs to expand overseas, and just as U.S. popular culture dominates the world, all of which is driven by U.S. leadership in the development and exploitation of new technologies.

Public apathy toward international news, however, may not actually be as deep as it seems. Today more Americans than ever are working, traveling, and studying abroad. Americans who want to engage directly with the broader world have more tools than ever to do so. Satellites transmit daily television programs from Europe, the Middle East, Asia, Africa, and Latin America to the growing ethnic markets in the United States. The proliferation of cable channels offers programs on the arts from many countries and foreign films, as well as new outlets for news and global business coverage. A discriminating, motivated viewer no longer needs to watch the traditional network newscasts to feel informed.

Each of the cable channels may have an audience that is one-tenth or even one-twentieth the size of an evening newscast (and Internet sites far fewer), but taken together they have been a major factor in reducing the networks' share of the television news market by more than 30 percent from their peak years. It is this decline in audience and market share that has pushed network television news producers to an apparently logical, if journalistically undesirable, decision: international news is expendable unless it is of clear and compelling interest to a mass audience. The current and future trend in television news is hardly different from that in most other industries in the evolving marketplace—as choice increases, power shifts from the producer to the consumer. Seen from a domestic perspective, the evening news producers, who are still chasing a mass (if diminished) audience, claim that they are focusing on their customers, or at least the great bulk of them. That strategy, though, amounts to an editorial downsizing, a narrowing of focus that gives viewers who are searching for a greater exposure to the world even less reason to watch the programs. It is a slippery slope that leads not only to smaller audiences but also to reduced relevance in the broadcast industry and in society.

The forces changing the network newscasts and the role of the foreign correspondent involve more than growing competition.

Television is the most expensive of news media, particularly in the reporting of international affairs. A correspondent for a newspaper, magazine, press agency, or radio is engaged, by and large, in one-man journalism. He or she can travel to the scene of a story alone, cover it alone, write it alone, and transmit it alone to a home office via phone, fax, or e-mail.

In television, however, the basic working unit consists of a correspondent, a field producer, a cameraman, and a sound engineer plus approximately five hundred pounds of camera equipment. If a report needs to be prepared for satellite transmission, an editor and an additional six hundred pounds of editing equipment is sent along as well. That can add up to half a ton of equipment packed in twenty-five or thirty cases. The cost of this journalistic extravaganza, including hotels, per diem, car rentals, and local support staff, begins at approximately $3,000 per day. Add in airfare and excess baggage charges, and the price of covering a story can reach $12,000 or more before the first videotape is put in the camera. On top of that are the satellite charges and, if needed, the rental and shipping of a portable ground station.

In a few years, no doubt, miniaturized cameras, editing equipment, and new transmission technology will reduce costs. But even with the blessings of the digital era the financial pressures on news organizations will inevitably increase as the news and information marketplace continues to splinter into ever more cable channels and Web sites. In this new television world, the only way a news organization can justify the expense of a costly worldwide news operation will be to have several news services that can help to amortize the cost of international coverage for audiences in the United States and abroad. That is what CNN has developed with its separate domestic, international, business, and Spanish-language channels. (MSNBC and the Fox news channels, on the other hand, do not currently have a major international news effort to match CNN.) And there is another trend to keep our eyes on.

The future of the television foreign correspondent, and of international news coverage in general, will be shaped by more than technology and budget constraints. With the merger of Time-Warner and Turner Broadcasting, which includes CNN (followed by AOL's purchase of Time-Warner) and Viacom's takeover of CBS, all of the major news divisions are now owned by large transnational corporations with many, and at times conflicting, interests. Deep pockets count for a lot in today's race to establish global television empires. However, it is that very drive to establish these empires, to penetrate new markets, that can pose serious concerns for international reporting and broadcasting. The news that is broadcast into these countries is frequently seen by the authorities on the receiving end as undesirable or even subversive. When there is a clash of interests, journalism is likely to be sacrificed.

CNN, because of its early penetration of the global television news market, has long been aware of the problem. To remain on good terms with governments around the world and of all political persuasions, CNN created *World Report*, a program that includes stories produced by state-controlled television services. If that is seen as an accommodation to local political sensitivities, the program at least has the virtue of truth in labeling: it states clearly that CNN is not involved in the content of the reports. That distinction has allowed CNN's international news coverage to maintain its accuracy and credibility. The distinction between journalistic integrity and business imperatives, however, can become problematic as media mergers turn news operations into ever smaller components of the ever larger companies.

When Rupert Murdoch purchased the Hong Kong–based Star

TV satellite system in July 1993, it was his major move to dominate satellite broadcasting from the Pacific to the Middle East. The main attraction was the booming economy and more than a billion potential consumers in China. However, Star TV carried BBC World, the British international television news service. Chinese authorities did not want BBC coverage, or indeed any autonomous outside television news service, entering China. Murdoch bowed to Beijing's pressure and dropped the *BBC News* from Star.

When the Walt Disney Company stunned the media world by buying Capital Cities/ABC in July 1995, Disney CEO Michael Eisner appeared at a news conference with Capital Cities/ABC management in an ABC studio in New York City. Eisner was asked by a reporter how he saw synergy operating between the two companies. His response took on a global dimension. "There are many places in the world, like China, India, and other places," he said, "that do not want to accept programming that has any political content. But they have no problem with sports, and they have no problem with Disney kind of programming." Political content, of course, is precisely what much of ABC News coverage is about. (Even in sports, as NBC discovered.)

On the opening night of the Olympic Games in Atlanta in 1996, NBC sports commentator Bob Costas angered the Chinese government as the Chinese team marched into the stadium. Costas said, according to an NBC transcript, "Every economic power including the United States wants to tap into that huge potential market, but of course there are problems with human rights, property rights disputes, the threat posed to Taiwan." Costas also described the achievements of Chinese athletes and referred to suspicions that performance-enhancing drugs contributed to some of those successes. China's state-run media and Foreign Ministry were swift and sharp in attacking Costas's comments. A month later NBC issued a statement, saying that "we apologize for any resulting hurt feelings." The statement continued, "The comments were not based on NBC beliefs. Nobody at NBC ever intends to offend anyone."

The television world was shaken again in September 1999 with the news that CBS, the most venerable of networks, had been bought by Viacom. Beyond the size of the $80 billion merger was the added irony that Viacom had been created as a spinoff of CBS when the network was forced by the FCC to divest itself of its television syndication business. Under its CEO, Sumner Redstone, Viacom had become the father to its parent. Redstone and Viacom, also for the first time, were the parents of a news division, CBS News, with a long and honored pedigree. On a visit to China less than a month after the purchase, Redstone was asked about possible conflicts between Viacom's commercial interests and journalistic practice. At a news conference he said, "Journalistic integrity must prevail in the final analysis. But that doesn't mean that journalistic integrity should be exercised in a way that is unnecessarily offensive to the countries in which you operate." Redstone was reading from the same corporate interest page as the earlier NBC statement regarding China. In the end who decides what is "unnecessarily offensive" to an objecting government: a news editor or producer, or a corporate chieftain?

"A chilling effect" is a term long used when commercial or other pressures have been applied against the independence of reporters and their employers. Increasingly, it will be the foreign correspondents and their editors and producers who will likely feel the chill as they report from countries where commercial markets have become free before the flow of information has. Unlike the reporters and editors who in the past needed only to climb a flight of stairs to discuss a sensitive issue with the publisher, the new owners are, by the very nature of their transnational organizations, more distant in place and priorities.

Censorship is nothing new for the foreign correspondent. But what is likely to develop in nations that seek the bounty of the global market without sacrificing political control can be just as effective if less visible: the potential for self-censorship. As GE tries to sell more jet engines to the Chinese, and Microsoft more of its software, how free or self-confident will NBC or MSNBC or CNBC reporters feel about interviewing dissidents? As Disney develops its giant theme park in Hong Kong, will ABC News producers and reporters have second thoughts about taping an investigative report on corruption among Chinese government and party officials? As NBC and Bob Costas can testify, these are no longer hypothetical questions, but pressures journalists will have to challenge head on. And who will be the journalists of tomorrow?

The probability that technology and information flow on the Internet will eventually overwhelm efforts to control it means that the traditional foreign correspondent will play a proportionately smaller role in the transmission of news and information. Anyone sending information or a story from one country to another will be a de facto foreign correspondent. With the global spread of computers and computer owners on-line, the number of people sending and receiving these foreign dispatches is increasing rapidly. Even in those countries where governments may try to control Internet traffic via telephone lines, ingenuity and ever smaller satellite dishes will enable some and eventually a lot of news and information to get through.

In a few years, when the Internet and on-line services offer full-motion video, network newscasts may feel even less compunction to provide coverage of foreign events to a mass audience. But what is lost will be more than matched by what is gained in the breadth and depth of choice. Those interested in what is happening abroad will find an ever broadening and deepening selection of information than is currently provided, even by cable news channels. The much promised multilayering of information—video, sound, text, and graphics—will offer the news consumer unprecedented choice and editorial control.

And the person providing this information could be a new type of foreign correspondent, or perhaps the old type resurrected. Instead of dashing about the world to provide an on-screen "presence," the correspondent will demonstrate the quality and depth of the expertise he or she possesses. Foreign correspondents will have to be versatile as well as informed journalists who can write scripts for video and radio as well as print. They will need to be knowledgeable specialists who stick close to a country, a region, or a specific topic. They will have to possess the skills to appear on camera or to go on-line to communicate unilaterally or interactively with an audience whose members will be informed, engaged, and demanding, far more so than today's passive television viewer. The result is that those Americans who actively seek more knowledge about the rest of the world and the place of their country or business in it could be better served than they have been in the past.

What is being lost, or at least eroded, is the role of network news as the unifying central nervous system of information for the nation. Some may mourn this, especially those who grew up in the age of network news. Social critics and viewers may debate whether what is being gained with the growing diversity and flexibility of news and information delivery outweighs what is disappearing or, indeed, has already disappeared as far as the viewing audience under age thirty-five is concerned. Quite aside from the fact that there is nothing that can or should stop the rising technological tide, the benefits measured in choice and content are clear and exciting. For the fraternity of foreign correspondents, it could eventually offer a road back to our traditional craft. In the future they may no longer speak to the mass audience they could command in the past. They may even discard their trenchcoats and safari jackets. In speaking to a more limited but highly motivated audience, the foreign correspondent will have to possess, and will take pride in possessing, a depth of knowledge and expertise needed to satisfy the increasingly demanding, informed, and technologically equipped consumer of the digital age.

Chapter 21

THE NOISE OF NEWS

ALL EYES WERE focused on the speed indicator in front of us. The numbers on the dial crept up, indicating the rapid acceleration of the plane. As the earth below slipped away, conversation in the passenger cabin was reduced to a few whispered comments as we awaited Mach 1, the speed of sound. We had been told that there would be no particular sensation as we sped through what had once been called, ominously, the sound barrier. Military flyers had been doing it for three decades, and now ninety-six civilians, sipping champagne in their narrow Concorde seats, were about to, as the saying goes, share the experience.

It was May 1976, the inaugural flight of the Concorde between Europe and the United States. Among the passengers was a contingent of two dozen journalists poised to report on this new era of intercontinental travel that would, we were assured, once again alter our sense of distance and time. There was, however, no sense of speed as the indicator in front of us passed Mach 1 and we began to race the sun across the North Atlantic.

I boarded the flight from London to Washington prepared to marvel at this latest advance in aviation while deploring the fact that it would now be possible to have a power breakfast in Europe and a business lunch in the United States. The space in the cabin was limited, especially for someone accustomed to the ample walking around roominess of a wide-bodied 747. On the Concorde we were pampered prisoners in narrow seats, and maneuvering our way to the Lilliputian lavatories was no comfortable stroll. Still, if you ignored the price of a ticket (and at first class plus surcharge, it was a lot to ignore), the advantage of the Concorde was self-defining. If you wanted to fly the Atlantic in under four hours, it was the only way to go.

What was remarkable about the flight was not the time spent in the plane. The surprise came after the flight, the sensation of having been instantaneously transplanted from Europe to America as if the intervening three hours and fifty minutes had not elapsed. I had walked into London's Heathrow Airport at twelve noon on a sunny spring day and walked out of Dulles Airport in Virginia at twelve noon on the same sunny day, with an exhilarating and yet unsettling sense that the sun overhead had been stopped in its tracks.

Several thousand people had turned out at Dulles Airport to watch the British Airways Concorde touch down, followed two minutes later by its Air France sibling. Europe, draped in the red, white, and blue of France and Great Britain, was making the point that it could still play in the technology game. The United States had put men on the moon, but Europe would send men and women hurtling across the Atlantic at twice the speed of sound while drinking champagne. Which was the more civilizing achievement?

It was not the time or place to debate the point as the Concorde taxied to a halt and the cabin door swung open. I grabbed my small carry-on bag and hurried to join the NBC camera team that was waiting inside the terminal to report on the "historic" event. A U.S. Immigration officer stamped my passport quickly and slid it back across the counter with a smile. "Congratulations, Mr. Utley," he said. "Congratulations for what?" I asked, curiously. "You are the first passenger to enter the United States on Concorde." For a brief moment I envisaged an appropriate recognition in the Smithsonian, but the idea passed.

The Concorde may create the sensation of time and distance being suspended, but it is only an illusion; time and distance only seem to shrink. Television, however, makes their destruction real and total. How real became clear during the Gulf War. I participated in NBC's coverage of the conflict, and on a Saturday morning, when young children were camped in front of television screens across the country, we devoted one of our special reports to calls from parents and children with questions about the war. Several parents reported that their small children were afraid of the Iraqi Scud missiles, which they saw exploding in Saudi Arabia and Israel. When asked why they were afraid, the children had told their parents that the missiles would strike their homes in Memphis or Sioux Falls. In their young minds distance had no meaning. The television screen was their window on the world, and danger was located on the other side of the glass.

For adults too the Gulf War signaled an important change in television news, one we were not fully aware of at the time, as we watched time and distance collapse. Vietnam had been the first war in which television pictures conveyed human experience, but it had been presented in a controlled, edited format and on a delayed basis. It was traditional journalism conducted in the past tense and adapted to the technology of the moving image. In 1991, however, Desert Storm was conveying experience in real, present-tense time. Live broadcasts of news events, of course, were not new. The Kennedy assassination, Neil Armstrong stepping onto the lunar surface, and other landmark experiences had been shared live and simultaneously by the public. But they were exceptional events, distinctively different from daily journalism, which involved an editorial process of balance, thought, structure, and confirmation of facts before the news was delivered.

In the Gulf War, the concept of broadcast journalism as a single, stable craft and discipline came under strain as the imperatives of broadcasting and the distinct rules of journalism pulled reporters as well as viewers in opposite directions. In a fundamental shift, live broadcasting was separating itself from traditional journalism right before our eyes. The television cameras showed the distant flash of a Scud missile exploding, but the television reporter next to the camera or back in a studio could offer no more information or confirmation of what had happened than the viewer at home could see. Later news reports could and would offer a fuller, more detailed picture of what had actually occurred. But the move to live, real-time, "event" news coverage was under way. Broadcast news, driven by CNN and the other twenty-four-hour news channels that would follow, was pushing farther into the arena of sensation and direct experience, an arena already occupied by sports, in which live coverage of a particular play or game is accompanied by the instant analysis and commentary of specialists covering the action.

Critics have argued that sports is not news, or at least not traditional news, and that news should not be covered like sports. The point is valid, but it is becoming irrelevant or at least is being ignored. On CNN, as on other twenty-four-hour news channels, the largest audiences are generally drawn to live coverage of news events. In addition to the importance and drama of the event, viewers can feel that they are plugged in to what is happening in the world. Not only have they become direct observers, but they may also feel that they are participating in the event just as a theater or movie audience participates in a collective experience. The second-highest-rated programs on cable news channels are often talk shows. Viewers can feel that they are present at a discussion or debate about what is happening in the news. To the extent that the viewer can (or feels that he or she can) phone in a question or e-mail a comment to the studio, that viewer becomes a participant in the national conversation.

The programs that usually attract the smaller audiences on cable news are newscasts—the highly crafted and more carefully considered programs that demand the greatest journalistic skill and effort. Catching up with the news is no longer an end-of-day experience, but increasingly a continuing process of updating oneself throughout the day. Indeed, it is not difficult to envisage a time when newscasts, as we have known them, will disappear. Viewers will compile their own "newscasts" by going to their favorite Web site and clicking on a video report of the story or stories they want to see. This is already happening on-line as individuals prioritize the news in text form according to their own tastes and interests. If this seems like another milestone in the information age, we might think of how we read our morning newspaper; some start with the front page, others with the sports or business section. Each reader makes a personal choice on what is most important or interesting. Just as newspaper editors provide choice, so too will television news on the Web, once ample bandwidth can deliver quality pictures to the screen.

The Noise of News

What is ending is television news as ritual. This is a significant loss because ritual strengthens commitment. Through most of the Cold War period the world seemed a more dangerous place to Americans, and following the news, being "an informed citizen," was seen as an aspect of civic duty. It was a responsibility, even if it entailed little more than scanning the morning newspaper or sitting down to watch the evening network newscast. For high school students it was a ritual faced in the classroom current affairs quizzes. The duty to "be informed," like brushing your teeth or washing behind your ears, did not mean that everyone did it. It did mean that everyone was aware of being supposed to do it. No more.

The new alliance of television technology, all-news channels, and Web sites and the competitive pressures driving them have changed television news forever and in many ways for the better (in the broader range of information and faster accessibility that is now available). This may be difficult to accept for those who suffered through the marathon coverage of the O.J. Simpson trial and the press frenzy of the presidential soap opera starring Monica Lewinsky. But we need to appreciate the significance and power of changing times, otherwise known as generation shifts.

Those known among demographers as the "mature" generation (older than baby boomers) grew up in an era and an environment that structured life more formally, paying greater attention and respect to individuals and institutions and authority. More than their children, research has shown, Americans born before 1945 prefer to receive their news in coherent packages (newscasts) from authoritative (anchormen and -women) sources. This generation interprets the incoherence of the news cacophony as dissonant noise, which is as grating to the traditional news viewer as atonal music was to the lover of the romantic sweep of Brahms or as acid

245

rock was to the fan of Sinatra's lyrical phrasing. But more than tonality and familiarity are at play here. Older news viewers came of age at a time when social and human virtues included personal restraint, self-discipline, and delayed gratification. If "less is more," as Mies van der Rohe proclaimed in his vision of modernism, we today can ask whether the reverse is also true. Twenty-four-hour news channels have not significantly expanded the breadth or depth of reporting as much as they have increased the number of broadcast hours. Any industry undergoing rapid expansion and facing limitations on the availability of top talent is bound to be diluting the quality of the "product" (to use the marketer's term), whether we are talking about expanding professional football and basketball franchises or expanding television news. More can be less.

Which means that news, the twenty-four-hour variety, can be boring, repetitive, superficial, and even gratuitous. As television news becomes more present time, rather than past time, it is moving further away from the values and disciplines of print journalism. But then television is not print. This exposes another uncomfortable trait of television: its reporters are, with few exceptions, not reporters to the extent our brethren in print are. What most television reporters are, and have always been, is compilers of information, manipulators of factual and visual information, and communicators of that information called news. It is an honorable calling, one that attempts to mold some coherence out of the chaos of life.

In nineteenth-century frontier America, a popular saying was that God did not make all men equal, but Mr. Colt (maker of the Colt .45) did. Today, the same can be said of the communications technology available to all. The institutions that used to control the microphones and loudspeakers (governments, television networks, established churches, etc.) have discovered that they are no longer soloists in the great oratorio of life but, increasingly, mere members of the chorus. Perhaps the problem of an overloaded cortex is caused not only by the rising flood of images inundating us but also by the sound, the voices, the changed aural landscape of life. It has become intrusive and is the result of a profound shift in power. For the first time in history, just about anyone can have access to a microphone and a loudspeaker, even if it is a small one in an Internet chat room. Today, individuals and institutions can be divided into two groups: those who have recognized and digested this irreversible shift in power and those who have not.

Bill Clinton was one of the first to catch on. By the start of his second term it became clear that something was missing from his practice of the presidency. He rarely spoke to the nation from the Oval Office. Older Americans, and even some not that old, grew up with the memory and the habit of listening to presidents address them directly. From Eisenhower to Reagan and Bush, presidents spoke several times a year from the Oval Office, usually at 9:00 P.M., eastern time. There was no escaping the speeches, since there were only three networks and the president was on all of them. An Oval Office speech usually meant a president applying subtle pressure on the viewing public, asking for support to send more troops to Vietnam or in Ronald Reagan's presidency, mobilizing backing to reshape legislation and society.

Bill Clinton, though, chose a different tactic. As a leading-edge baby boomer, he understood that authority figures in the 1990s no longer carried the weight, the authority, they once did. For that matter, no longer did television anchors, correspondents, commentators, or newspaper editorialists. Nor did traditional, mainstream preachers and ministers in their Sunday morning pulpits, who saw the public flocking to new megachurchs complete with upbeat contemporary music, show business effects, and a precise awareness of which emotional and spiritual buttons to push. From the pulpit to the White House, empathy was in and authority was out. President Clinton resonated with it and mastered it.

What we are seeing and hearing in this "age of the image" is a revival of the oldest and most intimate means of communication: the personality of the voice and the power of the individual's spoken word. In television, it began in the 1980s with the rise of the morning and afternoon talk shows, and on radio with the dyspeptic call-in programs. Talk is cheap; talk is direct and often emotional and therefore engaging. Above all, talk is interactive and gives the speaker, whose voice is being heard, a sense of power. The turning point, the moment when the talk syndrome arrived as the new model of the national conversation, came in the 1992 presidential campaign—the first one since the advent of television news not to be waged primarily on the evening network newscasts with ever shorter sound bites and ever more hyped photo "ops." In 1992 the candidates appeared in the more natural and informal environment of talk shows. Ross Perot took up residence on *Larry King*, Bill Clinton went on MTV, and all the candidates got up early to appear on the network morning programs, where they agreed to participate in lengthy interviews and take calls from the public. There were also the familiar series of debates in prime time. In 1992 we went from the era dominated by structured discourse (speeches, carefully planned sound bites, and political commercials) to the age of increasingly natural and often louder discourse that we live in today. And once again, the network newscasts, the most tightly structured discourse in television news, with stories and scripts controlled to the second, found their star dimming. They were no longer the dominant playing field in the election contest. They could and did perform the important role of campaign referee, assessing the accuracy of claims and political commercials of the candidates. But it was not the same as being in the middle of the field, at the center of the action.

Those who regret or resist this change in public life and wince at the rising decibel level may find some wisdom and solace in the slightly profane insight of a Marine Corps sergeant in the early days of the Vietnam War. Late one afternoon a marine platoon on patrol came under mortar attack from the Vietcong. Immediately the marines on the periphery of our column began shooting back into the woods where the Vietcong were hiding. The air was filled with the thunderous, disorienting, chaotic, and frightening noise of war. In Vietnam you often did not see the battle you were in; rather, you heard it. And since we could not easily distinguish the sounds of the marines' weapons from those of the enemy, the natural survival mechanism was to bury our noses, and as much of the rest of the anatomy as possible, into the ground. Which is what a good number of marines and I were doing. The shooting had raged for a minute or two when we heard the gruff voice of a sergeant approaching us. "Get up, you bastards, and move!" he barked at us. I looked up and saw him standing tall, and to this day I can hear his battlefield admonition, which I have carried through the din of modern life and broadcasting: "Remember, the noise can't hurt you. Only the bullets can!"

Chapter 22

PARTING COMPANY

O N   A   W A R M evening in July 1993 a small group of NBC journalists gathered in a Manhattan restaurant to pay tribute to one of our colleagues. There were fourteen of us seated around the table in a private dining room, our attention and words directed at the man who sat at one end, John Chancellor, who, as always, was enjoying the company of his fellow journalists. As each correspondent, producer, and former executive toasted him, he responded with anecdotes and shared incidents from his rich experiences in television news. Behind the familiar glasses, which gave him a slightly professorial air on the TV screen, his eyes spoke their own thoughts. They brightened at the memory of a particular story or person. They grew somber at the idea of what this evening meant. It was John Chancellor's retirement dinner.

He had prepared for it well. Following thirteen years of anchoring *NBC Nightly News,* Chancellor had negotiated a contract that allowed him to continue on the program as a commentator when Tom Brokaw succeeded him in the anchor seat. Now that contract was up and NBC News was changing. A representative of that change also sat at the table in the role of dinner host. Andrew Lack had been hired two months earlier as the new president of NBC News. His vision of the future of network news did not draw on its past. Magazine programs in prime time, he believed correctly, would become the major gatherers of audiences and revenue. The *Today* program and other morning programs would hold on to their audiences, but the half hour evening newscasts would continue to lose viewers. The consequences of this were clear: the gathering and reporting of news would be reduced as the production of feature stories and programs devoted to a "softer" (and broader) definition of news was increased. The business logic behind Lack's reasoning did not ease the disappointment felt by most of those at the table. The Chancellor era at NBC had started before there was network news, had arced through its three decades of preeminence, and now in the 1990s had accompanied it into unmistakable decline. For anyone with a life in television news and a strong sense of history (and Chancellor had both) what was happening was unavoidable, if not welcome. As I looked around the table and joined in the bonhomie I understood that my time at NBC had reached its end too.

The thought was not new. Over the previous year NBC had been slicing away the programs I was anchoring. *Meet the Press* had rekindled my interest in politics even as it confirmed my reluctance to be limited by politics, government news, and a life lived inside the Beltway, which is part of the job requirement for the host of that program. *Sunday Today,* which I had hosted from 1988 (first with Maria Shriver and then Mary Alice Williams), never established a clear identity, although we produced some fine reports and programs on serious issues and cultural subjects. *Sunday Today* was part *CBS Sunday Morning* with Charles Kuralt & Co. and part the usual television morning show fare. We were aiming too high for some of our viewers and too low for the rest. Near the end of our run I arranged for an interview and a profile of David Hockney to be taped in his studio in Los Angeles. The story would cover his life as a painter and, more recently, a stage design-er. When I told the executive producer of *Sunday Today*, Gerry Solomon, that we had the interview, he replied, "Great, we can run it during sweeps" (he wasn't kidding). The confusion over what *Sunday Today* was supposed to be continued under the new team. As my replacement NBC hired Scott Simon, a talented and sophis-ticated host from public radio. One year after taking over, Simon was back at National Public Radio, a wiser and happier man.

As part of my weekend grab bag of programs, the most suc-cessful in the ratings was the *Weekend Nightly News*, particular-ly on Saturday night, where we established ourselves as the audi-ence leader. Network management, however, cared little about weekend ratings one way or the other, and the newscasts were fre-quently cut short or preempted by sports events. Moreover, the weekend news was the time and place to try out and promote the next generation of anchors. It was not only people that the current news management at NBC wanted to change, it was also the look, the style, and the substance of network news. I did not fit into any of the categories, with the possible exception of foreign reporting. NBC did offer the top international job in London. But it was clear that foreign news was going to play even less of a role at NBC than at the other networks, and I turned it down.

At the end of the Chancellor retirement dinner, after the sto-ries were exhausted and the cognac glasses emptied, there were farewells and embraces. I took a long walk home. For over a year I had been thinking about what I wanted to do next (and what I could do). There had been informal discussions outside NBC about television projects. Irons were in the fire, but my contract would run out in three weeks, thirty years (to the week) from the day I had arrived in Brussels with a suitcase, a typewriter, and a job offer from John Chancellor. I was fifty-three years old and didn't see a clear future.

Fortunately unemployment was brief. Despite the general retreat at NBC from foreign news, ABC News still maintained its overseas bureaus with a full compliment of reporters, producers, and camera crews. In August 1993 the position of chief foreign correspondent based in London became open. An offer was made and quickly accepted. Unlike NBC, ABC still offered commitment and opportunities for covering international stories. Peter Jennings at *World News Tonight* had spent years reporting from abroad, Ted Koppel at *Nightline* was born and raised in Europe and had covered the State Department, and Roone Arledge, who had built ABC News, was determined to keep ABC at the top of the network news game. The job in London also carried a personal attraction. For several years Gertje and I had thought of returning to Europe to live, if work could be found or developed. ABC and BBC had just announced a new alliance for news coverage to replace the decades-old partnership between the BBC and NBC. The decision by Britain's (and, in many eyes, the world's) leading broadcast organization to switch to a new American partner not only confirmed the widespread belief of where NBC was heading but also offered the prospect of new international projects involving ABC and the BBC.

There was, however, a personal problem. Gertje had been studying art history at New York University and was well into the writing of a Ph.D. thesis on Pablo Picasso. Establishing a new home in London and reestablishing old friendships would delay finishing her thesis. We also knew that once again I would be flying off on assignments as I had twenty years earlier from London for NBC. Gertje came to London to set up house, but she kept her work in New York. For the next two and a half years intense periods of her work in New York were relieved by intense periods of personal life together in London. We were not alone. In my travels I was constantly meeting other husbands and wives who were leading divided married lives. It was the evolving nature of globalized business, marriages held together by love, cheaper telephone rates, frequent flyer miles, and the determination to make them all work.

In London in the mid-1990s the work of a foreign correspondent bore only a fading resemblance to an earlier broadcast age that stretched half a century from World War II to the end of the Cold War. The ABC news bureau occupied a seven-story building equipped with a large newsroom, studio, control rooms, state-of-the-art editing facilities, and 120 people who could have run a good-sized television station from it. Unfortunately many talented staff members were underused.

Soon after I arrived, it became clear to me that the appetite for foreign news was shrinking at ABC too. The big stories were still covered and got on the air. However, the definition of what constituted a "big story" was growing narrower, as it had at NBC and CBS. The frustration of correspondents and producers grew as reports were ordered and then not used. Just as unsettling were reports that actually reached the screen—after having been cut in length and often micromanaged by senior producers in New York. Foreign correspondents were losing much of their editorial independence. Still, I felt the eternal exhilaration of traveling, seeing places, and speaking with people who made news or whose lives were being changed by news in the 1990s. In Mexico workers were hoping that NAFTA would bring greater trade and prosperity. At a once secret Russian naval base north of the Arctic Circle I spent an evening with the commander of one of the large "Red October" class of nuclear submarines that lay idly in port. There was no money to put to sea, and the captain spoke of his life's dream to travel. Over the dinner table in his modest apartment in the middle of a crumbling naval base, he told us that he had circled the world three times, under water, but had never "seen" it. Now the greatest ambition of this officer, whose submarine and missiles could have destroyed a good portion of the United States, was to see the world ... from a sailboat.

Mexico, Russia, China, Europe, and the Middle East ... the datelines, old and new, still had their power of attraction. But there was something missing. Behind the effort and excitement of covering the news was the unsettling awareness of how long this type of reporting could continue. As the economics of foreign news coverage turned against the networks, the picture grew darker. There was no surprise when, four years after ABC was bought by Disney, ABC's London bureau was moved from its own building in the heart of London into the Disney corporate offices on the edge of the city.

In the early summer of 1996 I received a call from CNN in Atlanta with an offer. This was unusual. CNN had reshaped television news and had done so in its own way with its own people. With a few exceptions it did not look to the networks as a source of its on-air reporters, anchors, or producers. Now it was. The reason was the one that moves any company to act when it feels threatened: competition. When NBC and Microsoft joined to launch MSNBC and Rupert Murdoch joined them in the twenty-four-hour news battle with his Fox news channel, television news was irrevocably changed. News competition would no longer be at supper time, but all day and all night. It would be less between the three networks and more between them and the cable news channels. There was no doubt who would win. In establishing itself as the place to turn for live news coverage and constant updates, CNN had shown where the future of television news lay and also that anyone with the determination and financial resources could do the same. How many could do it and make money was a question for a another day. In 1996 broadcasters had their last chance to make the leap to cable. Two networks, CBS and ABC, did not. It was a particularly painful moment at ABC News. In 1982 ABC and Westinghouse Broadcasting had joined forces to launch SNC, the Satellite News Channel, to compete head-to-head with Ted Turner and CNN. Although cable was seen as part of television's future, network executives did not yet understand how large a part it would be, particularly in news. The cost of running SNC mounted quickly. Sixteen months after going on the air, ABC and Westinghouse sold their struggling channel for $25 million to Ted Turner, who closed his competitor down. It was the best deal Turner ever made. For ABC and Westinghouse (which later bought CBS) it was a sale each would regret.

Thirteen years later, in the summer of 1996, Roone Arledge hoped to start an ABC cable news channel along with NBC and Fox. But ABC brought too little too late into a crowded field. The BBC already had its BBC World television news channel competing with CNN outside North America. In theory a news channel combining the resources of the BBC and ABC News might have created a quick and effective competitor with CNN as well as the newer and weaker channels coming on screen in the United States. However, cultural differences between the BBC and ABC prevented the new partnership doing more than sharing tapes of news stories, when one or the other did not have a camera crew present. ABC still had the strongest of the three network news divisions. Its journalistic heart was still in the right place. But heart could not change the facts. ABC had missed the cable news boat, which could have accommodated and amortized the work of its experienced international staff. The future of any network foreign correspondent was threatened. We were now in the CNN era.

In fact we had been in the new era since the evening of January 16, 1991, in the United States. It was early the next morning in Baghdad when American planes and missiles launched their air strikes, lighting up the city with the explosive flashes of munitions striking targets and the streaking arcs of antiaircraft fire vainly searching the dark sky for something to hit.

In the United States viewers had the choice of ABC, CBS, NBC, or CNN to watch the war live via satellite. Once again the major networks, with their large audiences, were performing the familiar and trusted role as the place for the public to gather to live a moment of great drama. In the NBC news room and studio in New York the atmosphere crackled with the intensity of crisis coverage as entertainment programs were pushed aside to make way for television's second war. Neither Tom Brokaw at NBC, Dan Rather at CBS nor Peter Jennings at ABC, indeed none of us gathered in the network news headquarters, suspected that network television news was about to take a direct, devastating hit.

And then we saw it happen. We watched helplessly, along with our viewers, as the voice reports from the network correspondents in Baghdad were cut off. Suddenly there was nothing. Nothing to see, (there were no pictures that first night) nothing to show. Television's highest power, to transmit experience, had been neutered. With the loss of the visual images there were only the voice reports of the television correspondents left. But they too went silent at the networks, because the sound as well as the pictures were being sent through the now destroyed television station. CNN, however, had arranged for a separate voice link with the outside world. Its reporters could at least provide their commentary of what they could see and hear from their hotel, and those listening to the television would create their own mental images. In the NBC news room all eyes and ears were now directed on the CNN monitor and we knew that millions of viewers would soon abandon us and turn to CNN. The dilemma was clear, the remedy inescapable. With the approval of CNN executives in Atlanta, the networks were able to speak with three CNN reporters in Baghdad; Bernard Shaw, Peter Arnette, and John Holliman. It was a coming of age for the Cable News Network that, in its earlier years, had been dismissed by some at the networks as "chicken noodle news." When Tom Brokaw finished the live telephone interview, the NBC anchor faced the camera and said "CNN used to be called The Little Network That Could. It's no longer a little network." In the NBC news room the sense of history was exceeded by a mood of deflation. In one evening CNN had established itself as the place to turn to for breaking news. The age of dominance of network news was over.

Chapter 23

EMBRACING THE EPOCH

*What's the point of doing something worthwhile if there is
nobody watching? So, when people are watching it makes
you a better person. So if everybody was on TV all the time,
everybody would be better people [sic]. But if everybody
was on TV all the time there wouldn't be anybody left to
watch. And this is where I get confused.*

BUCK HENRY,
SCREENWRITER OF *To Die For*

JOSEPH DE MAISTRE is not exactly a household name in the
United States, nor was he one in late-eighteenth-century France.
Among the thinkers of his time he was known for his brilliant
mind and penetrating analyses, as well as his conservative beliefs,
which would put to shame contemporary political and social commentators such as Rush Limbaugh or Howard Stern. Maistre was
a royalist who opposed the slightest concession to democracy. He
believed fervently in the ideals and practices of the Spanish
Inquisition. While serving as a diplomat in St. Petersburg, he
wrote that the public executioner was one of the most important
public officials in Russia. Maistre, we can surmise, was not exactly a fun figure, but no doubt he could be counted upon to enliven
a conversation on *Larry King Live*.

Unlike so many of his fellow aristocrats, Maistre escaped the French Revolution and the terror that followed it with his head safely on his shoulders. In exile abroad, he continued to follow developments in France. However strong and extreme his beliefs, his cold, analytical mind could not remain blind to the harsh truth of what had happened to him and his country. He observed:

> For a long time we did not understand the revolution we are witnessing; for a long time we took it for a mere event. We were wrong: it is an epoch, and woe to those generations present at the epochs of the world!

Today, our social pundits appear in many guises to offer their insights into this new epoch. Among the most influential are those using images as well as words: film directors and writers who have tracked the changes in television journalism with entertaining and often painful accuracy. In the 1970s, *Network* painted a picture of a crazed anchorman whipping up public outrage while network executives negotiated with a terrorist group to star in a new television series. In the 1980s, *Broadcast News* asked pointed questions about the commercialization of news and where, if anywhere, the shifting line of journalistic responsibility was to be drawn. In the 1990s, *To Die For*, with Nicole Kidman, looked at the future of television in a marketplace that is fragmenting to the point of losing shape and coherence. Screenwriter Buck Henry, from whose gaze and word processor no social foible escapes, posed his pertinent and frightening question to broadcasters when he asked, Who will be left to watch television once everyone is on television?

Part of the answer to the question of where we are heading in television and on the Internet came a week after the death of

Princess Diana in 1997, a tragedy and a news spectacle that shift-
ed our perceptions of the world of media and experience and emotions. The public reaction to her death, and the ability of broadcast
journalists to feed the apparently insatiable hunger for "news"
about Diana, confirmed once again the dominant power of television news as it illustrated the declining image and influence of
those ultimate authority figures, the British royal family. In the
media tumult that followed the midnight accident in a Paris tunnel, the picture that lodged in my mind was not only a mangled
Mercedes but also an embattled Elizabeth II. When the queen and
her family returned to London from Balmoral Castle in Scotland,
where they had been in seclusion, she faced a gale of criticism that
the royals had shown neither themselves nor the appropriate grief
to the public in the days following Diana's death. Offering a gesture as their response, Queen Elizabeth and Prince Philip emerged
from Buckingham Palace to mingle with the vast crowd that had
gathered in front of the palace gates. On the surface, the scene was
no different from the carefully planned "walkabouts" the queen
performs on official occasions. But on this occasion the television
cameras sending the live pictures around the world and into our
CNN newsroom in New York were showing something quite different—a rebellion if not yet a revolution. In the past, in Paris or
St. Petersburg, revolution meant the crowd, the mob, storming the
palace or some other citadel of authority. But on that day in
London the crowd, and the public opinion it represented, forced
the monarch to come out of the palace and down into the street to
meet the people on their level. This shift in power from the palace
to the street was seen again later the same day when the queen
spoke to the nation on television from inside Buckingham Palace,
with the crowd outside gathered in front of the gates shown clearly in the background and therefore integrated into the event. The

video symbolism was crucial to protecting the royal family's fortunes among the queen's wavering subjects. The family's long and
fervently held belief that its authority was rooted in a mystique
that grew from, and indeed depended on, a deliberate distancing of
itself from the people was crumbling on the television screen.

At 10:00 A.M., London time, Saturday, September 6, 1997, the
procession accompanying the remains of the Princess of Wales
departed Kensington Palace for funeral services in Westminster
Abbey. It was 5:00 A.M. eastern time in the United States, and millions of Americans had set their alarm clocks early to watch the
final act of the drama and phenomenon that had gripped the attention of the nation and the world. A few days later, in preparing a
report on public reaction to Diana's death, I checked the CNN
audience ratings for that morning. What the ratings showed was
not surprising, and most likely prophetic. At five in the morning,
eastern time, the number of "hits" of people logging on to
CNN.com dropped while the size of the television audience
soared. Two hours later, as Diana's casket left Westminster Abbey
for burial on her family's estate and CNN television resumed its
normal programming, the viewing audience declined and the
number of people logging on to CNN's Web site increased marked-
ly. The reason behind these tidal shifts in the audience was as clear
as the picture on the screen. Going back to the death of John F.
Kennedy, no other medium could compete with television when
its cameras were showing an event and conveying an experience of
such emotional and popular magnitude. Nor could television compete effectively with other sources of information when it did not
have compelling pictures or experience to communicate.

The long anticipated and much promised convergence of all
media—the printed word, still and moving images, and sound,
pumped into our lives via satellite, on telephone and cable lines,

and through digital compression boxes—is upon us. And so are the consequences. For news and information that are not particularly visual we look first to text and graphics that we find in newspapers, magazines, and books, and on the Web. Although this news and information will in the future be delivered in text form to our television sets as well as our computers, it will not be the television of moving images. However, when we seek emotion or visual experience, which are the essential ingredients of entertainment (even news as entertainment), we will look to the power of moving images of events, whether they appear on television or on a computer screen. We will no longer talk about television and text (once known as print) as separate media, but rather as two aspects of one common, or converged, medium. The text and the moving image will likely follow the inevitable law of technology and business; each will be used in ways that give it the largest marginal advantage over a competing technology and business. Television, including television news, will be filled with programs that are driven even more by sensation. There will be more confessional talk shows, more Jerry Springers, and more fights and wrestling and tasteless acts on shows searching desperately for an audience, not to mention the megadollar quiz shows pushing the most common denominational button: financial wealth.

What will be the future of programs that appeal to the mind rather than to the gut? They will, as now, find it difficult to exert a prominent presence amid the incessant competition for a significant space in the commercial marketplace. Those interested in ideas and thought, who seek refuge from the excesses of television, will find solace and stimulation in programs catering to these tastes on the low-budget, minimal production model of C-SPAN. They will provide intelligent talk from interesting people, but with their small slice of the marketplace they will have a limited financial base to pay for significant productions, be they documentary programs or serious drama. Here is the heart of the coming paradox of television in the digital age. As the number of channels increases into the hundreds, there will be steadily increasing pressure to spend more resources (money) to produce better programs to attract an audience. However, as the number of channels rises to an eyeball-numbing level, the market share of each channel is bound to decrease, diminishing its income and its financial ability to invest in the better programs that are needed to stay in business. It can lead to a downward spiral in quality programming from which news can claim no immunity.

Already we can see one example of this shift in television news coverage as it is driven by the new market forces. A major story such as the death of Princess Diana or John F. Kennedy Jr., or the Clinton/Lewinsky ordeal, can drive almost all other news off the screen. It may not be good or balanced journalism, but it is a commercially effective use of television. Not only can a big story draw more viewers, but dwelling obsessively on a big story can make a big story even bigger. When a critical mass of awareness among the public is reached, a viewer tunes in to television news not to learn about a different event or number of events of the day but rather to learn how the already familiar story, the ongoing drama, has developed. The reporting of a news story becomes a drama with new chapters or episodes: from the mangled Mercedes to Diana's funeral, Kennedy's crash off Martha's Vineyard to his burial at sea, from the first Lewinsky disclosure to the Senate trial. There was a business rationale behind "all Monica all the time!" Radio talk show hosts learned about the audience-drawing power of news as ongoing narrative in the 1980s. Television learned it in the 1990s.

Once again we face the inescapable question: Should we be upset by these upheavals and disorienting changes? Or should we be excited by the promise of choice and access that lies ahead, particularly as the Internet becomes a more prominent and cost-effective deliverer of news? The new pressures of technology and the marketplace put new stress on traditions and habits as well as on values and standards, those unseen but deeply felt companions that at some point in the past joined our journey through life. The challenge and the trick for journalists and consumers of news is to understand the current news environment in which we live while maintaining as best we can the standards that reporter and viewer must share as their common currency of exchange and trust. Broadcast news today is not what it was in the 1940s and 1950s, when Edward R. Murrow and his colleagues were the gold standard. Network news can no longer be what it was in the 1960s and 1970s, when a Cronkite and a Chancellor, a Huntley and a Brinkley symbolized a more stable order. Nor will the network newscasts long outlive the retirement of the current troika of evening news anchors.

In 1963 a vexing question facing the producers of the new half hour news programs was whether there would be enough news to fill the program. The answer was clearly yes. Today the challenge is to find enough news to fill the proliferation of twenty-four-hour news and information services with meaning, and viewers see how often reporters and producers come up short. Does that mean that television news today offers less than it did in the 1960s, when the new half hour evening newscast was a novelty that became a necessity? Absolutely not. In fact, taking all news services including Web sites into account, it offers more in both breadth and depth. That is what makes the future in electronic and digital journalism so exciting.

Historians, therapists, and self-help gurus never tire of telling us that the key to progress in a society or in an individual is the ability to face the future with a healthy sense of reality and a good measure of flexibility. Americans have proven themselves to be self-taught masters of that resilience. It is imprinted on our cultural DNA. The excitement and the humor of our new epoch were brought home in an issue of the *New Yorker*, a journal of taste whose style and content have been bent more than once to fit the shape of new market forces. Along one side of a page a full-column advertisement caught my eye. It had been paid for by Modern Library, a publisher of some distinction. A first reading of the ad provoked a feeling of literary sacrilege. An immediate second reading raised the suspicion that it was a finely honed jest. Finally, a third, more reflective consideration led me to the conclusion that Modern Library, like it or not, was offering a realistic and therefore healthy (if grating) perspective on our multimedia future. The advertisement offered an 800 number and said, in its entirety: "Now that you have seen the acclaimed BBC/A&E production of *Pride and Prejudice* on television, order the companion volume. By Jane Austen."

And why not?

BEFORE we conclude this uncompleted journey of a television journalist, let's take one more step back, to a warm night in Rome.

Chapter 24

A DINNER IN ROME

T HE FIRST TIME I met O.J. Simpson he was having dinner with Federico Fellini.

WE NEED some breathing space after that opening sentence. It is what much of a journalist's life and craft are about. Indeed, it is, I suppose, why young people are still drawn by curiosity, as well as a hunger for adventure, to this old and honorable (though somewhat battered) profession. Only a few among the global multitudes of journalists may ever come face-to-face with the horror of war, the rage of revolution, or ethnic hate: the stuff of the darkest headlines and the most pulse-quickening television images. Yet reporters have all been given a professional key to the true drama of our world so often hidden in the small print of life—the surprise and paradox, and the sense of adventure and mystery, that hung over that dinner table in Rome. On one side of the table sat a hero of American football whose fame would turn to notoriety. Across from him sat a preeminent artist whose renown as a filmmaker had been painstakingly built over decades. What did O.J. Simpson and Federico Fellini have to say to each other? And why was Ava Gardner listening in?

The path to that dinner table in 1976 was accidental, or I should say coincidental. Neither my wife nor I was a stranger to Europe. But neither of us knew Rome or anyone living there, a glaring, not to say embarrassing, shortcoming for a foreign correspondent.

A one-week assignment in Italy had brought us to Rome, and we decided to spend the first weekend as tourists before beginning my work for the *Nightly News* broadcast the following Monday. On Saturday morning we donned our walking shoes, descended the elegant Spanish Steps under a cloudless blue sky, purchased a guide to the city at a corner newsstand, and sat down at an outdoor cafe to plan our pilgrimage through the Rome of the emperors and the Renaissance. Over coffee, and surrounded by a chorus of languages from fellow tourists drinking their cappuccinos, chance intervened. A friend from Paris, a writer of considerable charm and talent, spotted us from the street as he was walking by and now was striding toward our table with eyes sparkling and arms spread wide in greeting. Richard Grenier did not bother to sit down before announcing with appropriate authority, "This is your lucky day: you are going to have dinner with Fellini." Gertje and I exchanged a baffled glance. This was our first morning together in Rome. We had no contacts and no plans beyond sightseeing and the prospect of a romantic tête-à-tête dinner in an outdoor restaurant in the Trastevere quarter of the city. Who were we to hesitate even a second in seizing Richard's invitation?

The dinner, it turned out, was being given by Donald Sutherland. Grenier was preparing a magazine profile of the actor, who was filming *Casanova* with Fellini. Sutherland was living in a big house with a big dining table and two more guests would fit right in, Richard insisted. He wrote out the address and left with a cheery wave.

It was a big house, and the party was under way when we arrived. There were twenty-five guests or so, some working with Fellini and Sutherland on *Casanova* and, in what might be called a supporting role, the director and cast of another film that was also being made in Rome. It was *The Cassandra Crossing*, an adventure-thriller whose title sticks in the mind not due to any enduring merit but because of its cast, which included Sophia Loren (who alas was not at the dinner), Ava Gardner (who was), and O.J. Simpson.

That night Simpson was beginning a film career that did not take him as far as television commercials eventually did. Still, he was more than another face in a crowd of several famous faces. I was struck immediately by his eyes. In predinner cocktail conversation they would twinkle for a moment and then suddenly, like a dark cloud crossing the sun, the warmth would vanish. The smile of the soul in the eyes was never as radiant or as lasting as the one supported by the muscles of the face. An impression of strength radiated from him, but it was less the physical strength of a professional football player and more the aura of extraordinary discipline. Simpson was already well along his chosen path, shaping his public persona for a life in the public eye long after the NFL. It was an act of pure will, and at Donald Sutherland's party, as on the football field, he had the right moves.

Simpson and other cast members from the film were seated on one side of the long dining table, with Fellini, Sutherland, and the rest of the *Casanova* team facing them. Pasta was followed by veal served with copious amounts of Italian wine. Given the dynamics of the dinner, Fellini was the center of attention, a magnetic presence who had not been molded by an act of will but had emerged naturally through the years of creative struggle, like the layers of a fine patina building up on a precious antique table. As Gertje and I watched, we were struck by how each side in front of us represented two opposite and indeed incompatible approaches to telling a story through moving images. On the left, the young director of *The Cassandra Crossing* had the advantage of one clear goal: to use his multimillion-dollar budget and his stars to turn out a commercial success so that he would be given more millions to make another film. Across from him, Fellini was in a different situation, and he spoke about it over the dinner table with an air that was more resignation than complaint.

He too, he said, had to have money from financial backers, a few million dollars to put his unique visions on celluloid. He owed his backers a lot, at least the amount of their investment in him, and yet, he continued, he could not trim his cinematic sails to suit the prevailing commercial winds. If he did, he would not be Fellini. The pressure he felt not to compromise his ideas and instincts was greater than the pressure to accommodate to the commercial marketplace. How nice, he mused, to be a painter or a writer who could simply throw away a canvas or a piece of paper when a work did not turn out right.

The dinner was going well, although I noticed that Ava Gardner, a few seats to my left, was growing less animated in direct proportion to the wine being consumed. By the end of the main course she had begun to drift off in mid-conversation. Simpson had not engaged Fellini in the dinner talk, which continued in English and Italian. But when it came to helping an aging star in distress, he needed no director. Quietly, Simpson arose from his place and, with an air of dignified self-assurance, walked behind Ava Gardner's chair, leaned over, and whispered into her ear. She nodded and laid down her napkin as Simpson pulled the chair back, helped her to her feet, took her firmly by the arm, and escorted the Hollywood legend from the room. A minute later Simpson was back at the dinner table, where there was a sense of admiration among the assembled directors and actors who had watched the brief scene without breaking their conversation. In theater, as in life, it is far easier to stage a dramatic entrance than a dignified exit.

Coffee was served in the living room and the adjoining library as the guests broke up into small groups. In one corner Fellini and his wife, the actress Giulietta Masina, stood apart from the English-speaking crowd. Gertje and I went up to them.

"I am looking forward to seeing your next film," Gertje said as an unexciting but usually effective key to launching a conversation.

"Well, I am afraid you are going to be disappointed," Fellini replied, in French. "I thought Casanova would be perfect for me, but I didn't read up on him enough. The man does not equal his image. He actually is not that interesting a figure. My mistake."

There was an awkward pause as we all searched for a new direction to take the stillborn conversation. Then, with an Italianate shrug and a wave of the hand he relaxed, or perhaps decided to accept the fate he was certain awaited his film.

"But at least I am doing something," he added with life and energy returning to his voice. And then the man, the creative artist who had few competitors in turning his deep observations of human existence into compelling and moving images on a screen, said something so ordinary and even banal, and yet so profound, that perhaps only he could give it true substance and meaning: "At least I am working. I have to keep working."

INDEX

Index

and correspondents group in 1960s,
80
and coverage of Democratic national
convention of 1972, 137–38
and decision to not move to cable, 256
and mid–1960s straight-news style,
78–80
and morning breakfast-time program
of 1954, 4
and national radio network, 75–76
and purchase by Larry Tisch, 224
and takeover by Viacom, 234, 236
and use of Telenews newsreel
footage, 6
and Vietnamese bureau, 47
CBS Reports, 19
CBS Sunday Morning, 252
Censorship
by networks themselves for commercial reasons, 237
and "chilling effect," 236–37
Chancellor, John, 79, 140
as boss of Utley in Brussels, 11–16
as Clinton Utley's assistant, 7
and coverage of Democratic national
convention of 1972, 136, 138
and *NBC Nightly News*, 124, 130,
250–51
retirement dinner of, 250–53
Checkpoint Charley, 108
Chicago Cubs and Belize, 212, 213
"Chilling effect," 236–37
China
and Bob Costas coverage of Atlanta
Olympic Games of 1996, 235–36
and foreign news censorship, 235
Churchill, Winston, 3
Cierna, Czechoslovakia, 113, 115
Cigarette companies
and sponsorship of radio news programs, 7
and sponsorship of television news
broadcasting, 3–4
Circle Sportif nightclub, 168
Clarke, Arthur C., 209, 210, 212

and discussion of impact of global
television, 219–20
Clinton, Bill and news media, 247–48,
264
Club Med, 100
CNN (Cable News Network), 224, 234
and audience rating of major events
since 1985, 227–28
and establishment of full-time news
coverage, 256
and Gulf War and achievement of
dominance in news field, 257–58
and live broadcasts, 243–44
and news coverage of Princess
Diana's funeral, 262
and relationship with world governments and political persuasions,
234
and separate news channels, 233
Cold War
and concern about foreign issues, 231
and following news as "civic duty,"
245
Collapse of South Vietnam in 1975,
157–69
Columbia Broadcasting Network. *See*
CBS News
Computer education in the Soviet
Union, 206–8
Computers as new focus of information
age, 224
Concorde, inaugural flight of, 240–42
Constellation Hotel (Laos), 54
Correspondents, foreign. *See* Foreign
correspondents
Costas, Bob, 235–36, 237
Crillon Hotel, Paris, 106–7
Cronkite, Walter
and *CBS Evening News*, 12, 78, 80,
130, 224
and coverage of Democratic national
convention of 1972, 137–38
and popular and wide appeal, 140
and Winston cigarette commercials,
4, 7

275

Index

Index

Index

Index

Index

Newsreel, movie, compared to early television news, 5–6
New York Times
  and 1927 testing of television, 75–77
  and POW film story, 110
Ngo Dinh Diem, 38, 58
Nickless, Jim, 148–50
Nigeria, 175–83
Nigerian Broadcasting Corporation, 178–79
Nightline, 253
Nixon, Richard, 130
  and animosity toward network news, 131–32
  and attack upon news media, 132–34
  and coverage of fall from grace, 135
  and effective use of network news, 132
  and Republican National Convention of 1972, 138
  and visit to Cairo, 153
North Vietnam and Ho Chi Minh Trail, 54, 56
Nosovan, Phoumi, 54
Nuclear submarine commander, Russian, 255
Nuremberg War trials, 91, 92, 95

Office of War Information (O.W.I.), 65–66
Oil
  conferences regarding, 145–46
  and Nigeria and Biafra, 175–76
Ojukwu, Odumegwu, 177
Oldsmobile and sponsorship of CBS news, 4
OPEC. *See* Organization of Petroleum Exporting Countries
Opium and Laos, 55–56
Organization of Petroleum Exporting Countries (OPEC), 144
  and Vienna conference of 1973, 145–46

Palace of Congresses, Moscow, 199
Paley, William, 18
Paris, and Utley posting in, 121–24
Paris Peace Talks on Vietnam of 1968, 106–7
Perkins, Jack, 133
Perot, Ross, 248
Pettit, Tom, 133, 137
Philip, Prince of England, 261
Phouma, Souvonna, 53
Pilots in Pajamas documentary program, 110
Podgorny, Nikolay, 116
Political conventions
  of 1948 in Philadelphia, 2
  of 1972, 136–39
Politics
  and Olympic Games coverage, 235–36
  and television newscasts, 234–37
Power
  and shift from palace to the street, 261–62
  and the visual image, 44–45
Presidential election of 1992 and advent of talk syndrome, 248–49
Pride and Prejudice (Austen), 266

Quiz show scandals, 18–20, 21

Radio
  and the "big story," 264
Railroads
  and construction to and over Victoria Falls, 189–91
  and expansion of Africa, 189
  and freight traffic between Rhodesia and Zambia, 187–88, 192
  and station at Victoria Falls, 191–93
Rather, Dan, 80, 137, 257
Ratings mania, 78
RCA
  and NBC, 214
  and purchase of by General Electric, 223

Index

Index

Index

Index

PublicAffairs is a new nonfiction publishing house and a tribute to the standards, values, and flair of three persons who have served as mentors to countless reporters, writers, editors, and book people of all kinds, including me.

I.F. STONE, proprietor of *I. F. Stone's Weekly*, combined a commitment to the First Amendment with entrepreneurial zeal and reporting skill and became one of the great independent journalists in American history. At the age of eighty, Izzy published *The Trial of Socrates*, which was a national bestseller. He wrote the book after he taught himself ancient Greek.

BENJAMIN C. BRADLEE was for nearly thirty years the charismatic editorial leader of *The Washington Post*. It was Ben who gave the *Post* the range and courage to pursue such historic issues as Watergate. He supported his reporters with a tenacity that made them fearless and it is no accident that so many became authors of influential, best-selling books.

ROBERT L. BERNSTEIN, the chief executive of Random House for more than a quarter century, guided one of the nation's premier publishing houses. Bob was personally responsible for many books of political dissent and argument that challenged tyranny around the globe. He is also the founder and longtime chair of Human Rights Watch, one of the most respected human rights organizations in the world.

For fifty years, the banner of Public Affairs Press was carried by its owner Morris B. Schnapper, who published Gandhi, Nasser, Toynbee, Truman and about 1,500 other authors. In 1983, Schnapper was described by *The Washington Post* as "a redoubtable gadfly." His legacy will endure in the books to come.

Peter Osnos, *Publisher*